Hacking GPS

Hacking GPS

Kathie Kingsley-Hughes

Wiley Publishing, Inc.

Hacking GPS

Published by
Wiley Publishing, Inc.
10475 Crosspoint Boulevard
Indianapolis, IN 46256
www.wiley.com

Copyright © 2005 by Wiley Publishing, Inc., Indianapolis, Indiana

Published by Wiley Publishing, Inc., Indianapolis, Indiana

Published simultaneously in Canada

ISBN: 0-7645-8424-3

Manufactured in the United States of America

10 9 8 7 6 5 4 3 2 1

1B/QR/QT/QV/IN

For general information on our other products and services or to obtain technical support, please contact our Customer Care Department within the U.S. at (800) 762-2974, outside the U.S. at (317) 572-3993 or fax (317) 572-4002.

Wiley also publishes its books in a variety of electronic formats. Some content that appears in print may not be available in electronic books.

Library of Congress Cataloging-in-Publication Data is Available from the Publisher

About the Author

Kathie Kingsley-Hughes has written numerous books in the PC and programming fields and is comfortable explaining hi-tech concepts in an easy-to-follow way. Several of the titles that she has authored or co-authored are set books used in many U.S. and international colleges and universities. Writing in the technical arena has given her many opportunities to use hundreds of different gadgets and gizmos; and because she has a love of the outdoors, it was inevitable that she would become involved in GPS and digital mapping.

Kathie has been using GPS since its early days when the accuracy and quality of the receivers were poor. Even back then, however, she realized the potential of such devices and predicted that they would be a huge hit in the consumer arena.

Credits

Acquisitions Editor
Katie Mohr

Development Editor
Brian MacDonald

Project Editor
Pamela Hanley

Technical Editor
Joel McNamara

Copy Editor
Luann Rouff

Editorial Manager
Mary Beth Wakefield

Vice President & Executive Group Publisher
Richard Swadley

Vice President and Publisher
Joseph B. Wikert

Executive Editorial Director
Mary Bednarek

Project Coordinator
Erin Smith

Graphics and Production Specialists
Jonelle Burns
Lauren Goddard
Denny Hager
Heather Ryan
Erin Zeltner

Quality Control Technicians
Leeann Harney
Carl Pierce
Brian Walls

Proofreading and Indexing
TECHBOOKS Production Services

To my husband, Adrian—my inspiration

Acknowledgments

Extra special thanks to Katie Mohr for believing in this project and guiding it along from concept to completion. It's been a pleasure working with you on this project.

Thanks too to Chris Webb for all his feedback and help in molding the book into a workable project.

I also want to extend a sincere "thank-you" to the rest of the publishing team, both those I've dealt with directly and those who have worked hard behind the scenes.

Contents at a Glance

Contents

Part II: Software Hacks   123

Part IV: Playtime — 253

Chapter 11: Hacking Geocaching — 255

Chapter 12: GPS Games — 289

Introduction

People have always had a fascination with where they are in the world and where they are going in it. We began by looking to the skies before perfecting our skills with maps and compasses, so it is only right that once again we look to the skies to guide us — only this time we aren't looking at stellar constellations, but instead at a constellation of high-tech satellites designed for military use and later made available to the public.

This book isn't about the actual GPS system. I assume that you've been using GPS already and that you have an understanding of how your GPS receiver works and how to use it to get from one place to another. This book is different; it's about taking the unit that you have and making tweaks to it or adding new hardware.

In this book, we will be looking at a variety of modifications and hacks that you can make to your GPS. You'll learn how to alter the built-in software, how to make mobile power supplies, how to improve signal reception under tough conditions, and how to connect your GPS to a variety of other devices.

No matter what your interest in GPS or what you use it for, you are bound to find something useful in this book that will enhance your experience with your GPS.

Who This Book Is For

This book is aimed at GPS users who have a sense of adventure — but rather than a sense of adventure in the outdoors, this book is aimed at the reader who has a sense of adventure when it comes to experimenting, modifying, and improving technology.

Whether you use your GPS for hiking, sailing, in-car navigation, or sports, this book contains information that you won't find in a user manual or other GPS books.

What This Book Covers

No matter what you use your GPS for, you are bound to find ideas, hints, tips, and inside knowledge in this book that will make your GPS experience even more worthwhile.

Among other things, this book will show you how to do the following:

- Make custom cables for your GPS
- Power your GPS by a variety of means
- Get a better signal

- Upgrade and modify the firmware loaded onto the GPS
- Make modifications to your GPS to make it more robust and to protect it from the elements

It doesn't matter which kind of GPS receiver you use either; you will find dozens of hacks, tweaks, and modifications in this book that will enable you to do more with your GPS than before. And best of all, most of these tweaks will cost you nothing at all!

How This Book Is Structured

This book is divided into four parts, covering hardware, software, data, and just plain fun. Unless otherwise noted, the chapters are independent of each other and don't need to be read in order.

Part I: Hardware Hacks

In this part, you will look at how you can take control of your GPS by making additions, modifications, and improvements to the hardware. These improvements will help you to get the most out of your GPS and make it better and easier to use. You will also examine how you can make additional custom hardware for your GPS (such as cables, cases, and connectors) that you can't buy off the shelf.

Part II: Software Hacks

After looking at how you can modify the hardware, you will look in detail at ways to modify the software that you will be using in conjunction with your GPS. In this part, you will learn how to connect your GPS to various software packages, what communication protocols are used, and how to use this knowledge to improve the way that you use your GPS and troubleshoot problems that you might encounter.

Part III: Data Hacking

A GPS is all about data, and this part presents useful information about the structure that this data takes, how it is sorted, how to move it from the GPS onto a PC or handheld device, how to edit the data, and finally how to upload new data back into the memory of your GPS. This part also covers a variety of powerful software applications that enable you to make the most efficient use of the data that your GPS receiver collects.

Part IV: Playtime

This part looks at how GPS receivers have spawned a whole raft of new and exciting outdoor games, as well as infusing new life into existing games. These two chapters look at a variety of fun uses for your GPS, and offer numerous hints and tips that will give you an advantage over other players.

What You Need to Use This Book

To work through the projects in this book, you will need the following:

- A GPS receiver
- A PC (any 486-based PC or later will do, running Microsoft Windows 95 or later)
- A basic toolkit (screwdrivers, pliers, etc.)

Other items may be needed for individual projects. These are introduced as required.

Hardware Hacks

part

GPS Secrets

It's fun to uncover something that you aren't supposed to know about—
many software applications and movies on DVD contain what are known
as "easter eggs." However, imagine finding something that you aren't supposed to find that turns out to be useful and informative.

In this chapter, we are going to hunt for GPS easter eggs, delving into the
secrets that lie behind the standard menus on your GPS unit to find useful
features and diagnostic screens that can give you information about your
system and troubleshoot problems that you might have.

There's a lot of information to find — technical information, diagnostic
information, and more.

Let's begin our tour of the secrets of GPS units.

Hidden Secrets

Most electronic devices contain hidden diagnostic screens or setup menus
that are used by the manufacturer to diagnose faults and possibly remedy
them. GPS receivers are no different, but because of their limited number of
buttons, numerous complicated keystrokes are often needed to access such
menus so that users don't accidentally find them.

You are unlikely to get any tech support for any of the undocumented features of your GPS unit, and these screens offer plenty of opportunity to
cause problems and mess up your unit. Take care and don't make any
changes unless you are sure of what you are doing.

If you do make changes, take the following precautions:

- Make a note of the changes you are making — that includes any new
settings and their original values.

- Don't make too many changes at once. Better still, make one change
at a time.

- If the unit appears worse after the change you made, undo the
change immediately.

- If the unit doesn't allow you to reverse a change, you will have to
reset the device (details are provided later in this chapter).

Garmin Secret Screens

In this section, I show you the secrets that are specific to GPS units from Garmin. I cover the older units, including the GPS III and III+, all the way up to the modern eTrex and Geko lines. I also include some specialized units, such as the Forerunner, which is designed to be worn on your wrist for hands-free outdoor activities, and the iQue, which is a combination GPS and Palm PDA.

Hard Resets

A *hard reset* wipes out all the data in your GPS and returns the unit to its initial factory settings. If you're having trouble with your unit and a soft reset doesn't help, a hard reset may be your only recourse.

Most of the hard reset sequences are complicated, to ensure that you don't press them by accident. Some of these key combinations require an extra hand, or another person, to assist you.

To confuse the issue further, different models of GPS use different terms for a hard reset. Several models call it a *master reset*, for example.

The iQue 3600 is an exception. In this case, a hard reset wipes out all data on the iQue, but leaves any GPS-related data present.

Here are the hard reset keys for the various Garmin products.

Model	Hard Reset Key
iQue 3600	RESET + POWER
Forerunner	RESET + POWER
StreetPilot	Hold down the MENU and FIND and PAGE buttons and switch the unit on using the POWER button.
Geko	Press down all the keys except the DOWN key and hold that for 5 seconds.
eTrex	For units that don't have the click-stick, hold the UP and ENTER keys and then press the POWER button.
	For click-stick units, hold the PAGE button down while at the same time holding the click-stick in the down position and powering up the unit.
GPS 60/60CS	Hold down ENTER and the PAGE buttons while powering up.
GPS 76/76C/76CS	Hold down ENTER and the PAGE buttons while powering up.
GPS 176	Simultaneously hold down the button, the NAV button and the QUIT button and then tap the POWER button. Make sure that you continue to hold all the buttons until the unit switches on.
eMap	Hold ESC while powering up the unit.

Model	Hard Reset Key
GPS 76S	Hold down the DOWN button while powering up.
GPS III and GPS III+	Press the MENU button while powering the unit up.
GPS V	Hold down the ZOOM OUT and QUIT buttons while powering up. (This only works with units that run version 2.20 of the firmware and earlier.)

Soft Resets

A *soft reset* is a way to erase all the data in your GPS's memory and restart the system. Any settings you've changed are kept, but any waypoints, routes, or other data is deleted. You might want to do this when you're having problems with your unit. A soft reset isn't as destructive to the settings as a hard reset, so if you're trying to fix your unit, you should try a soft reset first.

Only the Garmin iQue 3600 and Forerunner models have a soft reset feature. On the iQue, a soft reset deletes all the volatile memory, but any data saved in applications is retained.

Here are the soft reset keys for the Garmin products that have this feature.

Model	Soft Reset Key
iQue 3600	RESET
Forerunner	Switch the unit off. Then press and hold down MODE + ENTER while pressing and releasing POWER. The screen should turn light gray. Continue holding the MODE and ENTER button until the startup screen appears.

Warm Resets

The *warm reset* feature is unique to the iQue 3600. It's less dangerous than a soft reset, because it is the equivalent of booting a PC and reloading the applications. Memory management on handheld devices isn't as good as on a desktop PC, and periodic warm resets help to solve problems and speed up operation. This type of reset can be useful for solving operating system issues with the unit. To perform a warm reset on the iQue, press RESET and SCROLL UP.

Full GPS Resets

The full reset is another function unique to the iQue. This reset wipes out all GPS data on the unit, but only GPS data. The PDA data remains intact. To perform a full reset on the iQue, press the RESET, ESC, and DateBook keys simultaneously.

Diagnostic Screens

The diagnostic screens on many GPS units give you access to an array of information about the unit. The screens available vary depending on which unit you have, but most of them will tell you the version of the firmware you're running and the battery voltage. Some will also tell you the temperature of the unit.

Here are the keys to access the diagnostic screens for the various Garmin products.

Model	Access Diagnostic Screens
Forerunner	Hold down ENTER and switch the unit on.
StreetPilot	Hold down the MENU and FIND buttons and switch the unit on using the POWER button.
Geko	Press OK while powering the unit on.
eTrex	If your unit doesn't have the click-stick, hold the UP and PAGE keys and then press the POWER button.
	If you have the click-stick, hold it in the down position and then power up.
GPS 60/60CS	Hold ENTER while powering up the unit.
GPS 76/76C/76CS	Hold ENTER while powering up the unit.
GPS 176	Hold ENTER while powering up the unit. (This only works with a limited number of firmware versions.)
eMap	Hold ENTER while powering up the unit.
GPS 76S	Hold OK while powering up the unit.
GPS III and GPS III+	Power up the unit while holding down the ENTER key.

Garmin GPS III Test Screens

The Garmin GPS III and GPS III+ have a number of test screens that warrant special mention here. As mentioned in the earlier table, you enter this mode by powering up the unit while holding down the ENTER key.

The test screen is used by Garmin for final testing and calibration of the unit, so if at all possible, only enter this mode when you can avoid getting a signal for the GPS satellites. The best place to do this is indoors away from doors and windows. Check for satellite coverage before entering this mode and bear in mind that satellites are continuously moving, so no signal now is no guarantee of no signal later during the day or night.

If your unit does pick up a signal, it's not the end of the world and no permanent harm will be done. The worst that can happen is that you may experience a little longer lockup times, or you might have to perform a full cold start to get it running again. You might also experience continued longer lockup times for a while until the unit recalibrates itself under use or from being left in the open while on.

Note The Garmin GPS III has a removable antenna, and unplugging it is a good way to ensure that no GPS signal lock can be obtained.

The test screen may also appear of its own accord — this can occur automatically if the unit detects a failure during power up.

You can use this mode to verify certain operations of the unit. For example, pressing each key will cause the corresponding key in the display to darken. Defective buttons won't cause this to happen.

Pressing the ENTER key twice in a succession will cause a graphic pixel test to run. This can be used to highlight any bad pixels on the display. Pressing the ENTER key again will further test the display. Pressing the ENTER key one more time will return you to the main test screen.

Pressing the POWER/LAMP key will show up onscreen and actually cause the backlight to illuminate.

Autolocating

Most units make the autolocate function a default feature. he autolocate feature deletes previous satellite data (the almanac) and downloads new data. It can sometime be very handy to force the GPS to download the almanac and "rediscover" where it is in the world. Some devices, such as the Garmin iQue 3600 and Geko, have an autolocate function that's plainly accessible to the user. Others have the feature, but it's hidden. The following table describes the keystrokes you can use to force autolocate for units on which it's hidden.

Model	Force Autolocate Key
Forerunner	With the unit off, press and hold down the DOWN key while pressing and releasing the POWER key.
StreetPilot	Hold down the PAGE and FIND buttons and then switch the unit on using the POWER button.
eMap	Hold FIND while powering up the unit.
GPS III and GPS III+	Press and hold down the PAGE button while switching the unit on.

Magellan Secret Screens

Magellan is the other primary manufacturer of GPS units other than Garmin. Almost all GPS units come from one of these two manufacturers. The different types of Magellan units have very different hidden screens, so I discuss them in separate sections.

Magellan Meridian Series

One of the most popular ranges of Magellan GPS units is the Meridian. This handheld GPS receiver is bigger and heavier than the Garmin eTrex, but it has a larger, easier-to-read LCD screen.

There are two types of secret menu for the Meridian: boot time screens, which you activate when you switch on the unit, and a secret menu that you can access while the unit is already running.

Boot Time Screens

These are screens that are accessed by pressing key combinations when the unit is switched on.

Function	Keys	To Exit
Force Off mode. Causes the system to shut down.	GOTO + ESC + ENTER	
Put the unit into software upload mode.	GOTO + ESC + PWR	Force Off
Switch the LCD off.	NAV + GOTO + ESC + PWR	Force Off
Carry out a burn-in test on the unit.	NAV + ESC + PWR	Press ESC
Access the hidden menu.	NAV + GOTO + PWR	Either press the power off button or use Force Off
Start a test of the display.	NAV + ZOOM IN + PWR	Force Off
Carry out a serial port test.	NAV + ZOOM OUT + PWR	Force Off
Clear the unit's memory.	ENTER + MENU + PWR	Press ESC

Access Menu (System On)

To access the secret menu, switch the unit on and press the following keys in order:

Note   Be very careful when using these menus, as making incorrect changes to the system can cause the device to become unusable.

1. Menu
2. Rocker pad right
3. Rocker pad left
4. Rocker pad right
5. Rocker pad left

6. Select the appropriate menu number (see the following table).

7. Press the Enter button.

Menu Number	Function	Exit By
00	Displays the firmware version	ESC button
01	Lists satellites	MENU button
03	WAAS status. Allows you to turn WAAS support on/off.	ESC button
09	Degauss sensors (factory use)	ESC button
10	Switches the unit off	
20	Satellite data	MENU button
21	Sensor degauss. Also begins compass calibration on the Meridian Platinum.	ESC button
22	Clears the sensor calibration information	ESC button
24	Clears the barometer calibration information	ESC button
30	Clears the unit's memory	ESC button
32	Clears all memory information	ESC button
38	Language select	ESC button
71	Creates waypoints for testing purposes	ESC button
82	Compensation offset	ESC button
86	Basemap upload (only via SD memory card). Rename basemap file to *basemap.img*.	ESC button
88	Firmware upload (only via SD memory card). Rename firmware file to *firmware.hex*.	ESC button
92	Change map menu	ESC button
93	Convert basemap name	ESC button
95	Erase all map data	ESC button
98	Map upload	ESC button
99	Software upload mode	Force off

Note   Menus 86 and 88 are only available on firmware versions 4.02 and later.

Magellan SporTrak

The SporTrak is another commonly seen GPS receiver. The following table provides some of the undocumented features of this unit.

Function	Keys
Clear memory	MENU + PWR
Burn-in test	ESC + PWR
Serial port test	OUT + PWR
Self test	IN + PWR

WAAS Switch On/Off

If you want to deactivate (or later reactivate) WAAS you can do so by following these steps:

1. Menu

2. Rocker pad right

3. Rocker pad left

4. Rocker pad right

5. Rocker pad left

A box containing "00" appears. Press the rocker pad up until you reach "03." Press ENTER to activate/deactivate WAAS. To exit, press the following:

1. ESC

2. ESC

3. PWR (to power off the unit)

Note Not following these steps to exit out of the menu can cause the SporTrak to lock up.

Magellan 300/330

The Magellan 300 was probably one of the first GPS units to hit the mainstream GPS market — many were sold, and if you go to geocaching events you will see plenty still in use.

The following table describes a few undocumented features of these units.

Function	Keys
Display software version	Press the left rocker pad key while starting the unit.
Delete memory	Press the right rocker pad key while starting the unit.
Display/keypad tests	Press the GOTO key while starting the unit.
Switch light on without icon	Press the LIGHT key while starting the unit.

After a Hard or Soft Reset

If you are unfortunate enough to have to perform a full reset on your unit using one of the sequences I've detailed in this chapter, you will need to allow the unit to download a full almanac from the GPS satellites before you can resume normal use.

To do this, you first need to place the unit in a location where a good satellite lock can be achieved. This process can take anywhere from 5 to 10 minutes, and I recommend doing this outdoors in a spot with a clear view of the sky. I also suggest that you keep the unit stationary, oriented vertically (upright) if it contains a helix antenna and horizontally if it uses a patch antenna (consult the manual for more details); otherwise, the process can take a lot longer.

After the first lock, you will need another 10 to 15 minutes to get the almanac reloaded. There's usually no onscreen indication that the almanac has been downloaded, but you can usually find out if it has been loaded by checking the date and time on the unit — if it is correct, or if the unit has a good lock on the satellites and is displaying location coordinates, then the almanac has been retrieved.

If your unit is a WAAS (Wide Area Augmentation System)–capable receiver, you will also have to allow the unit to download the WAAS almanac too. This can take some time; and if you are in Europe, you need to place the unit in a location where it has a view of the near horizon. Without the WAAS almanac loaded, the GPS will still report GPS positional information.

 Note Remember that the time will be shown as UTC time (or GMT) because your local time offset will have been lost in the reset.

Now you can reload all of your preferences into the unit, including data such as the following:

- Time zone information
- Daylight saving information
- Coordinate format
- Battery type

Finally, you will need to upload all your waypoints and saved routes to your unit, so it is important to keep a backup of your data.

Summary

This chapter provided you with a quick and easy introduction to the hidden features, menus, and diagnostic screens that are built in to many of the popular GPS receivers on the market.

I've not listed all of them here — that would take pages and some units are better documented than others. Try doing an Internet search using your favorite search engine, and keywords such as "undocumented" and your GPS brand and model to find out more.

In addition, if your GPS isn't listed here, try the key combinations for another receiver from the same manufacturer and you might get lucky. If you have a new, unlisted GPS, experiment with it and see what you find.

Building GPS Data Cables and Power Cords

A GPS receiver is designed as a standalone, mobile piece of equipment you can take with you in a car or on foot into the wilderness. It wouldn't be very useful if it needed a hard-wired connection — how often would you want to know the precise coordinates of your desktop PC? However, most GPS units can be hooked up via cables to other devices that enhance their functionality and add features that are not available on "out of the box" units.

Without cables, you can do a lot with your GPS unit; but with the right cables, you can do so much more. In this chapter, you'll learn how to combine power cords and data cables to reduce the clutter in your outdoor kit. You'll discover how to connect multiple GPS units to the same PDA. You'll even find out how to make your own cables, if you can't buy one that suits your needs.

Cables Demystified

Cables are available in numerous styles. Their differences reflect the different ways in which they are used. Typically, three types of cables are associated with GPS receivers:

- Data cables
- Power cords
- Combo cables

Note   Although most GPS units have an interface for a cable connection, bear in mind that not all do. This is especially true of some of the less expensive units. When in doubt, consult the manual.

In addition, when buying a new GPS receiver, it is generally uneconomical to choose one that does not have a cable interface, as the savings will be small, whereas the return from having an interface will be huge.

---

in this chapter

☑ The right cable for the right application

☑ Combining multiple cables

☑ Making your own cables

☑ Connecting to a PDA

No cable connection also means that you cannot update the firmware on the GPS, and thereby take advantage of bug fixes and new features released by the manufacturer.

How you acquire the cables is up to you. Shortly I will take you through the process of making them and you can also save yourself time (but not money unfortunately) by making these for yourself. The overwhelming advantage of making your own cables is that it offers you some practice with figuring out the wiring before progressing to more complex "multi" cables.

Let's take a brief tour of the different types of cable.

The Data Cable

A data cable is pretty self-explanatory — it is a cable that is used to transfer data between a GPS unit and another device. That other device is usually a PC or some form of handheld mobile device (such as a Pocket PC device like the HP iPAQ). When connecting to a PC, the port to which the cable connects is the serial port. The connector used is usually a 9-pin D connector.

Figure 2-1 shows a PC-to-Garmin eTrex data cable.

FIGURE 2-1: A PC-to-Garmin eTrex data cable

Note that not all data cables are the same. Not only won't a cable designed for the Garmin 76 fit a GPS from the eTrex range (as you will see shortly, the connectors on the interface are different), but a cable designed to fit a PC won't fit, say, an iPAQ. In other words, different devices need different cables to talk to other devices. The more GPSs you have, and the more varied the devices you want to connect them to, the more cables you will need. Figure 2-2 shows a data cable for an iPAQ Pocket PC.

Even with the widespread popularity of USB ports on PCs, most data cables still make use of older serial ports for data transfer. This can be a real pain on modern PCs (both desktops and laptops), whose serial ports have typically been replaced with the more versatile USB ports. If this is the case and you still want to make use of data cables, you will need to get a USB-to-serial converter and plug it into your USB port to create a serial port for the job. A good-quality and inexpensive USB-to-serial converter is available from pFranc (`http://pfranc.com/cgi-bin/P/USB_G4`).

Make sure that whatever converter you get has drivers to support the operating system you are running on your PC.

Bear in mind that there are several different kinds of GPS connector. Figure 2-3 shows two of the most common ones.

FIGURE 2-2: An iPAQ-to-Garmin eTrex data cable

FIGURE 2-3: Two GPS connectors

If you want to buy a cable for your GPS, most manufacturers make such cables available. They aren't cheap compared to making a cable yourself, but it is a quick option. Check the user manual for details — most accessories are listed there.

Power Cords

If you have owned and used a GPS for any length of time, you know how often the batteries need replacing just at a moment when you can't replace them, such as while driving.

Power cords differ from data cables in that they are used to transfer power to the GPS unit from a battery pack, a stack of batteries, or from an automotive circuit (commonly via the cigarette lighter). Using a power cord while using your GPS in the car (or while on the move, as I'll show you shortly) can dramatically increase the lifetime of the batteries in the device, saving you money (if you are using disposable batteries). It also reduces the load of spare batteries you have to carry for a particular trip.

You do need to be careful with power cords. The automotive system is a 12-volt system, and while some GPS receivers can handle this amount of power, some cannot.

Not all GPS receivers can handle a direct 12-volt power input and can be seriously damaged. When in doubt, check!

If you aren't sure, carefully check the documentation or user manual.

Don't assume that power cords are only useful in cars. Plenty of small 12-volt, lead-acid batteries available can be easily carried on a belt or in a backpack. You'll look at power cords in more detail later in this chapter, while Chapter 3 covers a few in-depth power hacks.

As with the data cables, if you want to buy a power cord for your GPS, most manufacturers make such cables available. Again, they aren't cheap, but it's quicker than making your own. Check the user manual for details.

Combo Cables

Combo cables, as the name suggests, are cables that combine the features of the data cable and power cord into a single cable. The result is a cable with the appropriate GPS connector for your GPS unit on one end, and at the other end a cigarette lighter adapter and a connector for your PC or Pocket PC. Figure 2-4 shows a combo cable.

The main advantage of a combo cable is that you can connect your GPS to a PC or other device while at the same time powering it from an available 12-volt system with just one cable. This can be extremely useful when you are using your system for in-car navigation.

Again, if you don't want to make a combo cable yourself, the manufacturer of your unit may have one. Check the user manual.

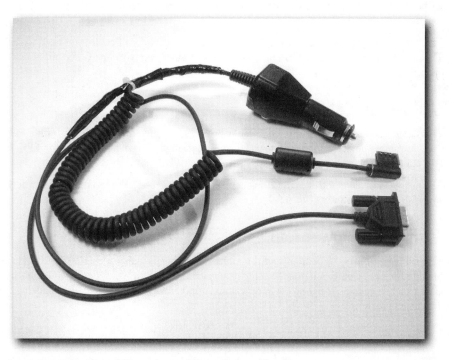

FIGURE 2-4: A combo cable combines data and power functions.

Combining Cable Types

So far, we've looked at one type of combo cable — a data/power combo cable — but there are many possible types. Here are a few possibilities:

- **Multi-GPS data cable:** A cable that can be used on more than one GPS unit
- **Multi-data cable:** A data cable that can connect to multiple devices
- **Multi-data/power cable:** A cable that can connect to more than one device and provide power
- **Multi-data/power/GPS cable:** A combo of all of the above

These cables aren't like any kind of cable you can buy off the shelf, and if you want cables like these, you have no choice but to make them yourself.

Multi-GPS Cables

A multi-GPS cable is a data cable that has a connector suitable for your PC or other mobile device at one end, while at the other end it is fitted with two (or more) connectors suitable for the GPS unit(s) that you have. This way, you only need to carry one cable, no matter what receiver or PC/handheld device you are using. An example might be a cable with connectors for both a Garmin eTrex and a Garmin 76 (one uses a square connector and the other uses a round one).

The advantage of a cable like this is that you reduce the number of cables you need to carry. The disadvantage is that you can only make a data connection with one GPS unit at any one time.

Multi-Data Cables

This cable is similar to the multi-GPS cable, but it has connectors suitable for both a PC and another mobile device you have. The usual combination is to have a connector for a PC serial port and a connector for a mobile device such as the iPAQ.

Again, the advantage of this is the convenience of carrying one cable no matter what device you wish to connect your GPS to.

Multi-Data/Power Cables

This cable combines the flexibility of the multi-data cable, but also adds a power connector suitable for a car cigarette lighter. It offers you great flexibility in what device you connect your GPS to while at the same time enabling you to supply power to the GPS, thus reducing the load on the batteries.

The main disadvantage of this kind of cable is that it is more complex, and has many unused ends and when in use need to be controlled, so as not to snag on anything.

Multi-Data/Power/GPS Cables

This is the ultimate GPS cable. It combines multiple GPS connectors, multiple device connectors, and includes the features of a power cord. This cable should cover all eventualities and all your needs. The disadvantage of this cable is that it can be a little bulky and cumbersome.

Making Your Own Data Cables

Now that you are familiar with the different types of cables that you can combine with your GPS, it's time to take a look at how to make some of them. I'll begin by taking you through the process of making a data cable. Specifically, this data cable is one for a Garmin eTrex GPS unit.

Materials You Will Need

To successfully build a data cable, you will need the following supplies and tools:

- A suitable connector for your GPS (these are available from www.pfranc.com or www.lynks.co.uk).
- A cable with a 9-pin D connector on the end — any old serial port cable will do, such as an old mouse or modem cable. Failing that, you will have to buy a cable).
- Soldering iron
- Solder
- Pliers/wire cutters
- Screwdriver (Crosspoint or Phillips)
- Electronic multimeter or circuit tester (if you have a multimeter, it will have an "ohms" setting — use this for circuit testing).

Cable Assembly
You assemble the cable as follows:

1. Take the wire with the 9-pin D connector at one end and cut off any connector at the opposite end.
2. Cut the outer sheathing off the trimmed end and expose the inner core of wires, as shown in Figure 2-5.
3. Strip the ends of the wires, as shown in Figure 2-6.

Figure 2-5: Exposing the inner core of wires

Figure 2-6: Stripping the sheathing off the end of the wire

4. Using a multimeter, you need to determine which wires corresponds to the *data in* and *data out* and *ground pin* on the 9-pin connector, as shown in Figure 2-7. To do this, set the multimeter to "ohms" (the 20 ohms setting will do just fine). Attach one probe to the bare wire; wrap a length of paper clip around the other probe, and probe the holes in the connector. Try them in turn; you are looking for a reading of zero, indicating that you have the right wire for the pin. The pins are as follows:

   ▪ Pin 2: Data out

   ▪ Pin 3: Data in

   ▪ Pin 5: Ground

FIGURE 2-7: A multimeter makes it easy to trace what wire goes to which pin.

Carefully note which wires correspond to each pin. If each is colored, make a note of this.

5. Trim back all the unneeded wires and cut the wires from pins 2, 3, and 5 to a length of approximately 1 inch (25 mm). Trim the sheath from these wires back about ¼ of an inch (6 mm), as shown in Figure 2-8.

Figure 2-8: Trimming back the sheathing

6. Now take a look at the pFranc eTrex connector shown in Figure 2-9. Notice that it has four pins. The pins are numbered 1, 2, 3, and 4, with pin number 1 being the pin furthest away from the cable. The pins are as follows:

   ▪ Pin 1: Power supply (+)

   ▪ Pin 2: RXD (data in)

   ▪ Pin 3: TXD (data out)

   ▪ Pin 4: GND (-)

7. Time to begin assembly of the pFranc connector. The connector includes five parts:

   ▪ Three plastic parts that make up the connector assembly

   ▪ One metal screw

   ▪ One strip of metal that has the four or eight pins attached to it (depending on the kit you receive), as shown in Figure 2-10.

FIGURE 2-9: The pFranc connector

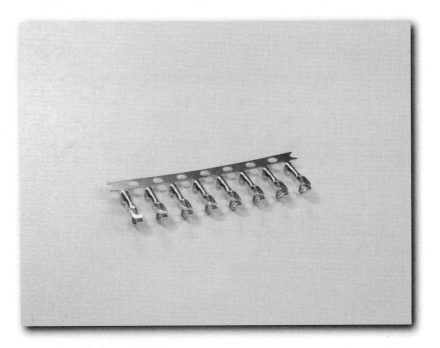

FIGURE 2-10: Metal strip with the pins

8. Carefully break off the pins (you only need three if you are making a data cable) from the sheet of metal by bending them off the metal strip. Take care and you will end up with four pins.

9. After breaking the pins free from the metal strip, bend them to 90 degrees as shown in Figure 2-11.

FIGURE 2-11: Bend the pins to the right shape.

10. Now it's time to solder the wires to the pins. At this stage, it doesn't matter which pins the wires are soldered to because you can rearrange them as necessary later.

After soldering, gently push each pin, one at a time, through the hole in the plastic piece with the large rectangle opening, as shown in Figure 2-12.

11. Now you are ready to place the pins in the proper position in the plastic holder (the base of the connector). The proper assembly is as follows:

   ▪ The wire corresponding to pin 2 (data out on the 9-pin D connector) connects to pin 3 (data out) on the GPS connector.

- The wire corresponding to pin 3 (data in on the 9-pin D connector) connects to pin 2 (data in) on the GPS connector.

- The wire corresponding to pin 5 (ground on the 9-pin D connector) connects to pin 4 (ground) on the GPS connector.

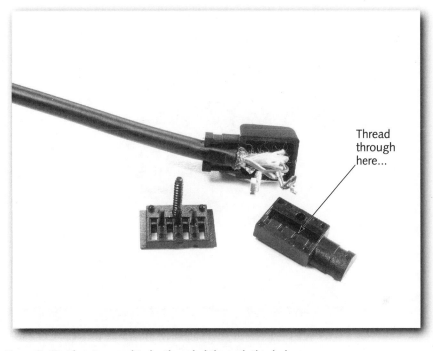

Thread through here...

FIGURE 2-12: The pins need to be threaded through this hole.

Note

The fourth pin is only required if you are making a power cable or a combo cable.

Note

If you're connecting to a 25-pin DB-25 connector, swap over pins 2 and 3 at the PC connector.

12. A clever way to hold the pins in place while assembling the connector is to use a piece of wire (or a needle) through the loops of the pins to hold them in place, as shown in Figure 2-13. This is the best hands-free way I've found of doing this.

FIGURE 2-13: Use a piece of wire to hold pins in place during assembly.

Note

Remember to remove the wire after assembly.

13. Bring the two parts of the connector together and then place the plastic hood on the connector. Make sure that all the cables seat properly and there is no chance of short-circuiting. Then add the screw and close the connector, as shown in Figure 2-14.

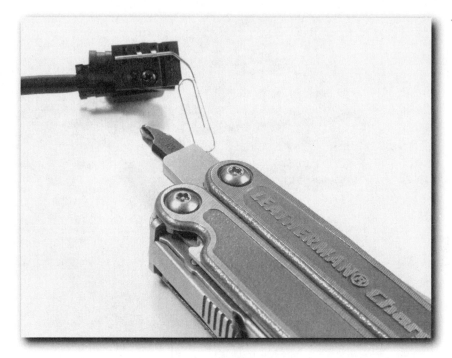

FIGURE 2-14: The single screw holds the connector together.

14. Remove the pin, needle, or wire used to hold the pins in place and the connector is finished.

Testing

You should always test your cables before first use to ensure that there are no short circuits or bad connections. Use a multimeter to do this, as shown in Figure 2-15. Make sure that each pin on the GPS connector corresponds to the appropriate pin on the 9-pin connector. Also ensure there are no short circuits to any other pins.

Note Refer to your multimeter's user manual for details on how to operate it.

After testing, you can connect the GPS to your PC.

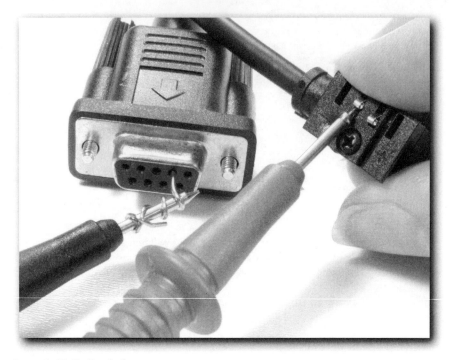

FIGURE 2-15: Testing before use

Don't Want to Buy a Connector?

If you don't want to buy a connector, can't get one, or are in a hurry, you have another option open to you if your GPS uses a flat connector, such as the Garmin eTrex.

You can use a piece of plastic (an old credit card is ideal), some small pieces of copper wire, and a marker pen to fashion a simple connector as follows:

1. Cut the plastic card into a small rectangle exactly 18 mm by 10 mm, as shown in Figure 2-16 (I've used diagrams here to make the process clearer).

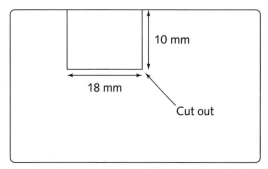

FIGURE 2-16: A corner off an old credit card is ideal for this.

2. Make three small holes down the middle of the plastic (along the long length). These holes should be made at 3.5 mm, 7 mm, and 10.5 mm from one end, as shown in Figure 2-17.

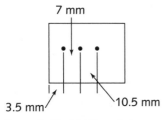

FIGURE 2-17: Add three holes.

3. Insert small lengths of copper wire through these small holes, as shown in Figure 2-18.

FIGURE 2-18: Insert the wires through the holes.

4. Solder these onto the wires from the 9-pin connector (in this setup, the wire coming out of the hole closest to the edge of the plastic is pin 4).

5. Holding the connector in front of you and facing away, with the pin nearest the edge to your left, write "TOP" along the top, as shown in Figure 2-19. This will help you orient your homemade connector properly when fitting it to the GPS (because a store-bought connector is keyed to prevent it being fitted the wrong way).

FIGURE 2-19: You want to know which side is the top of the connector.

6. Add a few dots of hot glue to the wires at the top to reduce the chances of short-circuiting, as shown in Figure 2-20. That's it! All done!

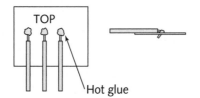

FIGURE 2-20: Hot glue keeps the wires in place.

Making Power Cords

Making power cords is similar to making data cables. The main differences between a data cable and a power cord are that you need a cigarette plug and you connect to different pins on the GPS connector.

There are some caveats to bear in mind. Not all GPS units can handle the full 12 volts from an automotive system. Connecting some units directly to the system can cause serious and permanent damage. The Garmin eTrex range and the eMap range take 2.5 volts, and 12 volts will seriously damage them. These all use the rectangular connector and as such are easily spotted. The Garmin Rino requires a 6-volt supply. Many others can take between 8 and 32 volts (usually making use of the round connectors) but there are notable exceptions — in particular, the Garmin GPS-12, GPS-38, and GPS-40, which can take no more than 8 volts.

If you have any doubt about the power range that your GPS can handle, consult the user manual. Specifications change regularly and it's better to be safe than sorry.

If your GPS cannot take a 12-volt supply, you will need a cigarette adapter that can step the voltage down. You can find plenty of cheap sources of these, in the form of old car phone chargers or chargers for other devices. You can also find variable chargers that enable you to control the output voltage. These are very handy, as they can be used for a variety of projects (as long as you remember to set the voltage properly before each use).

Once you have a suitable cigarette lighter adapter, making the cable is easy. The power inputs into a Garmin eTrex are pin 1 (+) and pin 4 (-), as shown in Figure 2-21.

Assembly is easy, as described in the following section.

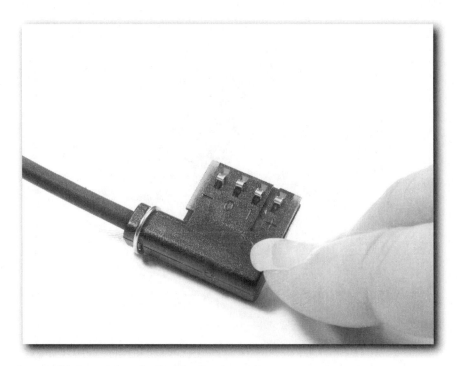

FIGURE 2-21: Power pins of a Garmin eTrex connector

Power Cord Assembly

If you managed to assemble a data cable, then building a power cord is just as easy. The main differences are how you hook up the pins. Pin 1 on the GPS connector is connected to the wire from the center of the cigarette lighter adapter (the power supply), while pin 4 is connected to the other wire (the ground). Remember that for most cars, the center pin in a cigarette socket is the positive terminal, while the outer is negative, as shown in Figure 2-22. If in doubt, check your vehicle's manual.

As a safety precaution, make sure that the cigarette lighter adapter is fused to protect both the GPS receiver from damage as well as the car from the risk of fire. If you are unsure, open up the connector and see if one is fitted. If it isn't, add an inline fuse (using a 5-amp fuse).

Testing

Make sure you use your multimeter to verify that the output voltages are correct and that there are no short-circuits that could blow the GPS unit.

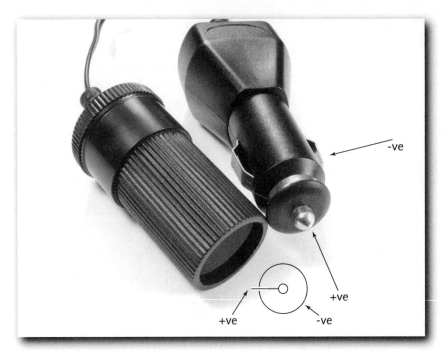

FIGURE 2-22: Cigarette socket detailed

When it's not plugged into a GPS, make sure that the cigarette adapter isn't plugged in, as that makes the pins of the GPS connector live. If those live pins come into contact with metallic objects, they could cause sparks, damage, and possibly a fire.

Note If you use a wire or needle to hold the pins in place while you assemble the power cord, it's particularly important to remember to remove it before use, as damage could occur.

Precautions

If you have more than one GPS unit and their acceptable voltage ranges are different, remember to carefully label which power cord goes with which GPS receiver. Carelessness to details here could cause significant damage to a GPS.

The best way to avoid confusion is to label the cables carefully, as shown in Figure 2-23, and keep the appropriate cable with the appropriate GPS. Remember to always double-check before using.

FIGURE 2-23: Label cables clearly to avoid confusion.

GPS/iPAQ Connections

Without a doubt, one of the most common GPS-to-device connections after the GPS-to-PC connection is the GPS-to-iPAQ connection. The iPAQ is a versatile companion to a GPS that, with the right software, enables you to do all sorts of things, from plotting your position on maps to planning and navigating a car journey.

The easiest way to connect a GPS to an iPAQ is using an appropriate cable that you can buy from the manufacturer. However, another great way to get a connection is to modify an iPAQ cradle to enable you to get a connection via the cradle.

Note A good source of cables is `http://pc-mobile.net/gps.htm`.

You could make the connection via the 9-pin D connector on the cradle (using the pins detailed earlier), but it's much more elegant if you make the connection an internal connection.

Cradle Modification

Here's how you carry out the cradle modification:

1. First, find your cradle! Once you've found the cradle, you need to open it. It's not held together with normal screws but with Torx screws. You will need a Torx bit or size T6 screwdriver (see Figure 2-24) to get inside the cradle. Don't try to use anything else or you will surely strip the screw heads.

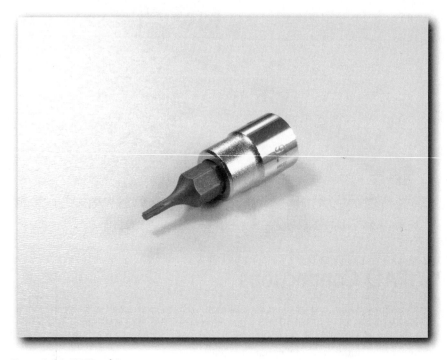

FIGURE 2-24: T6 Torx bit

2. Unplug the cradle from the PC. Undo the screws (see Figure 2-25) and be sure to keep them safe.

3. Once all four of the screws are out, start taking the plastic parts apart. This should be quite easy to do and requires no real force or pressure. Make a note of how it all comes apart for reassembly and be sure not to lose any of the springs.

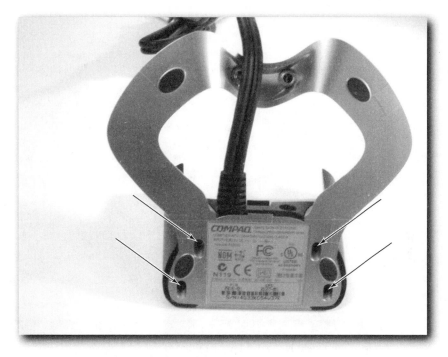

FIGURE 2-25: You need to undo these screws.

4. The bit inside that you are interested in is the little circuit board that plugs directly into the iPAQ serial port when it rests in the cradle. This is the green board with the black socket and USB cable connected to it.

5. Carefully free the board from the slot in the cradle so you can work on it (see Figure 2-26). Be very careful when you are handling it because the USB cable wires can easily break off of the board. If they do break, it's not the end of the world—you can easily solder the connections if it happens; but as always, it's better to avoid it.

6. You now need a cable with a GPS connector on one end. On this, three wires are of interest to you—from pin 2, pin 3, and pin 4. The goal is to solder these three wires to the appropriate pin on the cradle. At first, there may seem to be a lot of pins, but you will be relieved to know that only twelve are used, the rest being frame grounds.

7. The two pins that are of interest to us are pins 7 and 8, as shown in Figure 2-27. Pin 7 in the cradle needs to be connected to the wire from pin 2 on the Garmin eTrex connector, while pin 8 should be connected to the wire connected to pin 3. The easiest way to do this is by soldering the wire, but because the pins are so small and fragile, you do need to take care. It may test your soldering skills to get it right!

FIGURE 2-26: Carefully remove the circuit board from the cradle.

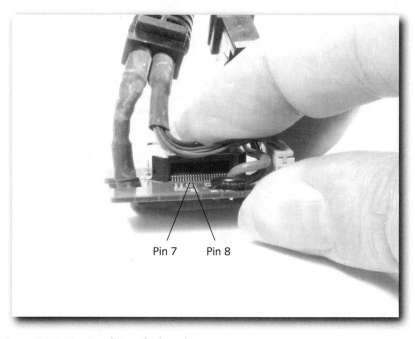

FIGURE 2-27: Pins 7 and 8 on the board.

Note

The easiest way to solder these is to heat up the wire from the cable, coat that in solder, and then put the coated wire against the appropriate pin. Using the soldering iron, heat up the appropriate pin in the cradle and when the solder melts, take the soldering iron away to fix it. This minimizes the risk of short circuits and splashing solder on something important.

8. Make a hole in the cradle exterior for the wire to come out of. Once you have done that, reassemble the cradle and then confirm that you can access your GPS from the iPAQ via the cradle.

Testing the Connection

The easiest way to test the connection is to use simple software, and software doesn't come much simpler than WinFast Navigator. This application is available free for download (the best, most reliable source for this can be found at www.pocketgpsworld.com/modules.php?name= Downloads&d_op=getit&lid=15) and can be installed and up and running on a Pocket PC device in minutes. Once installed, you should find Navigator showing on your Start menu.

Set your GPS to the NMEA data transfer protocol (more than 95 percent of units support this standard, and although it is old and a bit slow compared to the more modern SiRF, it is still likely to remain popular for a long time to come). Now connect the GPS to the cable connected to the cradle and seat the iPAQ in the cradle. Tap View and then Diagnostics. This will present you with another screen devoid of data, as shown in Figure 2-28. This is the diagnostics screen, and it's best to be sitting on this when you try to connect.

Note

You can find more information on these protocols in Chapter 9.

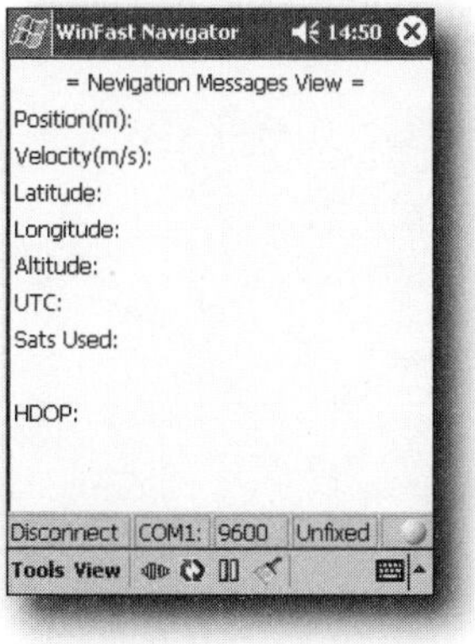

FIGURE 2-28: WinFast Navigator

If you don't see any data appear onscreen when connected, there is a problem somewhere — usually the wrong settings have been input. Connecting to the GPS unit can involve quite a lot of trial and error until you find the correct settings.

Now tap Tools followed by Settings and you will see the window shown in Figure 2-29.

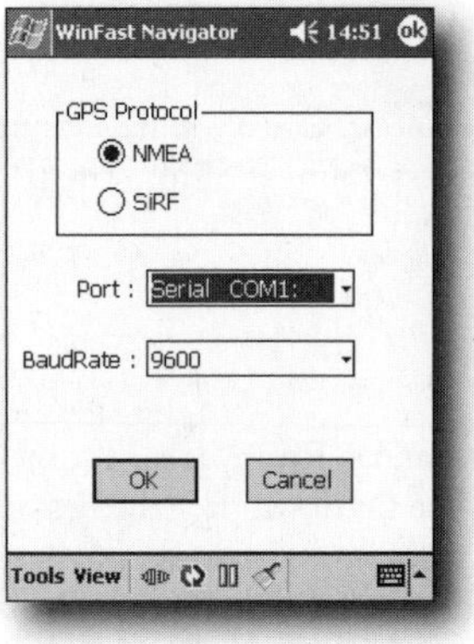

FIGURE 2-29: The settings window

This shows you the protocols available (e.g., NMEA and SiRF), the serial port on which you will connect, and the baud rate to use.

I recommend that you always try out NMEA first, so make sure this is selected. When it comes to baud rate (the rate at which communication should occur, measured in bits per second), generally NMEA prefers to use 4800, so make sure it's set to that.

For the Port setting, you know that you are connecting to a GPS receiver that plugs into the bottom of the sync port, and most of the time this is regarded as Serial1 COM1, so you can set it to this.

Tap the OK button. You should be taken back to the Development window in WinFast Navigator, where you should see a screen like the one shown in Figure 2-30.

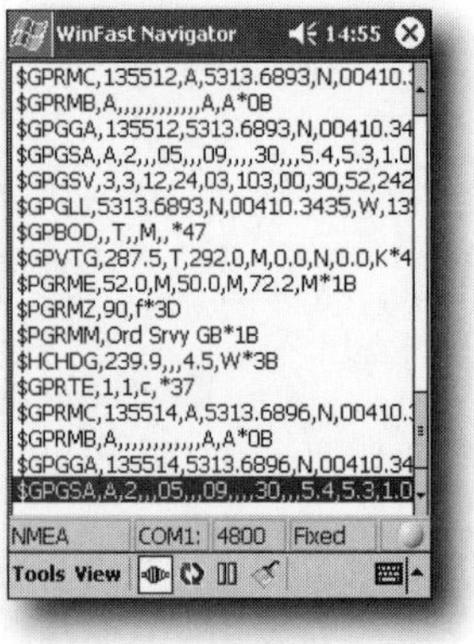

FIGURE 2-30: Development window in WinFast

If you don't, then you must have the wrong settings. Go back and try some alternative settings. Once you can successfully see data, you know it's working right.

Making Combo Cables

By now you've probably figured out how to make combo cables. First make one cable and then attach the other kind of cable to the spare pins, joining them together. It's really quite simple.

Many people seem confused about what to do with the two grounds that they end up with (a data ground and a power ground). The answer is simple: connect them together. That configuration works perfectly.

Another question that people have is how they should join the two cables together robustly, so as not to strain the joints. Over the years, I've found the best solution involves a combination of tape (both electrical and duct tape), followed by a few well-placed plastic ties (to take the strain). Another way to keep cables under control is to use a strip of shrink wrap.

Note that if you are making a combo cable, keep an eye on the wiring and make sure that it is both tidy and sound, as the last thing you want is a wire coming loose and causing a short circuit that could kill your GPS receiver.

Making Multi Cables

By now you also probably know how to make a multi-ended cable. All you need are the appropriate connectors and enough wire. The more you add, the more complex the cable will look, so you will need to keep track of which wires and parts go where — the last thing you want to end up with is a cable with a GPS connector at both ends (unless, that is, you want to transfer data between two GPS receivers).

I would suggest that for more complex cables, you make detailed notes and use your multimeter regularly during construction of the cable to ensure that everything works right.

Summary

This chapter has been all about cables — types of cables, making cables, and using cables. It's amazing what you can do with a GPS unit on its own, but add a cable and a PC or mobile device to the equation and the horizons really open up! In addition, GPS receivers need a lot of power, so making a cable that enables you to save a little battery power when you are in the car is always welcome. This enables you to save the battery power for when you are on foot and away from a 12-volt supply. In the next chapter, you'll find out that you are never too far away for a 12-volt supply, no matter where you are!

Have fun creating custom cables!

Power Hacks

Without power, even the best GPS receiver is nothing more than just an interesting box that does nothing. Given that a GPS unit has to pick up signals from satellites that orbit the globe at an altitude of 12,000 miles (19,200 km) and complete two rotations around the Earth every day, it's easy to see why there is a fair amount of power drain by the antenna in order to pick up and decode the signal. Add to that the power load of processing the data and displaying it, and you see that two or four small batteries aren't going to last too long under these conditions.

This chapter describes some power hacks you can do to your GPS to improve battery life, and how to extend battery life by making use of external sources.

Note GPS devices that contain a rechargeable Lithium-Ion battery are appearing on the market now. While this is generally an advantage, it can also be a disadvantage if it runs out in the field and you don't have access to a suitable charger.

GPS Power Needs

On the whole, battery lifetimes aren't that bad, depending on what batteries you use. Most GPS receivers use either AA or AAA batteries, but not all AA or AAA batteries are created equal, as you'll see in the following sections.

Note For more information on batteries, a good website to visit is http://michaelbluejay.com/batteries.

Alkaline Batteries

A fresh set of alkaline AA batteries (see Figure 3-1) in a receiver such as the basic Garmin eTrex will last approximately 22 hours, while the top of the range eTrex (the Vista) will go through the same two AA batteries in about 12 hours.

FIGURE 3-1: AA alkaline batteries

Use poorer quality alkaline batteries and you will see a drop of a few hours in these times. If you try using cheaper zinc-carbon batteries, you will see a huge decline in battery lifespan. A set of AAs might last only a few hours.

Note In high-drain devices (which a GPS receiver most certainly is) cheap zinc-carbon batteries are a false economy and offer very poor performance.

Compared to other types of batteries, alkaline batteries have greater availability, are reasonably priced, and have a consistent lifespan (when using good brands). They often have a warranty against leakage and damage, and are packaged with expiration dates (again, when using good brands). However, they are costly, have a short lifespan, and are wasteful (not to mention environmentally unsound).

Lithium Batteries

If you are willing to spend more and get a set of lithium AA batteries (not to be confused with rechargeable ones), as shown in Figure 3-2, you will see a huge increase in battery life (two or four times what you get from alkaline AA batteries). However, these batteries can cost two to four times as much as good quality alkaline batteries.

FIGURE 3-2: AA lithium batteries

Lithium batteries have an excellent lifespan in use, and a very long shelf-life. They also offer excellent cold weather performance, and are lighter than alkaline or rechargeable batteries. However, they're generally not widely available; and as mentioned above, they are very expensive.

Rechargeable (NiMH) Batteries

By far, the best way to invest your money is on rechargeable batteries. Get the best possible batteries, which means choosing nickel-metal hydride batteries (NiMH), shown in Figure 3-3, rather than the older and inferior nickel-cadmium (NiCd) batteries. In addition, choose the batteries with the greatest capacity (over 2000 mAh, preferably 2300 mAh or greater). The rule is that the greater the mAh (milliamp hour) capacity, the longer the batteries will last. These batteries will initially be more costly than alkaline batteries — especially if you figure in the cost of the charger too — but they can be recharged hundreds, if not thousands, of times.

Although some systems on the market claim to be able to recharge ordinary alkaline batteries, I don't recommend them. They are not recommended by battery makers; and not only do they invalidate any warranty on the battery (such as the leakage warranty), but they also increase the risk of the battery damaging your device. Play it safe and get proper rechargeable batteries and chargers.

FIGURE 3-3: NiMH rechargeable batteries

Compared to other types of batteries, rechargeables have a good lifespan in use, and can be recharged repeatedly. They're environmentally friendly, and you can recharge them while you're on the move, using in-car chargers or solar chargers.

Some drawbacks to rechargeable batteries are that they are not widely available and they are very costly. They generally have a shorter life than alkaline batteries, and they don't handle cold weather as well as alkaline or lithium batteries. They also require recharging before first use, which can be inconvenient. Finally, some rechargeable batteries can be slightly smaller (in length) than alkaline batteries, which can make the device cut out if subjected to shock or vibration.

You should be sure to get two chargers. Get a fast charger for when you want batteries in a hurry (see Figure 3-4), and get a slower charger that you can use occasionally to recharge and recondition your batteries. Alternating between a fast charger and a slow charger is good for battery health and will guarantee you the best performance and lifespan from your batteries.

Make sure that your charger matches your batteries. Never use a charger that's not designed for the batteries you are charging.

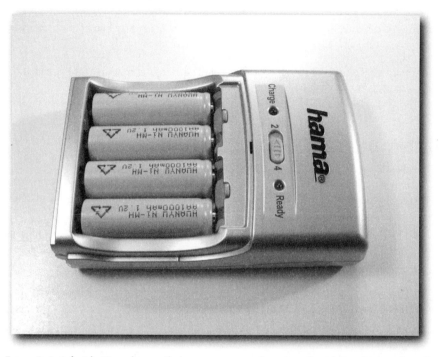

FIGURE 3-4: A fast battery charger that you can power from a wall socket or from a cigarette lighter socket in a car

For best performance and safety, never mix battery types. That includes mixing old and new batteries, different brands, and different types or capacities of rechargeable batteries. Mixing batteries can result in poorer performance and reduced lifespan, and creates a real risk of batteries exploding or rupturing.

Note A super battery-saving tip is to check the settings of your GPS. Look for an option or mode called Battery Saver or Low Power Mode. Not all receivers have this setting, but if yours does, it means that your GPS receiver consumes less power than normal, enabling it to last longer on a set of batteries than it typically would. The disadvantage of this setting is a slight decrease in accuracy because of the way in which the unit keeps a lock on the GPS satellites.

As for battery brands, there are plenty of good ones — Duracell, Energizer, Sanyo, Hama and Ansmann are all of excellent quality and backed by good warranties. Avoid buying cheap "no name" generic batteries, or batteries that are loose or out of blister packs — if these are DOA or leak all over your device, you are unlikely to have any warranty to fall back on.

Another thing to remember is that some GPS receivers contain a small button cell, similar to a watch backup battery (usually non-user replaceable), that is used to store some data in memory in case the main batteries are depleted or removed. However, if you store your GPS for a long period of time without batteries or with dead batteries, this can cause a drain of the backup battery. If this is battery is run down, then the device may not work properly and will need repairing. Therefore, when storing a GPS unit with this kind of backup battery, always be sure to fit new (or recently recharged) batteries and check them regularly.

Note Never put a GPS receiver that contains old batteries into long-term storage, as this increases the risk of damage from leaking batteries.

Battery Do's and Don'ts

The following guidelines will help you get the most from your batteries:

- Recharge NiCd and NiMH batteries as soon as possible after discharge to maintain peak performance.

- Never store batteries loose in a bag or pocket, which increases the risk of a short circuit that can result in fire or injury. Store batteries in a proper battery box or holder.

- Store batteries at room temperature. There is no need to store batteries in a freezer or refrigerator to maintain peak performance.

- Never use batteries after their expiration date.

- Never dispose of batteries in a fire, as this can result in an explosion and cause serious injury.

- Extreme temperatures reduce battery life. Keep battery-powered devices away from extreme heat or cold.

- Take care that you insert batteries properly into your device. Some devices that use three or more batteries might still function with one battery inserted incorrectly, but this can cause battery damage that can potentially damage your device.

- Dispose of used batteries responsibly. For online guidelines visit www.duracell.com/care_disposal/disposal.asp.

Power Hacks

There is no doubt that having auxiliary power (in addition to the internal batteries) is handy when out and about with your GPS. The easiest way to accomplish this is to carry a stash of batteries and replace them as they run out. This method, while effective, is very expensive and not very eco-friendly.

When in a vehicle, another option is to use a power cord that draws power from the automotive 12-volt system via a cigarette lighter socket. Chapter 2 describes these kinds of cables and how to make them.

Note Refer to Chapter 2 for details about how to build your own power cord cables.

But what about when you are on the move? How can you supply power to your GPS receiver when walking, hiking, or geocaching?

Carrying Your Own 12-Volt Power Supply

One thing that you can do is carry your own 12-volt power supply around with you. No, this doesn't mean having to lug a heavy car battery that can spill sulphuric acid all over the place! Other options are available to you.

One thing you can do is buy a portable lead-acid battery designed for large flashlights. They contain a cigarette lighter socket and often come with a case and belt loops. These batteries usually have fuses, as shown in Figure 3-5. They come in a variety of sizes; generally, the larger the battery the longer it lasts. The downside, however, is that the larger the battery, the heavier the battery.

These packs will give you hours of additional battery time and the batteries can be recharged when you get back to your vehicle by plugging them into the cigarette socket. Charging back at base is via a charger that plugs into a mains power outlet.

However, you might have handy batteries suitable for this job lying about. If you have an old PC uninterruptible power supply (UPS) unit lying around (the kind of thing that any self-respecting geek would have!), these typically contain a battery similar to the battery packs that you can buy for flashlights, as shown in Figure 3-6.

FIGURE 3-5: A fused 12-volt lead-acid battery

FIGURE 3-6: A lead-acid battery from a UPS device

Usually, you remove the battery through a hatch at the back of the UPS unit (remember to disconnect it from the mains power supply first). Once you have the battery out, you will need a few things to complete the build:

- Wire (automotive wire like the type used to wire in spot lamps is ideal)
- A cigarette lighter socket
- A fuse and fuse holder (such as those used in an automotive spotlight or in car stereo parts; a 2A fuse will do just fine)
- Connectors to fit the connectors on the battery (sizes will vary and depend on the battery)
- A small car charger (to charge the battery when not in use)
- Some sort of case for the battery (heavy-duty nylon or cordura(works just fine)

Assembly is easy. Wire the cigarette lighter socket to the battery, negative (–) to the frame of the socket and positive (+) to the center post, remembering to add a fuse holder with the fuse in the wire. Test the whole circuit with a multimeter before plugging a GPS power cord into the socket.

These small lead-acid batteries are extremely handy auxiliary power packs and keep their charge for a long time in storage (recharge them every three months when not in use). A sticker on the side of the battery (see Figure 3-7) is ideal for keeping track of charge dates!

Lead-Acid Battery
Charge history

Last charge . . . / . . . / . . .

Next charge . . . / . . . / . . .

FIGURE 3-7: Suggested information to keep on the battery

Caution

When you are outdoors, take great care when carrying a lead-acid battery. Any damage or crack in the battery will leak dangerous, corrosive sulphuric acid.

If you want an alternative to lead-acid batteries, the following section describes how you can make simple battery packs from ordinary batteries (or rechargeable batteries).

Battery Packs

Making a battery pack isn't hard. All you need is a holder for the batteries and some way to wire that to the GPS you use. The easiest way to wire it up is through the GPS connector.

Before continuing, however, first a little battery theory. If you take two AA batteries and put them in a circuit end to end (see Figure 3-8), the voltage will equal 1.5 volts plus 1.5 volts, resulting in 3 volts.

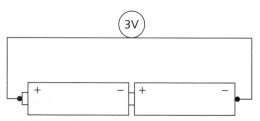

FIGURE 3-8: Two AA batteries end to end provide 3 volts

This is called putting the batteries *in series*. However, if you place the batteries in *parallel*, that is, take a wire and connect them positive to positive and take another wire and connect that negative to negative (see Figure 3-9), and then measure the voltage across the two wires, you will get a voltage measurement of 1.5 volts.

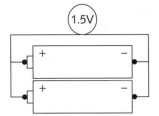

FIGURE 3-9: Two AA batteries
in parallel provide 1.5 volts

However, there is a side effect. The capacity of the batteries is increased. Therefore, if you take four AAs and put them into two pairs of two in series and join the two pairs in parallel, as shown in Figure 3-10, the output voltage would still be 3 volts, but the capacity (or how long the batteries would last) would be doubled.

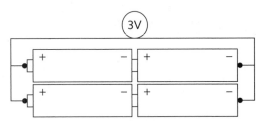

FIGURE 3-10: Four AA batteries arranged to provide 3 volts

As long as you have no more than two batteries in series, you can add a few sets in parallel to get additional power from the system. This is true no matter what kind of battery you are dealing with (although rechargeable batteries generally run at a lower voltage — about 1.2 volts — than alkaline batteries do).

Remember that you aren't limited to using AA batteries. The bigger the battery, the more power you'll get from it!

The power order of typical alkaline batteries is as follows:

Battery Size	Nominal Voltage (V)	Approximate Capacity (mAh)
AAA	1.5	1100
AA	1.5	2800
C	1.5	7500
D	1.5	15000
9V	9	580

As you can see, a typical alkaline D-cell battery has approximately six to eight times the capacity of a AA NiMH battery. The disadvantage is one of weight — twelve AAA batteries weigh about the same as one D-cell, but the D-cell has 14 times the capacity.

Now that NiMH AA batteries are capable of capacities of 2500 mAh, they are getting close to the capacities of their alkaline rivals.

What You Need

This section describes what you need to build a battery pack. Remember that there are many ways to build one and the final pack can be of any shape. The only important caveat is that you don't subject the GPS unit to too much voltage; if you stick to the normal battery voltages you'll be fine.

For example, a Garmin eTrex has two AA batteries and therefore runs at 3 volts, while a Garmin GPS III+ runs on four AA batteries, providing the operating voltage of 6 volts.

Note

Feeding more voltage through the GPS than it needs serves no purpose. If you feed it only what it needs, you avoid wasting batteries (and carrying extra weight), and supplying wasted additional voltage.

Batteries

A good battery to use is the AA battery because it is quite light and easily available. If you want greater capacity, then you might want to consider using D-cells, which have a far greater lifespan but are heavier to carry.

Battery Holder

Battery holders can be almost anything that can hold a battery. You can use a specific battery box (available from electronic outlets), a box you have lying around your home or office that you wire up, or something that you may already own that holds batteries.

A good example of something that already has a battery inside is a flashlight. Moreover, a flashlight has the added advantage of having a ready-made switch (although you may want to wire in a different switch because you might not want the flashlight on when you are running your GPS from the batteries).

Wiring and Connections

Figuring out the wiring and connections isn't hard if you follow the instructions in Chapter 2. All you need to do is hook up a connector suited to your GPS to a length of wire (covered in Chapter 2) and solder that wire to the connection in your battery pack, paying special attention to ensuring that you connect the positive and negative terminals correctly (see Figure 3-11). Load the holder with batteries and away you go!

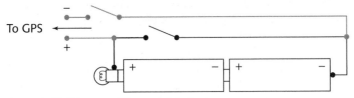

To GPS
−
+

FIGURE 3-11: Diagram of the completed setup

This kind of battery pack gives you great flexibility. You can either keep it in your pocket and use it only when needed or you can run your GPS from the battery pack and remove the pack once it is spent and switch to the internal batteries.

A Different Kind of Battery Pack

You can also use different kinds of batteries, and you're not limited to 1.5-volt batteries. A good battery to choose is the CR123A lithium cell (nonrechargeable) commonly used in photography (see Figure 3-12).

FIGURE 3-12: CR123A lithium cell

With two of these, a little wiring to put them in parallel, a connector, and a Kodak Advantix film canister (see Figure 3-13), you can create a small, simple, high-capacity battery pack.

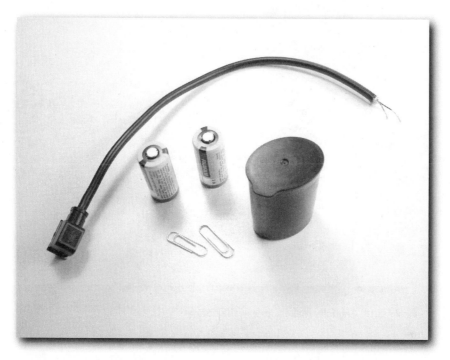

FIGURE 3-13: Simple starting material

Here's how you build this pack:

1. Take a Kodak Advantix film canister and make a small pinhole near the bottom on the side; as shown in Figure 3-14.

2. Put a small amount of modeling clay into the bottom of the film canister. You will need to experiment with the amount that you use here. This will be used to push the batteries up against the terminals. Figure 3-15 shows a cutaway of what you are aiming for here.

FIGURE 3-14: Carefully make a hole in the bottom

Cutaway of film pot

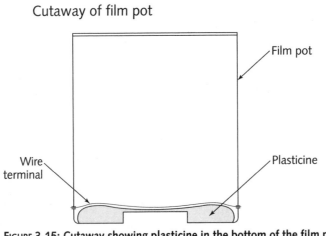

FIGURE 3-15: Cutaway showing plasticine in the bottom of the film pot

3. Take a paper clip and bend it as shown in Figure 3-16. This will act as the terminal connector for the battery's negative terminals.

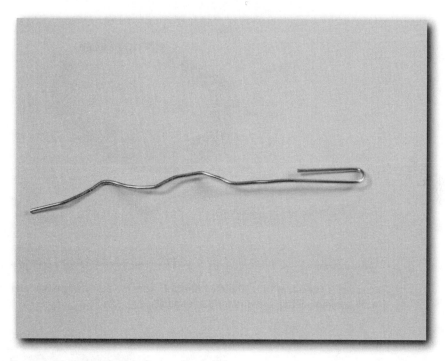

FIGURE 3-16: Terminal made from a paper clip

4. Now for the positive terminals at the top. Take the lid of the film pot and make two notches through the rim of it, cutting it at the narrow ends of the lid (at the points of the ovals in the lid). These notches will accommodate the terminal at the top of the pack.

5. Take a second bit of plasticine and another paper clip and repeat what you did at the bottom of the film canister, as shown in Figure 3-17. This figure also shows the notches cut in the lid.

6. Now you need a GPS connector properly wired to a suitable wire. Then, take the wire from the negative pin of the connector and solder that to the paper clip at the bottom of the film canister, as shown in Figure 3-18, and then solder the wire from the positive pin to the paper clip at the top. You will need to make a small hole in the lid to enable the wire through. Add a small drop of hot glue to make it waterproof.

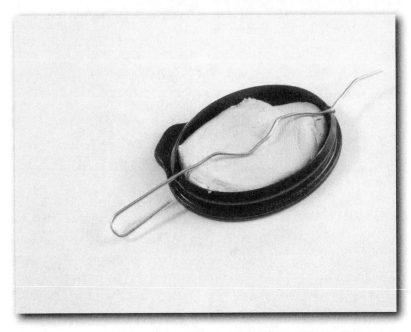

FIGURE 3-17: The top of the completed film pot. Note the notches at either end of the lid accommodating the wire for the terminals.

FIGURE 3-18: Hot glue for waterproofing

7. Finally, test the connections to make sure that they are sound, and add a small bit of tape around the base of the pot (to cover the paper-clip holes). If you want, you can wrap the entire pot in tape (as I've done in Figure 3-19).

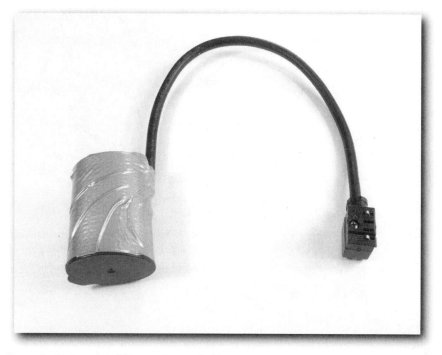

FIGURE 3-19: Completed film pot battery holder

That's it! Project done! These battery packs offer a great lifespan (a good 8 to 10 times the lifespan of normal alkaline AA batteries). Another advantage is that these batteries also perform well in cold conditions, and are far superior to alkaline batteries.

Alternative Power Supplies

What if you could carry something with you that could, under the right circumstances, give you unlimited power, a source that wouldn't run out. What am I talking about? Solar power, of course.

What you need to harness the power of the sun (apart from clear skies) is solar panels. Don't worry, you don't need an enormous panel like the kind on a satellite. In fact, you can find reasonably small, portable solar panels specifically designed to recharge batteries and power small devices. You can purchase a unit similar to the one shown in Figure 3-20 for under $50.

FIGURE 3-20: Solar charger

With these kinds of solar panels, you have power for a variety of applications:

- Charging batteries
- Outputting a 12-volt supply for use with a power cord, as shown in Figure 3-21
- Outputting a lower voltage

All you need, to have all the power you want, is sunlight. If you are traveling from and returning to a base camp daily, then you may be better off using the system to recharge batteries. You can also strap it to your backpack and use it on the move, as shown in Figure 3-22.

You can also use the solar charger system to power other devices too, such as cell phones.

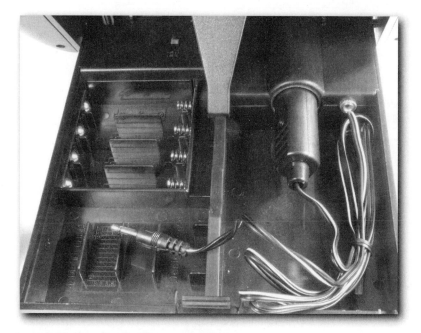

FIGURE 3-21: 12-volt output from a solar charger

FIGURE 3-22: Solar panel attached to a backpack. This is
an ideal way to position such panels when on the move.

Summary

This chapter described several ways to keep your GPS working for longer when in the field. You learned how to reduce battery consumption, how to build auxiliary power packs, how to use a 12-volt supply, and even how to use solar power.

This chapter has provided you with a variety of options for keeping your system going when the internal batteries are exhausted.

In the next chapter, you'll move on from powering your GPS to looking at antenna hacks.

Antenna Hacks

Making the most out of your GPS depends on getting a good signal from the satellites, which orbit the Earth at an altitude of around 20,000 kilometers (12,000 miles). This signal isn't a strong one; it's roughly equivalent to detecting the light from a 25-watt lightbulb from 16,000 kilometers (10,000 miles) away.

In other words, without a good signal from the satellites (at least three of them, preferably more), you aren't going to be able to use GPS at all, or the information it gives you will be erroneous. You can solve this problem by adding an external antenna to your GPS unit.

This chapter examines the GPS antenna and how you can maximize a weak signal when you are on the move.

The GPS Antenna

One part that all GPS receivers have in common is the antenna, whose job is to receive the signal from the satellites and pass that signal on for processing.

The signal the antenna picks up is a UHF signal with a frequency of 1575.2 MHz (this is the civilian, unencrypted frequency; the military signal uses 1227.6 MHz). This frequency offers all-weather navigation capability, but is blocked by walls, ceilings, and even trees.

GPS receivers usually come with one of the following antenna types attached:

- Quad-helix
- Patch

Receivers such as the Garmin III (shown in Figure 4-1), and most Magellan units, make use of the quad-helix style antenna, while units such as the Garmin eTrex (see Figure 4-2) use the patch antenna.

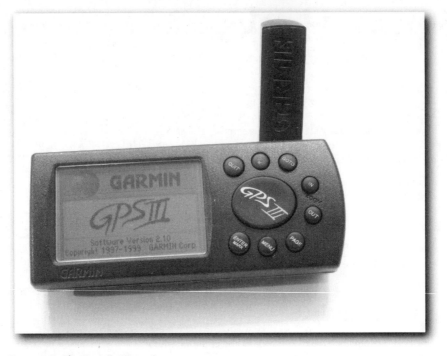

FIGURE 4-1: The Garmin III receiver

The debate as to which is best is a complex one, and there are pros and cons to each:

- Patch antennas are smaller.

- Patch antennas draw less power.

- Quad-helix antennas are usually bulky and generally protrude from the unit.

- Quad-helix antennas are less prone to having the signal from the satellites blocked (or *masked*, to use the technical term) by the receiver and the person holding the GPS.

- The surface of the GPS over the patch antenna is prone to catching rain and losing the signal (simply because it is a flat surface).

A lot of myth and rumor surrounds antennas. Many people believe that quad-helix antennas offer greater performance under tree cover and are less prone to signal loss in valleys and in urban areas. However, based on personal experience, I've not found this to be the case. Usually, such phenomena can be attributed to the particular GPS unit, assuming that your course and speed are unchanged and retaining a false signal lock.

FIGURE 4-2: The Garmin eTrex receiver

A good discussion on antenna sensitivity can be found at www.gpsinformation.net/
main/gpsant.htm. Generally, I don't really think it matters much which type of antenna
you use, but the one difference between the two types of antenna is how you hold them.

Quad-Helix Orientation

A quad-helix antenna works best when the antenna is placed in the vertical position (as shown
in Figure 4-3). This gives the antenna the greatest sky coverage and offers the best signal
reception.

Some GPS receivers allow you to place the antenna at odd angles, which enables you to get the
antenna in the right orientation no matter how the GPS is being held or how it is mounted.
However, make sure that the antenna is always vertical and not at odd angles (such as the one
shown in Figure 4-4).

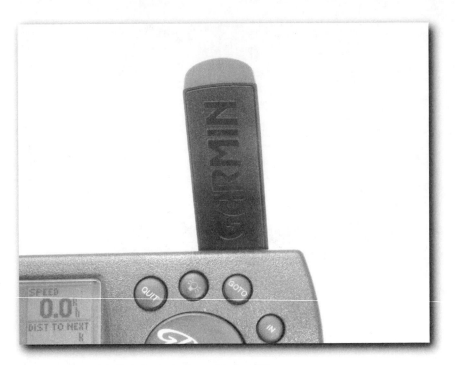

FIGURE 4-3: A quad-helix antenna in the vertical position

When you are holding the GPS on the move, try to hold it with the antenna as vertical as possible and as far away from the body as comfortably possible to reduce the degree to which your body shields the signal.

Note | The human body is very effective at shielding the microwave signal from GPS because your body is largely made up of water, and water is an effective absorber of microwave frequency electromagnetic radiation.

Patch Antenna Orientation

How you hold a patch antenna is completely different from how you hold a quad-helix antenna. To get the best out of these antennas, you want to hold them so that they are *horizontal* to the ground (see Figure 4-5).

This is by far the best orientation for patch antennas — the closer they are to being vertical, the less efficient they are. This may be a big part of the reason why some people think that the quad-helix antenna is better than the patch antenna. People have a natural tendency to hold a GPS receiver in a vertical position.

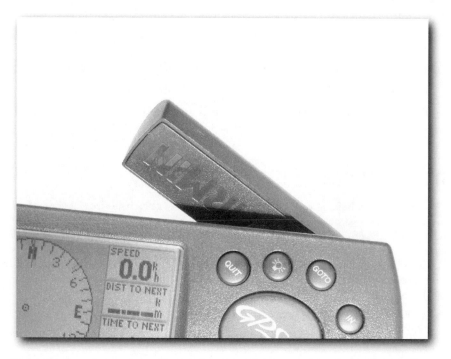

FIGURE 4-4: An antenna at an odd angle is not as effective as one in the vertical position.

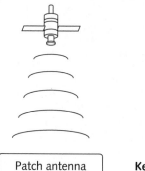

| Patch antenna | **Keep level** |

FIGURE 4-5: Horizontal is the best orientation
for a patch antenna.

Best Performance Summary

Before moving on, let's look at a quick "best performance summary" for built-in antennas for
GPS receivers:

1. Hold the antenna as far away from your body (and other human or animal bodies) as possible and away from other electrical devices, as these can all degrade the accuracy of your receiver.

2. If your GPS uses a patch antenna, keep it as close to horizontal as possible.

3. If your antenna is a quad-helix antenna, keep it as close to vertical as possible.

4. Whatever type of antenna you use, keep it as dry as possible — a coating of water droplets will severely affect performance.

External Antennas

One problem with holding your GPS in a nearly vertical or nearly horizontal orientation is that it can quickly become uncomfortable and cause you to start walking oddly. If you are in a vehicle, then the problem isn't one of orientation but actually getting the signal to the GPS, as most receivers find it hard to get a lock to the satellites when inside a car or boat. A far better idea is to place the antenna away from the GPS receiver. Some GPS receivers come with either a removable antenna or a socket that enables you to hook up an auxiliary external antenna to the device.

Figure 4-6 shows a Garmin III GPS receiver with the original antenna removed.

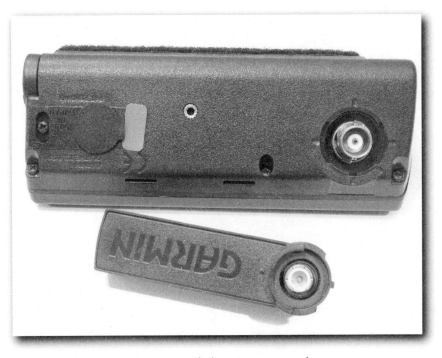

FIGURE 4-6: A Garmin III GPS receiver with the antenna removed

The connector shown in Figure 4-6 is called a BNC connector, and you can get many types of external antennas that connect to this port. Figure 4-7 shows a Lowe external antenna attached to the Garmin GPS III.

FIGURE 4-7: Lowe external antenna attached to the Garmin III

This antenna has a magnetic base, and draws power from the GPS unit itself. It is a patch antenna and offers better performance than the original antenna.

The antenna also has a strong magnet at the base (see Figure 4-8) that enables it to be firmly attached to a metal surface (such as the roof of a vehicle).

The BNC-style connector isn't the only style of external antenna connector available. Figure 4-9 shows the connector on a Garmin 76 GPS receiver. This is called an *MCX connector*, and it is much smaller than the BNC connector.

But they get even smaller! Figure 4-9 shows the connector on the Haicom Compact Flash GPS receiver. This is an MMCX connector (or Mini MCX or MicroMate). This connector is much smaller than the MCX connector, but smaller also means that the threads on the connectors are more delicate and prone to damage.

FIGURE 4-8: The external antenna has a strong magnet at the base for affixing to a car roof.

These antennas either replace the existing antenna on the unit or they bypass the built-in antenna after they're attached.

External antennas enable you to place the antenna in a different location than the actual receiver. This means that you (or whoever is holding the unit) will obscure the signal a lot less. It also means you can take the unit into an area with poor signal coverage and put the antenna where reception is better.

Some applications ideally suited to the use of an external antenna include the following:

- **Indoor use:** If you want to bring a GPS signal indoors, an external antenna is a great way to do it with little fuss.

- **Car use:** If you want to use a GPS in a car, especially a car that has metalized glass installed that blocks microwave radiation, an external antenna might be a possible solution that will enable you to use a GPS.

- **Boat use:** The antenna can be attached outside and the GPS kept inside, away from exposure to the elements.

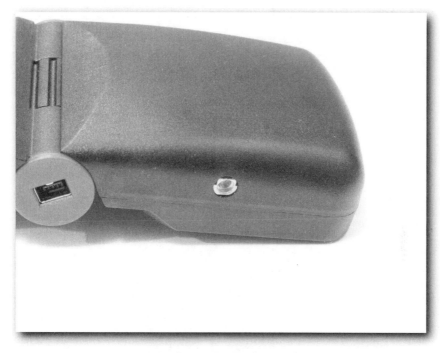

FIGURE 4-9: MMCX connector on a Haicom Compact Flash GPS

- **Mobile use:** Place the external antenna in the top of your backpack while out and about. This can really help to boost the signal! Usually, the higher the antenna, the better the signal.

As with most things, there are disadvantages to using external antennas:

- **Clumsiness:** All the additional cables can be a pain, as they can easily get in a tangle.

- **Power:** External antennas draw more power from the GPS unit. More power means the batteries don't last as long. Some external antennas come with their own power source, but remember that this means you have something else to keep charged up while on the move!

- **Antenna loss:** If the GPS has a removable antenna, make sure that you don't lose the original!

- **Cable length:** The longer the cable you have attached to the antenna, the greater the signal loss. This isn't a problem when you are routing the cable over a short distance, but if you are routing the cable over a long distance, then this could be a problem. Keep cables as short as possible; and above all, avoid keeping unnecessary loops of cable in the setup.

Antenna Placement

Where you place an external antenna is just as important as how you hold a GPS receiver. When using a fixed or semi-fixed antenna, you need to carefully consider where you place it in order to get the best coverage.

On a car, place the antenna as high as possible. The roof is the best place for it, while the hood and near the flat glass panels are worse. The area around the hood has high electromagnetic interference, while glass and flat metal surfaces cause signal reflections and signal loss (see Figure 4-10).

FIGURE 4-10: Good and bad placements for antenna on a car

Another possible area for placement is inside the front or rear plastic bumper, although bear in mind that small impacts can damage the antenna.

The problem with in-car use of GPS is that most people think that because they can get a satellite lock on their GPS when it is in their shirt pocket, in the car, they don't need to worry about antenna placement. The truth is that poor antenna placement in a car, especially using a GPS signal from inside the vehicle that has traveled through the metal skin of the vehicle, is likely to result in a very inaccurate signal. If your vehicle has tinted metalized windows, this can severely degrade the GPS signal you receive, and an external antenna becomes a must.

For trucks and vans, the best place for the antenna is going to be the cab or trailer roof. Both of these offer fantastic views of the sky.

Around buildings, keep the antenna away from walls. If possible, either put the antenna high up or at least well away from walls and obstructions. Keep the antenna away from trees (see Figure 4-11).

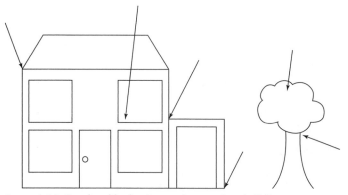

FIGURE 4-11: Good and bad antenna placement on buildings

In urban areas that have a large number of tall buildings, higher is better because it eliminates multipath errors caused by signal reflection (see Figure 4-12).

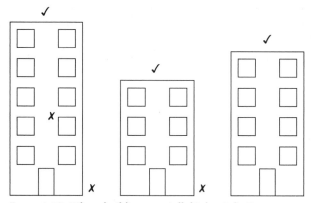

FIGURE 4-12: Where buildings are tall, higher is better.

Note one problem with the "higher is better" rule: lightning. A single lightning strike can completely destroy a GPS receiver. This is especially a problem with placing antennas on buildings.

If you are going to have a permanent antenna fixed on your building, then prevention is far better than the cure. You are safer if you attach lightning *arrestors* to the line.

There are several manufacturers of lightening arrestors. Here are a few to get you started:

- **Symmetricom:** www.symmetricom.com
- **PolyPhaser:** www.polyphaser.com
- **Radiall:** www.radiall.com
- **LightningMaster:** www.lightningmaster.com

This solution may seem pricey for something that may never be needed, but if you live in an area where lightning is common, consider how much it will cost you if your antenna is hit and you lose your GPS.

In addition, it's not just the GPS that you can lose — if your GPS happens to be connected to a PC at the time of the strike, you could also lose the PC and possibly even others connected on the same network if you happen to use one.

Other Things to Avoid

Here are a few other things that you should avoid when it comes to using external antennas:

- Knots and kinks in cables damage the interior of the coax and can cause signal loss. Keep the cables as straight as possible, and if the cable does have to travel around corners, don't make the loop too tight.

- Be careful about bringing cables in through windows and door frames, as crushing can severely damage the cable.

- Another way to damage a cable is to stretch it, so take care to avoid this. If you install the cable in warm weather, make sure you leave additional slack in the cable, as it will contract when the temperature drops.

- Keep the cable short and reduce the number of connectors: The greater the length of cable and the more connectors and joints you have in it, the more signal loss you will experience.

Reradiating Antennas

Another type of antenna you will come across is called the *reradiating antenna*. This is a combination GPS antenna and retransmitting unit.

It works as follows:

1. The main antenna picks up the GPS signal just like any other GPS antenna.

2. This signal is fed down a cable to a signal reradiator.

3. The signal reradiator takes the signal and reradiates it. This signal is then picked up by the antenna on the GPS.

This sequence is summarized in Figure 4-13.

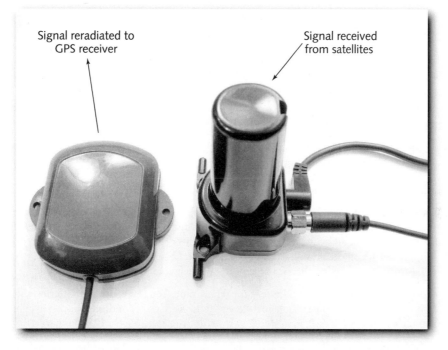

Signal reradiated to GPS receiver

Signal received from satellites

FIGURE 4-13: Reradiating antennas catch and retransmit the signals received from the GPS satellites.

There are two types of reradiating antenna:

- Personal reradiating antenna
- Communal reradiating antenna

Note Remember that a reradiating antenna can only pick up satellites that are above the horizon and not obscured by buildings or rock faces. Reradiating antennas can't perform the impossible, they are just able to make better use of the existing signal.

Personal Reradiating Antenna

Personal reradiating antennas have a short-range reradiator that can re-transmit the GPS signal over a relatively short distance (between 40 and 60 centimeters). The reradiator is usually fixed to the GPS close to the antenna on the device. Usually, it is fastened on with Velcro fasteners and can be removed when needed. These antennas are great for in-car use or other applications for which you only want the signal to be transmitted over a short range.

Communal Reradiating Antenna

The communal reradiating antenna reradiator can transmit the GPS signal over a larger range than the personal reradiating antenna. Usually, these reradiators are capable of transmitting over a range of three to four meters.

Reradiating Antenna Considerations

The following sections describe some considerations for you to bear in mind when you are choosing and using reradiating antennas.

Power

Reradiating antennas require power. This power supply usually needs a 12-volt DC source, and a lead-acid battery is normally ideal. In a car or on a boat, you can tap into the existing electrical system. This will give you an almost unlimited power supply (given fuel and no mechanical failure). If you are on the move, you can use a portable 12-volt lead-acid battery. If your antenna uses AA or 9-volt batteries, then make sure that you have an ample supply of these.

You don't have to use a lead-acid battery the whole time. You can use other batteries, such as AA or even D cells in series, which enables you to make a lighter and safer pack. If you use rechargeable batteries, it isn't as wasteful and you don't need to have a 12-volt charger.

Another power option is to use a solar charger to top up a battery pack. One such system is the SmartSolar solar panel and battery pack shown in Figure 4-14.

The 10 NiMH batteries provide a 12-volt power supply and can deliver 1 Ah of power. This is enough to keep a reradiating antenna working for several hours without recharge.

Range

If you want to use a reradiating antenna with more than one GPS unit, you will need the communal type that can serve more than one GPS. Technically, there is no limit to how many GPS receivers a single reradiating antenna can serve — as long as they all fall within the range of the re-transmitting antenna.

Remember that reradiating antennas can mask the proper GPS signal for those around you who may need to use it.

Tidiness

Reradiating antennas are made up of a lot of cables, including the cable taking the power to the reradiator and the coaxial cable to the antenna. Keep these cables tidy to prevent damage and tangles.

FIGURE 4-14: SmartSolar solar charger and power pack

Setting Up a Reradiating Antenna in a Car

This section describes how to set up a reradiating antenna in a car. Before you start, you have to make some decisions:

- Consider how you are going to power your reradiating antenna and your GPS while it's in the car. If your car has a 12-volt cigarette adapter, then that can be used (add a splitter if you need to double up on the sockets available). If you need to tap into the power supply to hardwire the power supply, remember to add a fuse to the circuit (2A will work).

- Consider antenna placement carefully. The best place is the highest point on the vehicle. Normally, the spot that has the best exposure to the sky is the roof, but if you usually have a roof rack, then this might need to be reconsidered.

- Is the antenna going to be permanently fixed to the vehicle or is it temporary? If it is going to be a permanent addition to your vehicle, I suggest you attach it using stainless-steel screws or bolts, and use silicone to waterproof any holes you make. You can achieve a temporary setup with a magnetically mounted antenna. These antennas often have a low profile, so they can be left attached and will withstand normal driving speeds and high winds. For a permanent antenna, you should take the cable into the vehicle through a hole near the antenna. For a temporary job, it's a better idea to take the cable in through the door frame. There is usually enough give in the rubber seal, and as long as you don't route it at the top of the door, it is unlikely to let in water.

- Consider where you are going to place the reradiator. The usual place for this is on the front windshield, attached using the suction cups that are supplied with most reradiating antenna units.

After you have answered the preceding questions, you can set up the reradiating gear:

1. Place the antenna in a suitable spot. Whether you plan to fix the antenna permanently or temporarily, attach it temporarily initially so that you can test the location before drilling holes in the bodywork.

2. Route the cable. The passenger door is the typical route into the vehicle (unless you are planning on a permanent connection — but even then, don't drill the holes just yet!). Tape can be used to fix the cables and keep them in place, as can cable ties. Don't use wire — this can cut through the cable. Route the cable from the antenna to the location you have chosen for the reradiator (on the front window).

3. Sort out the power. Route the wiring to the spot where you plan on putting the reradiator.

4. Add the reradiator. Attach this securely using the suction cups and loop any remaining cables tidily to keep them under control.

Testing the System

Now it's time for a test drive with the GPS system running. This can be a simple test in which you drive around and examine your route afterwards or you can plot a few different routes and see if the GPS will take you there.

Also test the reception from the reradiator at various points in the vehicle. Remember that the signal from the reradiator is the same frequency as the signal from the GPS satellites (just brought a lot closer) so obstructions, especially people, can adversely affect the signal. If you find that the placement is less than ideal, try raising it higher.

If you have installed a temporary reradiating antenna system, you are not done. After your first drive around, you might decide that you want to make a few adjustments to the setup (moving the antenna or rerouting the cables differently).

Making the System Permanent

Now's the time to make the setup permanent (if that was what you had planned in the first place). Ensure that you're happy with the placement of the various antennas and cabling, and think about any changes or additions you might want to make to your vehicle in the near future that might mean undoing any work you do now. Moving something held in place with a suction cup is one thing; moving something after you have drilled holes for it is another.

Carrying a GPS Signal via Cable

You've already learned that cables that are too long or have unnecessary connectors cause signal loss—but how much signal loss? The following sections outline some of the variables that affect the answer to this question.

How Much Signal Do You Need?

Before we look at the losses, let's look at how much signal you need to get to your GPS in order for it to work.

For a high-gain (high-sensitivity) antenna (roughly 35 dB), most receivers can function properly with 12 dB +/- 2 dB attenuation (signal loss) from the antenna to the receiver input.

For a lower-gain (low-sensitivity) antenna (those in the 26 dB region), most receivers can function normally with 6 dB +/- 2 dB attenuation from the antenna to the receiver input.

Cable Losses

There is significant signal loss through a cable. What we are interested in is the signal loss at 1575.2 MHz. The following list of four different cable types shows the average signal loss you'll encounter (derived from data on www.belden.com):

- RG8 (Belden 9913F), 100ft: 7.5 dB attenuation

- RG213 (Belden 8267), 100ft: 12.0 dB attenuation

- RG142 (Belden 84142), 10ft: 2.0 dB attenuation

- RG58 (Belden 8919), 10ft: 2.7 dB attenuation

Therefore, putting the preceding information into context, the following table shows the maximum length of cable that you should be able to use.

Cable	Max Length Using High-Gain Antenna (feet)	Max Length Using Low-Gain Antenna (feet)
RG8	150	80
RG213	100	50
RG142	60	30
RG58	40	20

The better quality cable (generally, "more expensive") you use, the lower the attenuation and the less the signal loss. However, higher-quality cables cost more. If you want less attenuation over greater distances, the only option available to you is to spend the money.

You can also find rigid and semi-rigid cables that have better specification, but these will undoubtedly cost extra and the gains you get aren't going to be massive.

For more information on Belden cable, check out the Belden website at `http://bwccat.belden.com/ecat/jsp/index.jsp`.

Note Many people don't realize that lower-loss cable usually means thicker cable. The thicker the cable, the harder it is to get it around bends.

Connector Losses

It's not just the cables that attenuate; the connectors do too. Generally, each connector adds about 1.5 dB of signal loss into the system. However, if you are using cable with 75-ohm resistance on a 50-ohm system (these figures will be marked on most cables that you use, while connectors are sold with a particular resistance value stated), then this figure goes up to 3 dB. This combination is therefore considered to be a poor match and not recommended for GPS.

Note One example of a 75-ohm cable from Belden is the RG59.

Adding a connector at each end of the cable means you are looking at a minimum of 3 dB attenuation of signal, which alters the maximum cable lengths that you can have. Depending on whether your cable/antenna setup has one connector or two, you can figure this value into your calculations directly, as shown in the following table.

Cable (with connectors)	Max Length Using High-Gain Antenna	Max Length Using Low-Gain Antenna
RG8	110	45
RG213	75	35
RG142	40	15
RG58	30	<10

Note Splitters don't normally add to the total attenuation in the system because they generally contain signal boosters to compensate.

As you can see, even with the best cable, 100 feet (33 meters) is probably the best you can do if you want to ensure that you get a useable signal.

You can find numerous types of cable out there (many more than I have listed), so you might find the following website useful:

`www.timesmicrowave.com/cgi-bin/calculate.pl`

This site enables you to work out attenuation for a variety of cables at a variety of lengths and frequencies quickly and easily.

Using a Signal Repeater

Another way to bring a signal indoors — for example, into an office building in which you want to set up a PC time sync system on each floor — is to use a GPS *signal repeater*.

Note GPS signal repeaters are also great idea on bigger yachts and boats too.

For specific information on splitters and repeaters, helpful websites include the following:

- Coverage Solutions: www.coveragesolutions.net/gps.htm
- GPS Source: www.gpssource.com

A GPS repeater kit usually consists of an amplifier with a power supply and a passive antenna assembled on a mount for easy roof installation. The input from an active GPS roof antenna is amplified and retransmitted into the building.

These kits usually have an indoor range of about 250 feet (80 meters) and are easy to fit.

Installing these kits is easy because they are packaged with everything you need. All the parts are properly weatherproofed and all the attenuation measurements are predetermined. The GPS repeater kits normally include a preassembled pedestal GPS amplifier antenna assembly. This is mounted indoors in the room or building into which you want to bring a GPS signal. The best placement is in a corner, about 8 to 30 feet (2.5 to 9 meters) high. This is then connected via the GPS cable to the GPS roof antenna, which has been positioned in a suitable spot. The amplifier antenna assembly is then used to retransmit the GPS signal within the building. The repeater antenna can be adjusted for best coverage within the building.

Building Your Own Mega GPS Antenna

Before closing this chapter, let's take a look at how you can create your own GPS quad-helix antenna.

Materials

To build your GPS antenna, you need the following items:

- **Ground plane:** This is the base of the antenna. For this you can use pretty much any sheet metal you can find. Aluminum, brass, steel, and stainless steel all work equally well. Thin (0.08 inch or 2 mm) sheet aluminum is probably the cheapest and best sheet to use. Get a sheet approximately 12 inches (30 centimeters) square.

- **Helix coil tube:** Two-inch diameter PVC pipe has a circumference of 7.4 inches (or 19 centimeters), which is to all intents and purposes an exact match of the GPS wavelength, making it ideal for an antenna. Two-inch diameter gray plastic electrical conduit also has these same dimensions, and while this costs a little more, it looks a little better.

- **Helix wire:** 16-gauge copper wire is ideal for this project. Get several yards of it.

- **Antenna connector:** What you choose here depends on the GPS to which you want to connect the antenna. You can either use a compression fit or solder it directly.

Building the Antenna

This antenna is based on an design by Walter Gulley, and the original can be seen at www.ggrweb.com/article/gulley.html.

Here's how you assemble your antenna:

1. Build the ground plane: This is the base of the antenna, and you make it by cutting a 19-centimeter (7.5 inch) diameter circle out of the middle of the sheet metal (see Figure 4-15). If you are using thin metal, then you can use an old pair of scissors to do this, but a thicker metal or stainless steel will require shears. Drill a hole in the center of the metal circle so that the coaxial cable can be passed through. A grommet (or a liberal application or hot glue or silicone) can be added to protect the cable if you are going to solder the coaxial outer directly to the ground plate. If you don't want to do any soldering, then you can attach the coaxial connector to the ground plate, making an ideal connection. No matter which method you sue, this connection is required; without it, the antenna won't work.

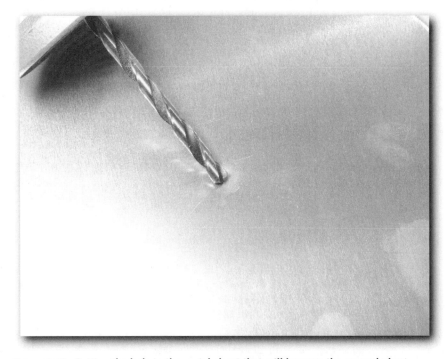

FIGURE 4-15: Cutting the hole in the metal sheet that will become the ground plane

Note

Aluminum and stainless steel are tricky to solder. If you want a material that is easy to solder, then select copper.

2. Build the helix base: Cut a 40.6-centimeter (16-inch) length of any nonmetallic material tube to form the base of the helix (see Figure 4-16). Plastic tubing is ideal for this because you can expose it to the elements without it degrading. If you want, you can also add an end cap to the base to keep out water and inhibit corrosion. If you are going to do this, then remember to add 25 millimeters (1 inch) to the length of this tube. Make sure you cut the ends of the pipe square and flat so it will lie perpendicular to the ground plate when it is mounted. Smooth it off with some sandpaper to make sure that it is true.

FIGURE 4-16: Building the helix base

3. Create the helix coil: The best way to wrap the wire around the base is to first clamp a ruler to the helix coil base (the pipe) and use that to draw a line from one end to the other, parallel to the center line of the tube that you are using. Along this line, measure intervals of 2.3 centimeters (⅞ inch) from one end (this will become the base of the tube that you will later attach to the ground plate), and place a mark for the beginning of the first turn of the helix winding. From this first mark, and along the line you drew, measure

and mark eight points that are each exactly 4.75 centimeters (1 ⅞ inches) apart (see Figure 4-17). These have to be as accurate as you can manage because this is key to the antenna picking up the right frequency.

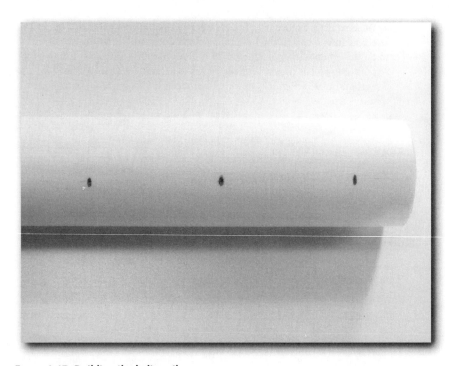

FIGURE 4-17: Building the helix coil

4. Drill the helix coil base: To do this you can either use a ¹⁄₁₆-inch bit to drill a hole at the last mark nearest each end of the helix coil base or you can use an awl to work through the plastic pipe.

5. Now you are ready to connect the helix wire to the antenna connection. If you are using a coaxial connector, all you now need to do is solder the end of the wire to the center of the connector. This will give you a robust and secure connection. If you aren't using a connector, then just solder the helix coil wire to the center wire of the cable you are using. Pass the free end of the wire from the inside of the tube through the hole located ⅞ inch from the base end of the helix coil base.

6. Now you need to attach the helix coil base to the ground plane. The easiest way I've found to do this is to use epoxy resin to attach the pipe to the ground plane. This ensures that the pipe is perpendicular to the ground plane. The epoxy resin also provides a robust and weatherproof joint. Another good way to create an effective joint is to use hot glue, although this doesn't give you as much of a chance to get the coil perpendicular to the ground plane (see Figure 4-18).

FIGURE 4-18: Epoxy resin is great for attaching the helix coil base to the ground plane.

7. Make sure that you pull the helix wire tightly through the hole in the helix coil base before you begin to wind the helix wire around the base or the coil will quickly loosen. Start to wind the wire, working slowly and carefully. Wind it counterclockwise around the helix coil base, making sure that it is smooth and even on the tube. Use a dot of hot glue periodically to keep the wire in place (although don't use too much hot glue). As each turn is completed, make sure the wire passes over each of the reference marks you made, and attach it in place with more hot glue. The partly completed helix coil is shown in Figure 4-19.

FIGURE 4-19: Partly completed helix coil

8. Continue winding all the way to the top, taking care that the coils are equally spaced and smooth, and add hot glue to keep it in place as you go. When you get to the top, pass the wire through the hole and back inside the tube. Use pliers to pull the wire tightly through the hole, and bend it up toward the top of the pipe (see Figure 4-20). Secure this in place with more hot glue. Cut the wire off, leaving about 6 millimeters ($\frac{1}{4}$ inch) from where it makes the turn inside the pipe so it will stay in place.

9. Connect the antenna to the GPS and test it for proper operation.

10. Optionally, glue the cap to the top of the antenna and ensure that all your joints, connectors, and glued parts are sound.

A diagram of the finished antenna is shown in Figure 4-21.

You can now think about attaching the antenna. No matter what you do, however, don't attach anything metallic to the ground plane (use glue or nylon nuts and bolts).

You can add glue some rubber-covered magnets to the base for automotive use. Make sure that these are strong magnets and test them to see how secure they are.

FIGURE 4-20: Holding the wire in place at the top

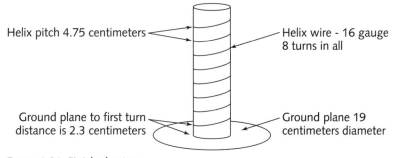

Helix pitch 4.75 centimeters

Helix wire - 16 gauge
8 turns in all

Ground plane to first turn
distance is 2.3 centimeters

Ground plane 19
centimeters diameter

FIGURE 4-21: Finished antenna

Summary

This chapter examined external antennas and how to use them. You looked at antennas that you can attach directly to a GPS via a connector, and reradiating antennas that take a signal and pipe it to a location that can't receive it.

You also learned how you can make a large and effective quad-helix antenna for your GPS out of plastic pipe, some sheet metal, wire, and a few connectors!

Hopefully, this chapter has you thinking carefully about GPS antennas—without a good antenna that has a clear view of the sky, you can forget about getting accurate information from your GPS. Believe me, a good antenna can make all the difference!

Protecting and Mounting Your GPS

A GPS represents a significant investment as a single electronic device that you're going to take into the outdoors, expose to the elements, and possibly treat roughly. While modern GPS units are quite robust, they are still electronic devices made of plastic, and as such dislike getting wet and knocked about. Moreoever, you may take PDAs and other mobile devices with you that are far happier in the office than on the trail. Even though GPS receivers are waterproof to a certain extent (most to IPX-7, which means that they can handle submersion to a depth of one meter for 30 minutes), they can benefit from a little bit more protection just to err on the safe side.

This chapter examines the steps you can take when you're outdoors to protect your devices from minor cosmetic damage such as scuffs and scrapes, and more extreme treatment such as impacts and submersion. You also look at ways to mount your GPS, both in the car or on foot.

Screen Damage

The screen on a GPS or other electronic device is obviously a highly vulnerable point. Not only is it more easily broken than the rest of the device, it is susceptible to minor but annoying cosmetic scratches. In fact, the screen picks up scratches easily, as you can see from Figure 5-1, which shows a well-cared-for (well, reasonably well-cared-for!) Garmin Vista.

If you are taking along PDAs that have touch-sensitive screens, such as the iPAQ, these are even more prone to screen damage. In fact, it only takes a small amount of pressure on the screen to totally destroy one. When it comes to screens, there's no such thing as a small amount of damage.

The following sections describe some simple steps that you can take to protect the screen on your GPS unit.

FIGURE 5-1: Normal wear and tear can take its toll on a GPS.

Screen Protectors

One of the simplest ways to protect your screen from minor damage is to apply a thin plastic screen protector to it. These screen protectors protect PDA screens from minor scuffs and scratches picked up during use. A screen protector set is shown in Figure 5-2.

Chances are good that you won't find a screen protector exactly the right size for your GPS, as most are designed for PDAs. Buy some that you can use for a PDA, and you can cut them down to fit the GPS screen.

The trick to applying screen protectors effectively is to first clean the screen surface thoroughly. It helps if the screen isn't too scratched to begin with, but protecting a slightly scratched screen and preventing it from getting any worse is better than doing nothing at all. Clean the screen with nothing more than a slightly damp cloth, as solvents or detergents can cause the material to cloud over or even melt. Make sure that you get into any scratches on the screen—a Q-tip is ideal for this. Also get into the edges with a Q-tip or toothpick. I'm using a Q-tip in Figure 5-3.

After you've thoroughly cleaned and dried the screen, you can apply the screen protector. The trick to attaching a screen protector is to work slowly and methodically, taking care to eliminate air bubbles from within the plastic sheet as you go.

FIGURE 5-2: Commercial screen protectors

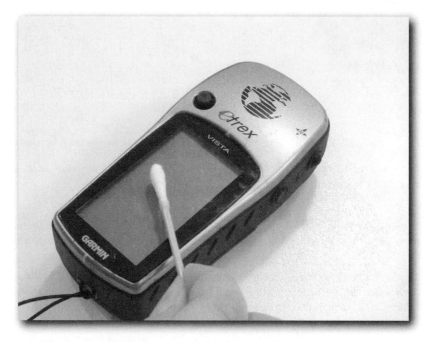

FIGURE 5-3: Carefully clean the screen before applying the screen protector.

Your screen protector set should contain the following:

- Screen protector sheets
- Plastic applicator card

This is the best way I've found to apply a screen protector:

1. Start peeling the backing off of one of the screen protector sheets, as shown in Figure 5-4. Start from the narrow end so you can work along the screen. You only need to peel off 5–10 mm of the backing at this time.

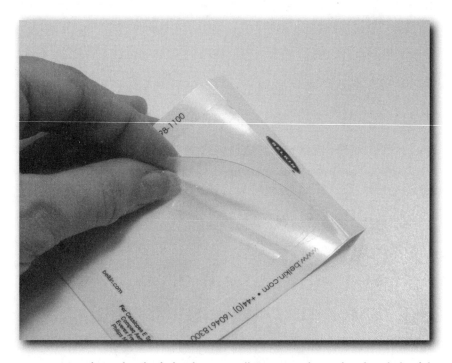

FIGURE 5-4: Start by peeling back the sheet a small amount—don't whip the whole of the backing off at once.

2. Stick the screen protector to the top of the screen as shown in Figure 5-5. Make sure the protector is applied well and that there are no bubbles in the film that will obscure the display.

3. Slowly work your way down the screen at a rate of about 10 mm at a time. Peel the backing a bit and use the plastic card to scrape the film onto the screen surface, as shown in Figure 5-6. This method is the one that give you the best results.

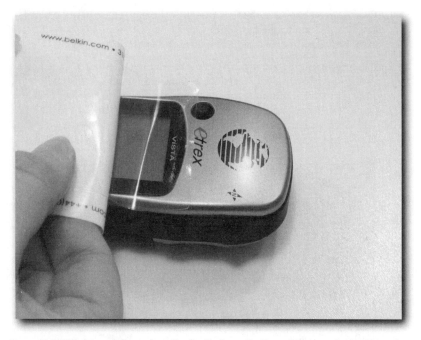

FIGURE 5-5: Work carefully and methodically from the top of the screen downward.

FIGURE 5-6: Using the plastic card to work out bubbles in the plastic film is vital.

4. If you do get a bubble in the film, peel back the film a little past the bubble and use the plastic card to scrape the film again. Don't worry about peeling back the film; you can do this quite a few times without affecting the adhesive.

5. After you've covered the screen, it's time to trim the film. Use a sharp knife or scissors to do this and follow the edge carefully, as shown in Figure 5-7. Carefully work your way around the screen, trimming the film as you go. Be careful not to scratch the screen in the process! If you've already made a screen protector, then you can peel the old one off and use that as a template for the new one!

FIGURE 5-7: Carefully cut around the edges of the screen protector.

Note

Never trim a screen protector that's attached to a touch-sensitive screen, as this will severely damage the screen.

6. And there you have it — a protected screen! The finish won't be perfect if the screen was already scuffed (as mine was), but it will help to protect it from further scuffs, scrapes, and scratches.

Note

A low-cost alternative to commercial screen protectors is to use a self-adhesive plastic film such as "Frisket" film.

More Screen Armoring

Screen protectors offer you some protection against screen damage, but don't expect miracles — all you've done is apply a thin film to the screen, which a rock or sharp edge can easily penetrate. Figure 5-8 shows the damage sustained by a screen protector when it was scratched against a rock — that would represent pretty severe damage to your unit.

FIGURE 5-8: Screen protectors really do offer good protection against scratches.

The best way to protect your screen is to take steps to prevent impacts from reaching the screen. The following sections describe some simple steps you can take to help achieve that.

Rubber Bumpers

One way to help protect a screen is to apply a few rubber bumpers to the screen. This won't protect it against all forms of damage, but if you use your GPS for work or in extreme sports such as kayaking, then this can certainly give it a fighting change of survival.

A simple way to do this is to squeeze out a few blobs of silicone sealant onto the corners of the screen. This is what I've done to a Garmin 76 in Figure 5-9.

This is a simple technique that helps to prevent damage. If you want, you can take this a stage further and add ridges of silicone to the screen, running along the edges as shown in Figure 5-10.

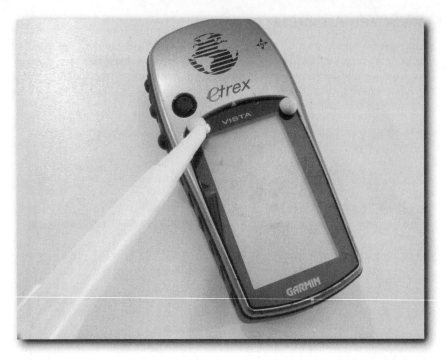

FIGURE 5-9: Apply a few blobs of silicone to the edges of the screen—waiting for it to dry before using.

The great thing about using silicone sealant is that you can remove it once it gets a bit rough and add some more. These bumpers won't last forever and usually come loose after a few weeks or months, so you will need to replace them regularly.

> **Note** Some people make more robust rubber bumpers by using hot glue from a hot glue gun instead of silicone. I don't suggest this because the heat from the glue can crack the screen or damage the underlying LCD display. The risks outweigh the benefits, and the objective is to protect the screen, not subject it to possible destruction.

Wire Bumpers

Another option is to create wire bumpers for your GPS. This mimics the protectors used on some sports watches to protect the LED from damage.

These are quite easy to make. All you need are the following:

- A few big paperclips (shown in Figure 5-11)
- A pair of pliers with wire cutters
- Silicone tubing (as used in a fish tank aquarium to pipe the air)

FIGURE 5-10: Ridges offer greater protection against scratches and bumps.

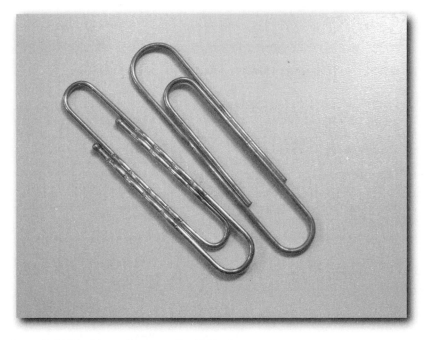

FIGURE 5-11: The bigger the paperclips the better.

Creating the wire bumpers is easy, and there are no real hard and fast rules as to how to do it—it will vary for each GPS. To help you complete this small project, you will need a good pair of pliers that have wire cutters on them. I find that a multitool such as the Leatherman Charge Ti (shown in Figure 5-12) is ideal for this.

FIGURE 5-12: The Leatherman Charge Ti—the ideal hacking companion!

1. Straighten out a few of the paperclips to give you the tough but flexible wire that you'll need. Don't remove all the bumps in the paper-clip wire, just straighten them out as shown in Figure 5-13.

2. Take the tubing and thread it over the wire to give it a quick and easy rubber coating.

3. In Figure 5-14, I've cut the tubing so that it extends a little beyond the end of the wire for safety. This is especially important if you have to cut the paper clips and expose a sharp end.

FIGURE 5-13: Straighten out the major bends and curves in the paper clip.

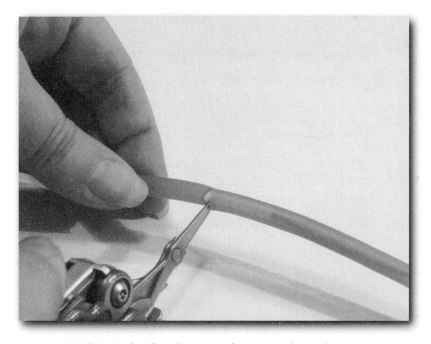

FIGURE 5-14: Make sure that the tubing extends over any sharp edges.

4. Take the silicone-coated wire and wrap it around the GPS. Try to avoid covering the battery compartment, so you can still change the battery without first removing the bumpers. Sometimes this is not possible, forcing you to choose between convenience and protection. Figure 5-15 shows a completed set of bumpers.

FIGURE 5-15: Completed set of bumpers

5. Figure 5-16 shows a close-up of one of the ends of the silicone-rubber-covered wire where I've overlapped the end to prevent the wire from poking through.

And that's it — done! Depending on how you arrange the wire, you can offer more protection to some areas on the GPS than others.

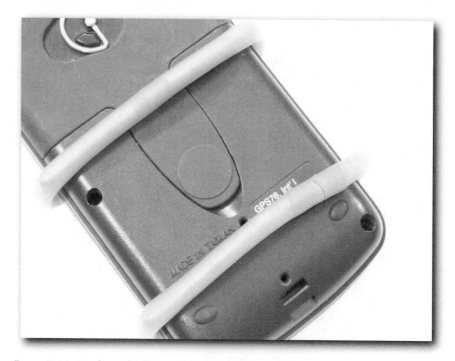

FIGURE 5-16: Overlapped tubing covers sharp edges.

Commercial Protection for GPS and PDAs

If you have spent hundreds or perhaps thousands of dollars on your electronic equipment, you might choose to protect it with some of the commercial protectors available. Inexpensive cases also exist for your GPS. These cases are similar to cases used to hold cell phones, but they can only be relied upon to offer the bear minimum of extra protection. Nonetheless, these cases are ideal for storing your GPS when at home or in the car, and do prevent scratch damage from keys and coins when in a pocket.

Here is a quick tour of some of the commercial protection solutions available that enable you to take your precious gear out of the safety of your home and into the outdoors.

Storm Case

The Storm Case by Hardigg is the ideal way to package your gear for transportation. These cases can really take a battering while still offering excellent protection to the equipment they contain. Figure 5-17 shows the smallest case in the Storm Case range — the iM2100.

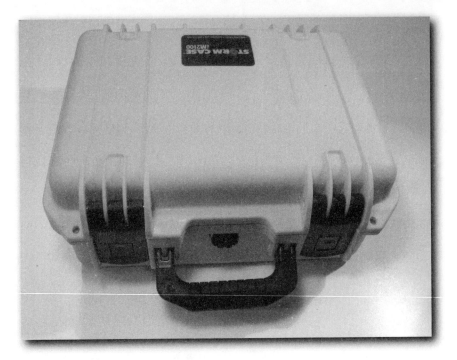

Figure 5-17: Hardigg Storm Case iM2100

These cases are crush-resistant, shatterproof, dent-resistant, watertight, airtight, and virtually unbreakable—everything electronic devices need. They are also equipped with a pressure-equalizing valve (see Figure 5-18) that accommodates pressure changes and prevents burst seals when the pressure increases or drops (handy for aircraft travel).

The inside of the case is lined with special shock-absorbing foam (see Figure 5-19) that cushions and protects what you keep inside.

The trick when using a case such as the Storm Case is to pack it so that nothing touches the edges of the case and no items touch one another, as shown in Figure 5-20. This arrangement offers the contents the best chance of survival if worse comes to worst.

For more details on the Hardigg Storm Case range, visit www.stormcase.com.

Aquapac

A great way to protect your GPS or PDA when on the move is by using an Aquapac carrier. A small one suited to GPS receivers is shown in Figure 5-21, while a bigger one for an iPAQ is shown in Figure 5-22.

FIGURE 5-18: Pressure-equalizing valve

FIGURE 5-19: The cases are lined with shock-absorbing foam.

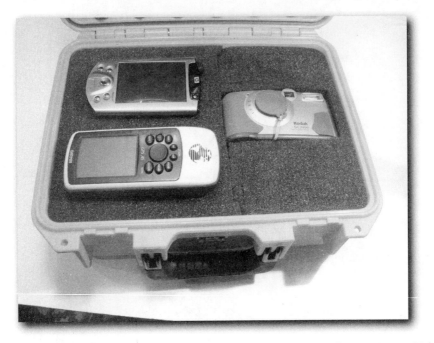

FIGURE 5-20: This is a good arrangement that offers good protection when carrying multiple devices.

FIGURE 5-21: Aquapac suitable for a GPS receiver

FIGURE 5-22: Aquapac suited to an iPAQ

Some carriers are soft PVC cases that have a special closure at the top to prevent water and dirt from reaching your device (see Figure 5-23).

These are very effective and both water- and dirtproof. If you want the capability to run cables to your GPS or PDA, you can get an Aquapac with a special cable port, which is also waterproof and dirtproof. Figure 5-24 shows an Aquapac containing a cable-connected PDA, sealed in safely from the environment.

The Aquapac doesn't offer much in the way of damage protection, but it does offer a great defense from the environment. It also offers the added advantage that you can still use your device while it is in the case.

In addition, if you drop a GPS inside an Aquapac into water, the whole package will float, giving you the chance to retrieve it before it sinks to the bottom.

Note These cases come with a lanyard designed to be worn around the neck. Personally, I don't like this because of the danger posed by the cord snagging on undergrowth and choking you. In addition, if you trip or fall, the device is in a prime position to take the brunt of the fall.

For more details on the Aquapac range, visit www.aquapac.net.

You might also be interested in checking out Voyageur bags, which are similar to the Aquapac. See www.voyageur-gear.com for more details.

FIGURE 5-23: The Aquapac closure is effective at keeping out water, dirt, and dust.

FIGURE 5-24: This Aquapac has a special cable port that enables you to have a cable connected to the iPAQ while in the case.

Otter Box

Another way to protect your devices from the elements is to enclose them in a box or case. The usual disadvantage of this option is that normally you can't use or interact with the device while it's in the box.

Otter Products have solved this problem with their Otter Box range designed for PDAs. They come in a variety of shapes and sizes. The Otter 2600 shown in Figure 5-25 is a basic case designed to offer good protection from the elements.

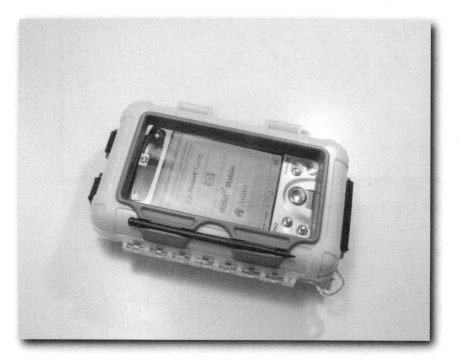

FIGURE 5-25: The Otter 2600

A more sophisticated case is the Otter 3600 case shown in Figure 5-26. This case offers excellent protection from the elements and from damage sustained from knocks, falls, and even being driven over!

The great thing about the Otter cases is that you can still use your device while it is in the case. This is made possible through the use of the thin, flexible plastic film on the face of the case. It is especially useful with a Bluetooth-enabled GPS and PDA combination. Figure 5-27 shows a close-up of the front of the Otter 2600.

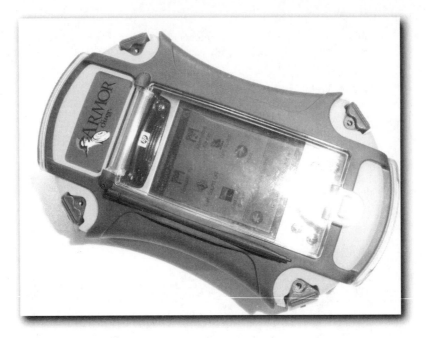

FIGURE 5-26: The top of the range Otter 3600

FIGURE 5-27: The flexible plastic film on the front enables you to use your device while it is still in the case.

This can be considered a weak point of the case, and an impact in the right (or wrong) spot could break the screen. The Otter 3600 gets around this problem with the addition of a tough plastic cover that flips down over the screen (see Figure 5-28). It can be flipped up out of the way when you need to interact with the PDA.

FIGURE 5-28: The well-armored Otter 3600 has a flip-down polycarbonate covering to shield the plastic film on the front.

The Otter 3600 also has clear windows at the top and bottom on the case (see Figure 5-29) that enable you to send and receive data via the infrared link, and optional extras enable you to run cables into the box without diminishing the protection it offers.

For more details on the Otter range of products, visit www.otterbox.com.

FIGURE 5-29: These removable clear windows enable you to use the infrared connection while the PDA is in the case. They can also be removed and replaced with extension ports (for large expansion cards) or cable input ports.

Mounting GPS

When you are on the move, it's good to have your GPS fixed to something so that it's not loose. A loose GPS in the car or while walking puts the GPS at risk as well as any devices attached to it via cables.

Car Mounting

An unsecured GPS in a car is also a bad idea because the movements can put stress on cables, connections, and the device itself. In an accident, an unsecured GPS could be turned into a lethal missile, which makes securing it doubly important.

A good, yet simple way to affix a GPS is to use a commercial mount. Some of the best mounts that I have found are made by RAM. Not only do they offer a great range of mounts for a variety of devices, but they are also very versatile because the same mount can be used for a variety of applications (attached to a bike clamp, suction cup, or special car mount). You have many options for securing the GPS in the car. One of the easiest ways to attach the GPS is via a RAM mount that has a suction cup attached to it (see Figure 5-30). These suction cups are extremely powerful and don't require the use of any adhesives or the drilling of any holes.

FIGURE 5-30: The RAM mount suction cup

RAM mounts are great because the fitting is a swivel mount and can be adjusted so that the GPS is oriented correctly for your seating position. This is possible through the use of two ball joints on the swivel arm (see Figure 5-31).

You can also connect a cable to the GPS while it is in the cradle. Figure 5-32 shows an eTrex in a RAM mount and attached to a cable.

Note   Choose a good spot to mount your GPS. You want a position that enables you to see the GPS but that doesn't obscure your vision while driving. Experiment with different locations until you find one you like. If you are using cables to antennas or power supplies, use cable ties to keep these under control. Wherever you choose, avoid areas on your dashboard that incorporate an air bag.

FIGURE 5-31: RAM mount swivel arm

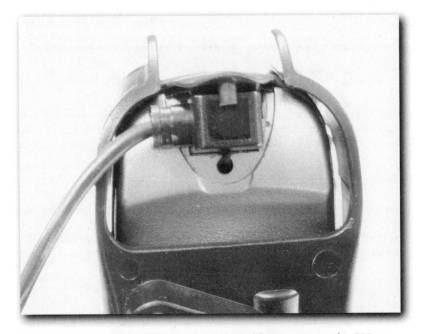

FIGURE 5-32: This cradle enables you to attach a cable connector to the GPS, an option not available with all mounts.

For more details on RAM mounts visit www.ram-mount.com.

RAM isn't the only maker of GPS mounts — most GPS manufacturers also make mounts for their GPS receivers. Your user manual will likely list the accessories that match your GPS receiver.

Other alternatives include the use of Velcro strips and beanbags to hold the GPS — personally, I don't find that these offer enough in the way of support. I prefer a more robust way to hold the receiver in place.

Mounting a GPS for Biking, Hiking, and Skiing

You can also mount a GPS on your bike if you purchase a bike RAM mount. These are easy to fit. To mount a GPS onto a ski-pole or hiking stick, all you need is a RAM mount that is designed to be attached to a bike. Figure 5-33 shows such a RAM mount.

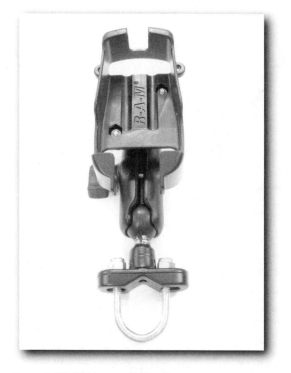

FIGURE 5-33: RAM mount bike clip

The U-shaped bolt that is designed to enable the RAM mount to be attached to a bike frame or the handlebars is also ideal for the diameters of most walking sticks, both wooden and metal. Figure 5-34 shows the mount attached to an aluminum ski pole.

FIGURE 5-34: Bike mount attached to a ski pole

Be careful not to tighten the nuts on the U-bolts too much, as that could crush the metal and damage the walking stick. This is especially true if the hiking stick is telescopic.

To ensure that the U-bolt is secure without having to tighten it too much, put a few layers of electrical tape underneath the bolt before securing it, as shown in Figure 5-35. This enables you to tighten the clip against the tape, putting less stress and pressure on the metal itself.

Never drill into a ski pole or hiking stick to attach anything, as this will dramatically weaken it and could cause you great harm should it break in use.

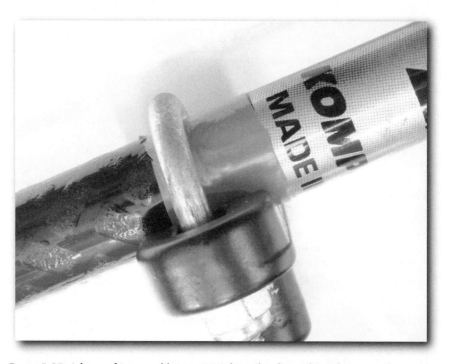

FIGURE 5-35: A layer of tape enables you to tighten the clip without damaging the metal. Even with this protection, however, remember to take it easy when tightening the nuts.

Making a Personalized Case

To close this chapter, I'm going to take you through the steps necessary to build your own GPS holster. In order to build this type of holster, you will need the following materials:

- Kydex or Concealex sheet (12 inch × 12 inch square). This will cost a few dollars (see www.sdplastics.com/kydex/kydex.html).

- A belt clip (under $10; see www.blade-tech.com)

- Chicago screws (used in leatherwork extensively; see www.eleathersupply.com/fasteners.shtml)

- Closed-cell foam

- Sharp knife and scissors

- Hair dryer/hot-air paint-stripping gun

- Access to an oven

- Heat-resistant gloves
- Workbench
- Vice/clamps
- Teflon-coated tray or baking sheet
- Sandpaper (various grades)
- Damp cotton rags
- Electric drill and $\frac{1}{16}$ size drill bit

Kydex and Concealex are types of plastics called high-performance thermoplastics that are supplied in sheet form. Concealex is tougher and more robust than Kydex because of the carbon fiber reinforcement it contains.

Both of these plastics can be heated up and molded to form all kinds of shapes. Figure 5-36 shows a sheet of Concealex. Both of these materials have been used extensively in the automotive and aerospace industry, but are nowadays also used to make holsters for firearms and sheathes for knives.

FIGURE 5-36: A sheet of Concealex

These materials can be purchased in a variety of sheet sizes, thicknesses, and colors. The best thickness for our purpose is 0.06 or 0.093 (measured in inches).

Note

The best way to buy it is to search the web for a nearby retailer or a mail-order supplier.

You are now ready to start making the holster for your GPS. Because Kydex and Concealex are both thermoplastics, the plastic needs to be heated in order for it to become supple enough to be molded. The following table shows the typical temperatures to which you need to heat the plastic in order to make it moldable.

Thermoplastic	Celsius	Fahrenheit
Kydex (0.06)	154	310
Kydex (0.093)	163	325
Concealex (0.06)	around 70–120	around 160–250
Concealex (0.093)	around 70–150	around 160–300

You will have to experiment with the temperature to get it right, and you should expect some failures.

Note

Kydex is easier to work with than Concealex, and as such, I would recommend that you start off with that, rather than Concealex. However, if you plan on using your GPS in cold conditions, Kydex can become brittle at temperatures below 32° Fahrenheit (0° Celsius).

Here's the procedure for creating your own thermoplastic holster:

1. Gather all your materials together. Make sure that you have a clear access from the oven to your work area. Remove any clutter and give yourself a clear work area.

   After you have done that, set the oven to the right temperature and let it heat up. Oven temperature sensors are notoriously inaccurate, so if you have access to a temperature probe, use that in conjunction with the oven temperature gauge. Figure 5-37 shows a multimeter that also has a temperature probe.

Note

Heating thermoplastics releases minute quantities of hydrofluoric acid, so I wouldn't recommend cooking anything in the oven while it is being used to heat up the plastic.

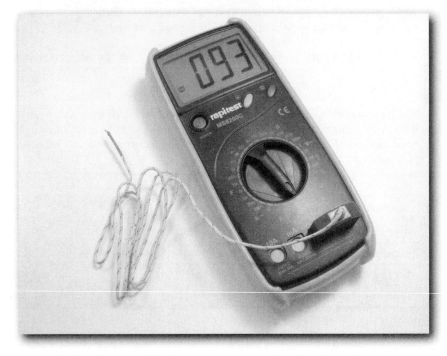

FIGURE 5-37: A multimeter with a temperature probe makes the job much easier.

2. Cut the thermoplastic into a shape for the holster. This shape will depend on the GPS for which you are making the holster, so I would experiment by making a template from cardboard and seeing how it fits. The thermoplastic can expand or contract after heating, so make the template a little larger initially because you can always cut it down and sand it to size.

Figure 5-38 shows a template that I made for the Garmin eTrex Vista.

3. Use your template to cut out a portion of the thermoplastic sheet to the shape you want. Take care when cutting the plastic, as it is quite dense and hard. The best way to cut the plastic is to score it before the final cutting, as shown in Figure 5-39.

4. Take the sheet of thermoplastic and place it on a clean baking sheet in the oven or use a portable toaster oven (which you could take outside to minimize the smell generated from heating Kydex). This will take several minutes to heat up. Don't rush this process because repeatedly heating and cooling the plastic will cause it to thicken significantly.

5. After the plastic reaches the required temperature, remove the baking sheet and take it to your work area. This is where heat-resistant gloves come in handy. Be quick, however, as you have about a minute before the Kydex cools too much to mold.

FIGURE 5-38: Garmin eTrex template

FIGURE 5-39: Score the Concealex before cutting it. If you make a mistake, you can just rescore it and cut along the right score, ignoring the mistake.

6. Place the GPS face down on the workbench and lift the warm plastic off the sheet, placing it on the back of the GPS receiver and molding it around the GPS. This is shown in Figure 5-40.

FIGURE 5-40: Mold the warm Concealex on the GPS.

Heating the thermoplastic to too high a temperature can not only damage the plastic but also damage the GPS itself. Keep the temperatures to those listed in this chapter and keep damp cotton cloths handy to cool the plastic quickly as it molds. If you overheat a sheet of Kydex, it's best to throw it away and start with a new piece.

7. Gloves and a piece of closed-cell foam can help you to press on the plastic to mold it around the GPS receiver better. Use the damp cotton rags to cool the plastic down selectively as shown in Figure 5-41.

8. Remove the GPS. You can now use a hair dryer or hot-air heat gun (or you can use boiling water) to heat up small parts of the plastic to help you finish the molding process (see Figure 5-42). Take your time at this stage because going too fast could result in a mistake that takes you back to Step 1.

FIGURE 5-41: Damp cloths enable you to selectively cool down areas of the plastic quickly, minimizing the time you have to hold it in place.

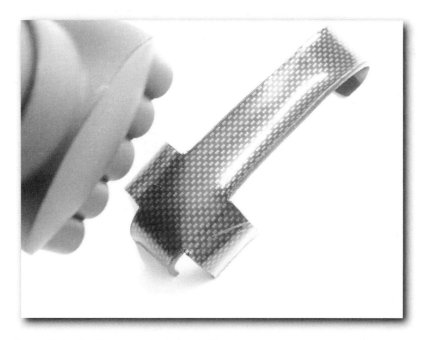

FIGURE 5-42: Heating up parts of the plastic

9. After you have finished the molding and shaping process, you should have a holster that enables you to easily access or remove your GPS (see Figure 5-43).

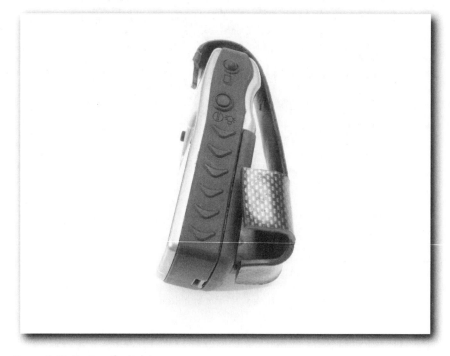

FIGURE 5-43: Testing the holster

10. Finish off the edges with sandpaper to remove any sharp edges that might be on the holster.

11. Now that the thermoplastic forming is completed, it's time to add the fittings. Figure 5-44 shows a belt loop called a Tek Lok (see www.blade-tech.com).

12. To fit the Tek Lok, decide where you want it (I left a space for it on the template) or you can create a new piece and attach it with Chicago screws. Now mark (see Figure 5-45) and drill the holes for the Tek Lok.

Figure 5-44: A large Tek Lok clip

Figure 5-45: Drilling the holes to attach the Tek Lok

13. Now fit the Tek Lok with the fitting provided and there you have it — a finished holster, as shown in Figure 5-46.

FIGURE 5-46: The finished holster

Summary

This chapter described several ways to protect delicate electronics while outdoors using a variety of products, both commercial and homemade.

You've looked at a variety of commercial products that can protect your GPS, PDA, and other delicate electronics from the worst that the environment can throw at them. Using some of the products, it is even possible to use a GPS/PDA combination while they are still in the protective case.

You've also looked at many homemade solutions to help make your GPS more rugged and robust and, if nothing else, protect it from scuffs and scrapes that it will otherwise pick up in use. They might even save you having to open your wallet and part with dollars unnecessarily.

Software Hacks

part

Hacking the Firmware

One guaranteed way to personalize your GPS is to update and modify the firmware that controls the actual running of the device. In this chapter, we'll be looking at how you can modify your GPS at a fundamental level.

Firmware

Firmware is the software that controls how hardware works and responds to inputs. It's called firmware instead of software because users generally aren't supposed to play around with it. But you're not just any old user, are you? Almost all electronic hardware contains some form of firmware. A television remote control contains firmware that controls what signals are sent via IR depending on what button is pressed. A cell phone contains a lot of firmware controlling cell access, phone books, security, and much, much more.

A GPS contains *a lot* of firmware controlling many of the key functions of the device (as shown in Figure 6-1):

- Reception of satellite data
- Decoding of positional information
- Processing of data
- Conversion of data into different formats
- Interpretation and display of information
- External communication with devices
- Storing and managing route/waypoint data

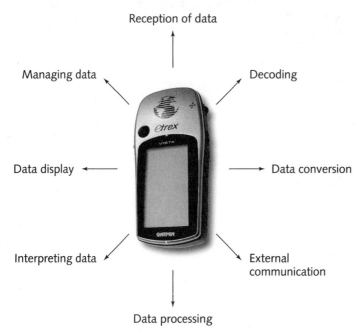

Reception of data

Managing data

Decoding

Data display

Data conversion

Interpreting data

External communication

Data processing

FIGURE 6-1: The basic functions of a GPS receiver

As you can see, being able to influence the firmware means you have influence on the actual workings of the GPS receiver itself. Not only can you make alterations to the text that is displayed on the screen of the GPS, you can also hide features that get in the way (such as startup screens). You can also add your contact details to the GPS in such a way that would discourage theft of your unit and encourage its return to you if it were found.

But you have to be careful . . .

Updating Warnings

You must be careful when making any changes or modifications to the firmware of your GPS because there is a risk that things can go wrong and render the GPS inoperable. Problems are rare, however, and you can take steps to reduce, if not eliminate, firmware update problems:

1. Make sure your GPS contains a new set of batteries. Batteries suddenly dying mid-firmware updating could cause big problems. Add fresh or recently recharged batteries, fire up the GPS, and confirm that the power levels are high. Figure 6-2 shows a healthy battery level in the lower-left corner of the screen on a Garmin eTrex.

2. Because you will be using a PC to do the update, it is better if the PC is connected to a UPS (uninterruptible power supply) battery backup, because the PC shutting off mid-update can be just as bad as the GPS battery dying. If you are using a laptop, power it from the mains supply or make sure the battery is fully charged.

FIGURE 6-2: Healthy battery
level on a Garmin eTrex

3. Shut down any running applications, including screen savers that will appear if the system is left unattended.

4. Make sure the cable connection is sound. If you have a screw-in com port connector, attach it securely.

5. Don't use the PC during the update—just in case it crashes and hangs the firmware update. Step away from the keyboard!

6. Finally, don't jolt or shake the GPS while the firmware update is being piped to the device, as this can cause the connection to drop or the device to cut out.

Before making any changes to the firmware, I strongly recommend that you visit the website of your GPS's manufacturer and download the latest firmware update and keep it handy.

Here are the websites of some of the most popular manufacturers:

- www.garmin.com
- www.magellangps.com
- www.delorme.com
- www.lowrance.com
- www.laipac.com
- www.haicom.com.tw
- www.navman.com
- www.miogps.com
- www.emtac.com.tw
- www.trimble.com

If things do go wrong, there is a good chance you will be able to reload the firmware and get the GPS receiver unit back up and running.

Caution Messing with the firmware of a GPS receiver is likely to invalidate the warranty, so take great care and weigh the benefits against the potential drawbacks. Everything described in this book has been tested by many people, but there is always a chance that things can go wrong.

Updating the Firmware

Updating the firmware on a GPS unit is a relatively easy process that takes only a few minutes. It varies slightly from unit to unit and maker to maker but usually the process is as follows:

1. Download the latest version of the firmware. A download package is shown in Figure 6-3. Make sure that the firmware that you download is the right firmware for the unit you are updating. Downloading and loading the wrong firmware onto a GPS unit is guaranteed to cause problems.

FIGURE 6-3: A firmware
download package

2. Downloads are usually available in a zipped, or compressed, file. Uncompress the file and extract the contents. The file for an update to a Garmin unit is shown in Figure 6-4.

3. Connect the GPS unit to the PC using the appropriate cable, and switch the GPS receiver on.

4. Run the main executable file that you extracted. This will begin the firmware updating process, as shown in Figure 6-5.

5. The firmware updating application will keep you posted as to the progress of the update.

6. After the update is complete, disconnect the GPS from the cable and switch it on — the system should fire up with the new firmware installed.

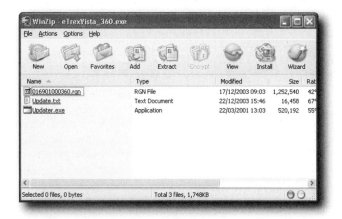

FIGURE 6-4: Files contained in the update

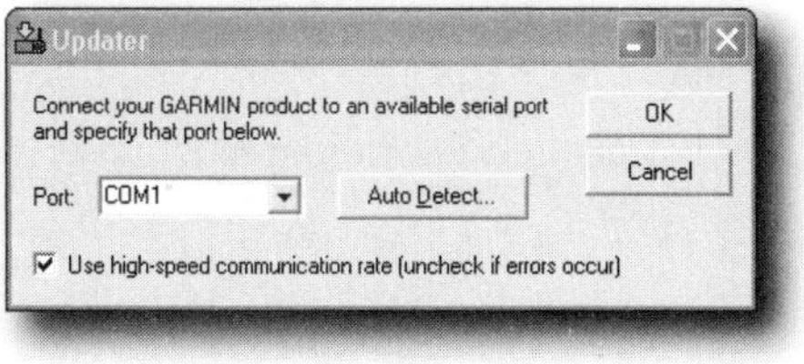

FIGURE 6-5: Beginning the firmware update process

That's all there is to it! I suggest you read any material that accompanies the update (especially any README files contained in the download package) to familiarize yourself with any new features of the firmware and to get any late-breaking information. Many vendors add new features to their GPS units well after release through firmware updates. Be careful about installing updates that have only just been released. Generally, I wait a week or two before updating so that if any bugs are found in the firmware update, they can be fixed before I install it.

Of course, uploading new firmware to a GPS is not hacking the firmware at all, so let's move on to actual firmware hacking!

Hacking GPS Firmware

The following sections describe how you can hack and tweak the firmware on a GPS unit. In this section, you will learn how you can bypass the startup screen on three different GPS receivers.

Note You won't be able to get any support from the manufacturer for altering or modifying the firmware. In fact, having modified firmware on the device may well invalidate your warranty.

Bypassing the Garmin eTrex Vista Startup Screen

One annoying feature of the eTrex range is that when the unit starts up, it takes you to a startup screen. This means you have to press buttons or wait for the satellite screen, which I find really annoying. There is a way around this, but only using an older firmware version (2.28 as opposed to the latest 3.60). However, using older firmware does mean that you lose any new features introduced (such as the JumpMaster feature — however, this particular feature is only relevant to experienced parachutists).

Here's how to bypass the startup screen:

1. Download a copy of the latest firmware from the Garmin website (www.garmin.com). Keep this just in case of problems.

2. Download a copy of the 2.28 version firmware for the Garmin eTrex Vista from www.gpsinformation.org/perry/vista/Vista_2_28.exe (read the agreement at www.gpsinformation.org/perry/agree.html first).

3. The download comes in a compressed file. Uncompress the file and extract the contents.

4. Find the file called 016901000228.RGN, as shown in Figure 6-6.

016901000228.RGN

FIGURE 6-6: The main file that contains the firmware information

5. You now need a program called a hex editor. I'm using one called UltraEdit, available from www.ultraedit.com (shown in Figure 6-7), but many are available on the Internet so fire up your browser and do a search for "hex editor." You need to open 016901000228.RGN and make a few small edits to it.

6. Go to the address 00024024 (there is a *go to* function in most good hex editors) and change F5 to 6D, as shown in Figure 6-8.

7. Go to the address 00024025 and change 24 to BA, as shown in Figure 6-9.

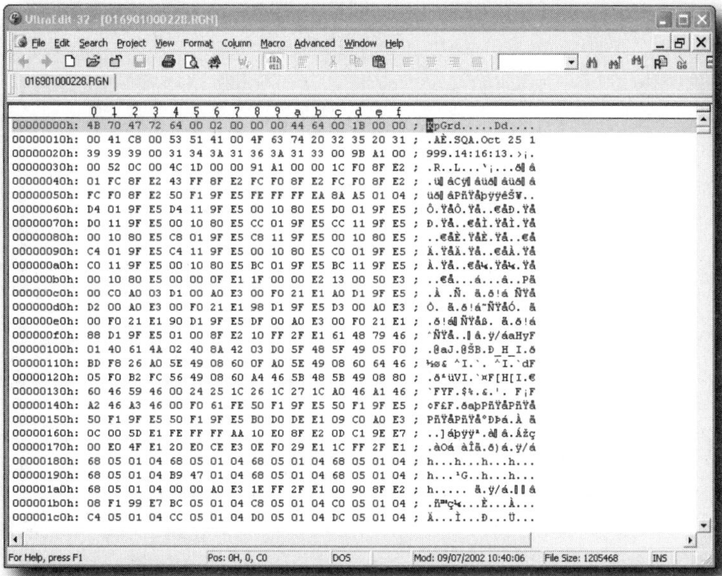

FIGURE 6-7: UltraEdit in action

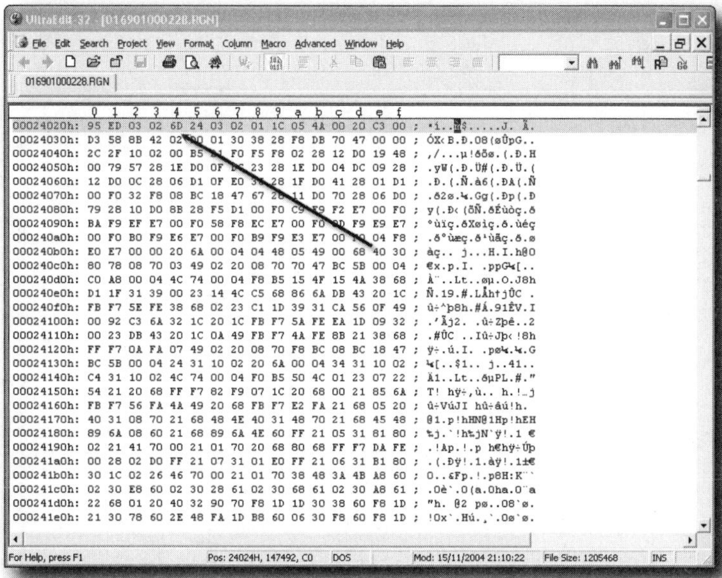

FIGURE 6-8: Make a change to the firmware.

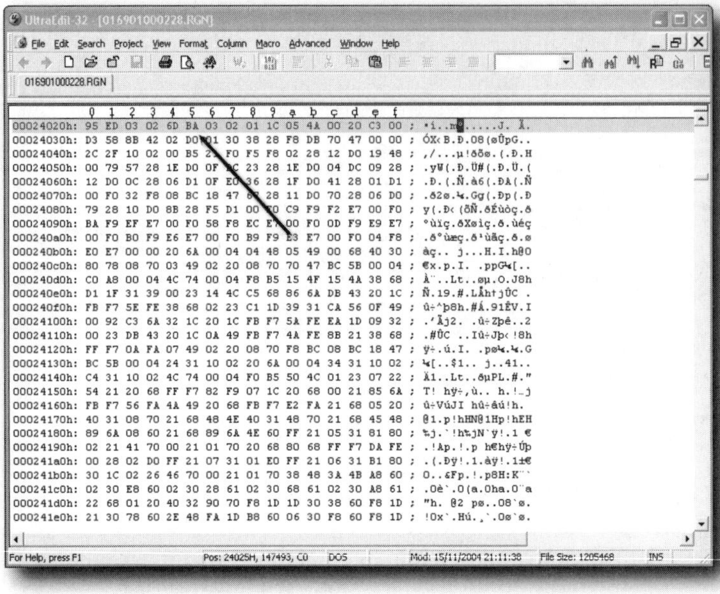

FIGURE 6-9: Make another change.

8. Go to the address 00024026 and change 03 to 04, as shown in Figure 6-10.

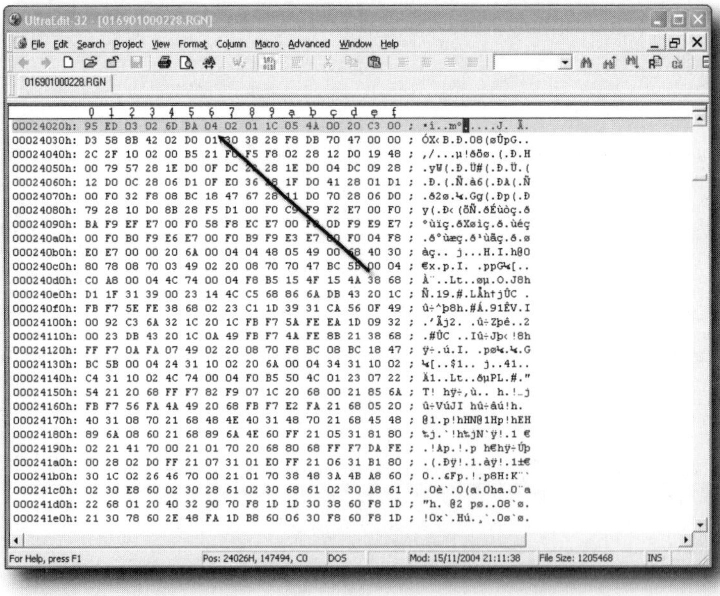

FIGURE 6-10: The final change!

9. Connect the GPS unit to the PC using the appropriate cable and switch the GPS receiver on.

10. Run the main executable file that you extracted. This will begin the firmware update process.

11. The firmware updating application will keep you posted as to the progress of the update. The process will complete reasonably quickly and the GPS will be ready for use.

Bypassing the Garmin eTrex Legend Startup Screen

The Garmin eTrex Legend suffers from the same problem as the Vista in that is has a startup screen that you must wait to get past. There is a way around this, but only using an older firmware version (2.41 as opposed to the latest 3.60).

This example uses UltraEdit as the hex editor.

Here's what you do:

1. Download a copy of the latest firmware from the Garmin website (www.garmin.com). Keep this just in case of problems.

2. Download a copy of the 2.41 version firmware for the Garmin eTrex Vista from www.gpsinformation.org/perry/legend/Legend_2_41.exe (read the agreement at www.gpsinformation.org/perry/agree.html first).

3. The download comes in a zipped, or compressed, file. Uncompress the file and extract the contents.

4. Find the file called 017901000241.RGN.

5. Open 017901000241.RGN in a hex editor and make the following changes to it.

6. Go to the address 000229DC (there is a *go to* function in most good hex editors) and change 91 to 49.

7. Go to the address 000229DD and change DE to 39.

8. Go to the address 0011CB07 and change 91 to 7E.

9. Connect the GPS unit to the PC using the appropriate cable and switch the GPS receiver on.

10. Run the main executable file that you extracted. This will begin the firmware update process.

11. The firmware updating application will keep you posted as to the progress of the update. The process will complete reasonably quickly and the GPS will be ready for use.

Bypassing the Garmin eTrex Venture Startup Screen

Just like the Garmin eTrex Vista and Legend, the Venture also suffers from the same problem as the Vista in that is has a startup screen that you have to get past.

Like the other models, the way around this uses an older firmware version (2.34 as opposed to the latest 3.70).

Here's what you do:

1. Download a copy of the latest firmware from the Garmin website (www.garmin.com). Keep this handy just in case of problems.

2. Download a copy of the 2.34 version firmware for the Garmin eTrex Vista from `www.gpsinformation.org/perry/venture/etrexventure_mariner_234.exe` (read the agreement at `www.gpsinformation.org/perry/agree.html` first).

3. The download is packaged in a compressed file. Uncompress the file and extract the contents.

4. Find the file called `015401000234.RGN`.

5. Open `015401000234.RGN` in a hex editor to make the following changes.

6. Go to the address 0001F4DC (there is a *go to* function in most good hex editors) and change E1 for C9.

7. Go to the address 0001F4DC and change 99 to FE.

8. Go to the address 0001F4DE and change 02 to 01.

9. Go to the address 000D002F and change A7 to 5B.

10. Connect the GPS unit to the PC using the appropriate cable and switch the GPS receiver on.

11. Run the main executable file that you extracted. This will begin the firmware update process.

12. The firmware updating application will keep you posted as to the progress of the update. The process will complete reasonably quickly and the GPS will be ready for use.

MeMap Personalization

An interesting way to personalize the text that displays on your Garmin eMap and eTrex range GPS is to use a program called MeMap. The MeMap firmware editing package is available for download on the web from Ido Bar Tana's site at `www.geocities.com/etrexkb/textpatch.zip`. More information about the application can be found at `www.geocities.com/etrexkb/textpatch.htm`.

MeMap enables you to search for text strings within the firmware so that you can edit them with your own strings.

Note   MeMap was written by Gilles Kohl (`http://ourworld.compuserve.com/homepages/gilles/memap/index.htm`).

This product is free, so it won't cost you anything if you want to experiment.

Note While this software does what it says it does, it can be a little quirky at times and your initial efforts may not work. If this is the case, revert to the original firmware and try again.

One possible quirk you might come across is that the preview screen displays the text upside down and left to right. This is because of the way that certain firmware versions store the text within their code. If you see this, don't worry; things should work out for you fine anyway.

The Garmin eTrex range includes the following units:

- Basic yellow
- Camo
- Legend
- Venture
- Summit
- Vista

Before you start, you will need the following:

- Garmin eTrex range GPS
- A cable to connect the GPS to a PC
- A PC running Microsoft Windows on which to run the software

The process involved is a simple one. Here's what you need to do:

1. Download the software from www.geocities.com/etrexkb/textpatch.zip. The zipped file is shown in Figure 6-11.

textpatch.zip

FIGURE 6-11: The compressed application

2. Extract the contents of the file to a convenient folder on your PC. The contents of the file are shown in Figure 6-12.

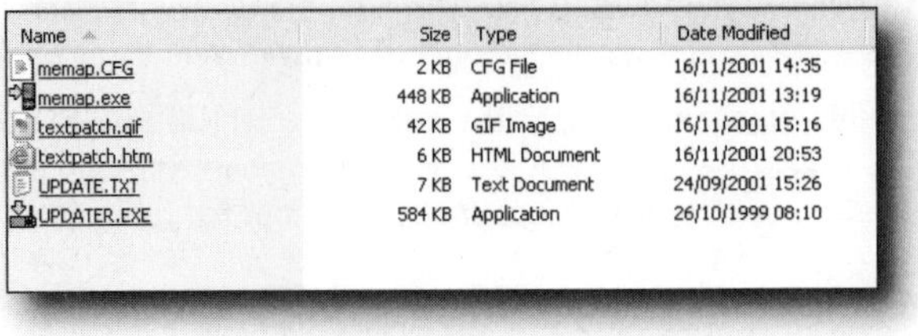

Name ▲	Size	Type	Date Modified
memap.CFG	2 KB	CFG File	16/11/2001 14:35
memap.exe	448 KB	Application	16/11/2001 13:19
textpatch.gif	42 KB	GIF Image	16/11/2001 15:16
textpatch.htm	6 KB	HTML Document	16/11/2001 20:53
UPDATE.TXT	7 KB	Text Document	24/09/2001 15:26
UPDATER.EXE	584 KB	Application	26/10/1999 08:10

FIGURE 6-12: Contents of the MeMap download

3. Because the software works on a firmware file (files that have the extension .RGN), you should now download a copy of the appropriate firmware for your device from Garmin (www.garmin.com/support/download.jsp).

4. Extract the files from the firmware download into a convenient location.

5. Copy the .RGN file from the location in which you extracted the firmware and copy it to the location of the MeMap application.

6. Now run the MeMap application (memap.exe). After a few seconds, the application will start and you will be presented with the main screen, as shown in Figure 6-13.

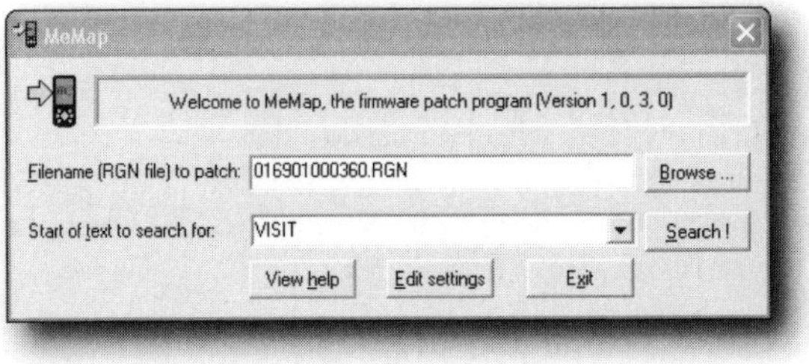

MeMap

Welcome to MeMap, the firmware patch program (Version 1, 0, 3, 0)

Filename (RGN file) to patch: 016901000360.RGN   Browse ...

Start of text to search for: VISIT   Search !

View help   Edit settings   Exit

FIGURE 6-13: MeMap main screen

7. You can now start searching for strings to replace. A good one to start with is "WARN-ING," as shown in Figure 6-14.

MeMap

Welcome to MeMap, the firmware patch program (Version 1, 0, 3, 0)

Filename (RGN file) to patch: 016901000360.RGN   Browse ...

Start of text to search for: WARNING   Search !

View help   Edit settings   Exit

FIGURE 6-14: Searching for the word "WARNING"

8. Click the button marked Search! This will take you to the first instance of the string found in the firmware. This is shown in Figure 6-15.

FIGURE 6-15: The first instance of the word "WARNING" in the firmware

9. You can now either choose to make edits to the text at the location of the word you searched for in the firmware or you can click the button marked Find Next to find the next instance of the string in the firmware. The string to be replaced is shown in the upper-left window, while the text to replace it with is in the lower-left. Figure 6-16 shows some edits I have made.

10. When you have finished making edits based on a particular keyword, click OK to take you back to the main screen.

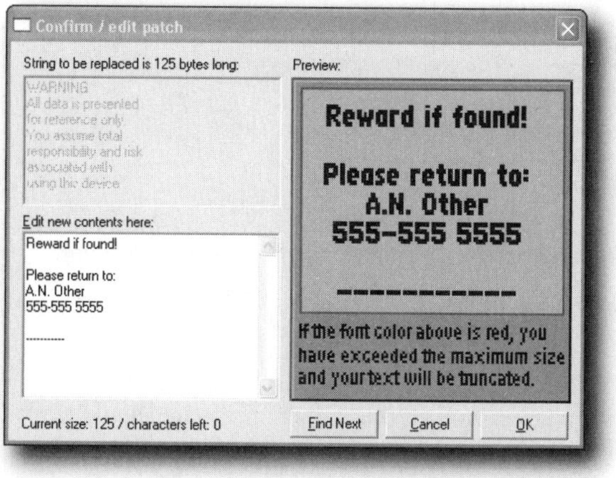

FIGURE 6-16: Making edits to the firmware

11. You can also search for your own strings using the box at the bottom of the main screen. In Figure 6-17, we are searching for the string "GPS".

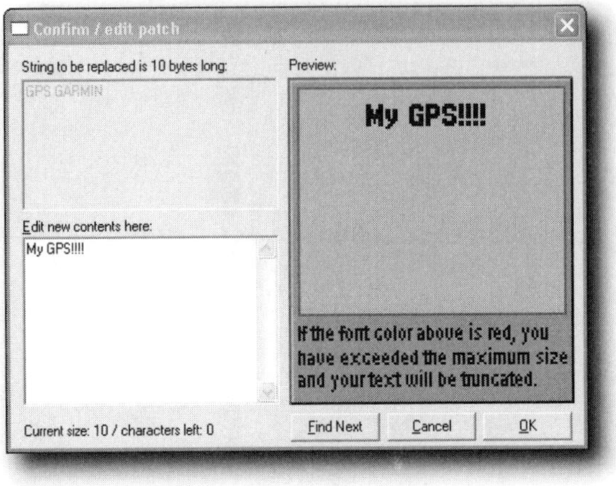

FIGURE 6-17: Searching for the term "GPS"

12. The longer the search string that you search for, the better. If you search for a small string, you will find many instances of them, whereas longer strings narrow the search better (see Figure 6-18).

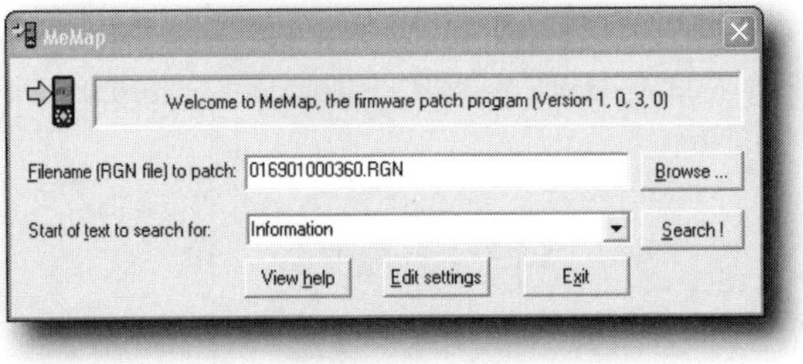

FIGURE 6-18: Longer strings provide better results, as short search strings return a large number of results.

13. After you are done making changes, click OK to close the edit window.

14. Now click Exit to close the application, and then click Yes to save the changes (see Figure 6-19).

15. All that remains for you to do now is to take the firmware and load it onto your GPS and try it out. If everything has worked thus far, the firmware should work — if you have problems, reload the original firmware on the device and try again.

FIGURE 6-19: Exiting the application

Using MeMap can be a little tricky, and because all firmware versions are different, there are no hard and fast rules as to what you can and can't do. Be careful and take your time. Mistakes can happen, but you should be able to either rectify them or reload old firmware that will restore your GPS to the condition that it was in before you attempted the changes. Because MeMap only works on text within the firmware, the danger of a mistake causing major problems other than just odd text on the screen is small.

Here are a few tips for you to get good results from using MeMap:

- The most common edit that you will probably make is replacing an entire line of text in the firmware. To do this, your search must start with the first character found in the firmware. This is normally straightforward, but some lines begin with the copyright symbol ©. In this case, you need to search for that. To do so, use an application that comes with Windows called Character Map. Select Start ➪ Run, type in **charmap,** and then click OK. Find the © character, select it, and copy it. Then switch to MeMap, select the search text, and then paste the © in by holding down the Ctrl key while pressing the V key.

- Uppercase characters are generally easier to read than lowercase characters.

- To center a line of text, add spaces in front of the text.

- Try to use the same number of lines of text that were originally used in your existing firmware, as this reduces the potential for problems.

Manual Firmware Editing

You don't actually need a special application to help you alter the firmware to customize the text that is displayed on the GPS. All you need for this is a hex editor. A hex editor is a program that enables you to open and edit a file represented in hexadecimal format.

I will be using a hex editor called UltraEdit available from www.ultraedit.com. UltraEdit is a shareware application (a very good one in fact), but if you want something free instead, you could try XVI32, available from www.chmaas.handshake.de.

Hexadecimal is a counting system that counts from zero to 16 instead of zero to 10, as in the base 10 decimal system that we're familiar and comfortable with. Counting to 16 is useful in computer applications because it enables you to represent any byte (we'll get to that in a moment) with only two characters.

This process isn't as straightforward as using MeMap, but it does take you closer to the code of the firmware and enables you to do more than you can with MeMap.

Before we go further, let's have a quick tutorial on the basic data structures in computers and look at how hex and bytes fit in.

A byte is composed of eight bits. A bit is the most basic unit of data in a computer. Bits can be either on (1) or off (0). These are the basic units of the number system known as *binary*. For example, if you have eight bits that are all on, you could represent the number 11111111. This same number would be FF in hexadecimal because hexadecimal uses characters to count past 9: A, B, C, D, E, and F.

Putting this all together, the binary notation for the largest number a byte can represent would be 11111111, which is equal to 256 in decimal and equivalent to FF in hexadecimal.

Fortunately, you don't really need to know that much about bits, bytes, or hexadecimal to modify the GPS firmware.

Note   If you want to experiment with binary, decimal, and hexadecimal numbers, fire up Windows Calculator, which enables you to work with all three formats.

The text strings that appear on the screen of your Garmin eTrex or eMap are stored in the firmware as text, which means that it is relatively easy for you to search for, find, and replace these strings of text using a hex editor, as shown in the following steps:

1. Open the firmware file in your selected hex editor. This is usually done by selecting File ➪ Open and searching for the appropriate file (see Figure 6-20).

   Garmin eMap and eTrex firmware files have a .RGN file extension so they are quite easy to find.

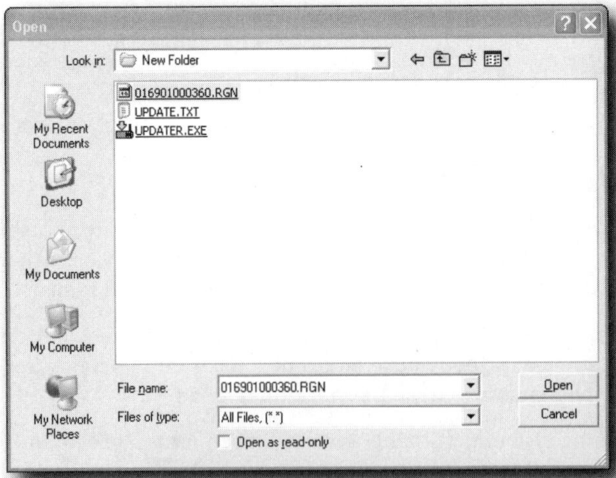

FIGURE 6-20: Search for the appropriate file.

2. The version 3.60 firmware for the Garmin eTrex Vista is called `016901000360.RGN`. After the file is loaded into the hex editor, you need to carry out a search for the text string "WARNING" (see Figure 6-21).

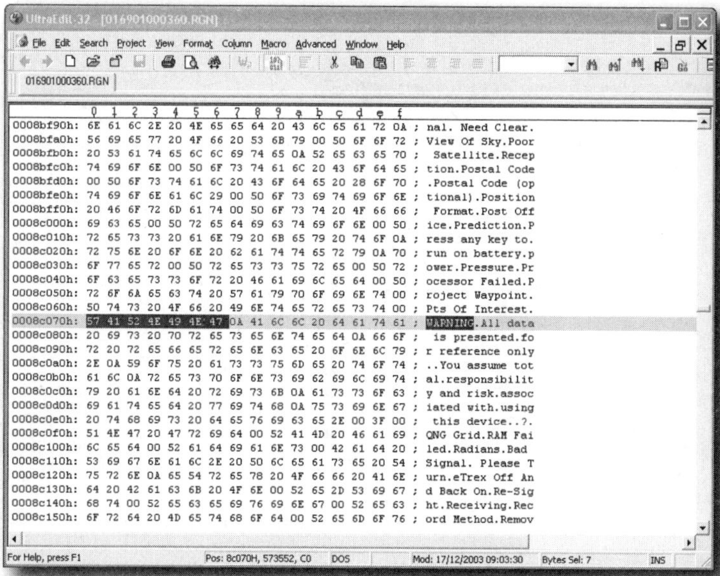

FIGURE 6-21: Searching for the word "WARNING"

3. Now select Search ⇨ Find (see Figure 6-22), which brings up the Find dialog box (see Figure 6-23).

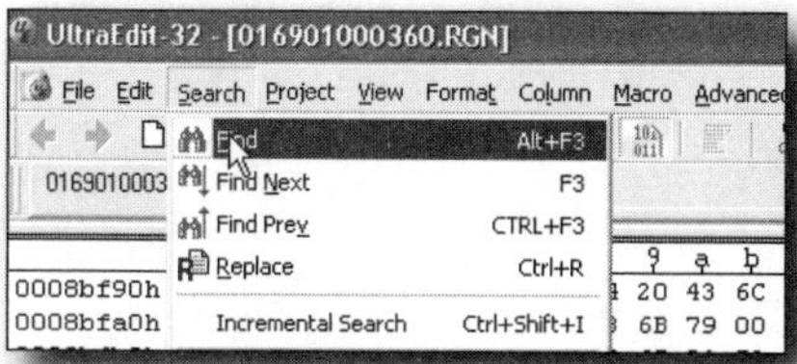

FIGURE 6-22: Select Find from the Search menu.

4. In the Find What text box, enter the text that you want to search for, as shown in Figure 6-24.

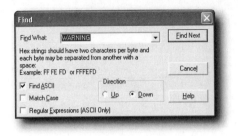

FIGURE 6-23: The Find dialog box

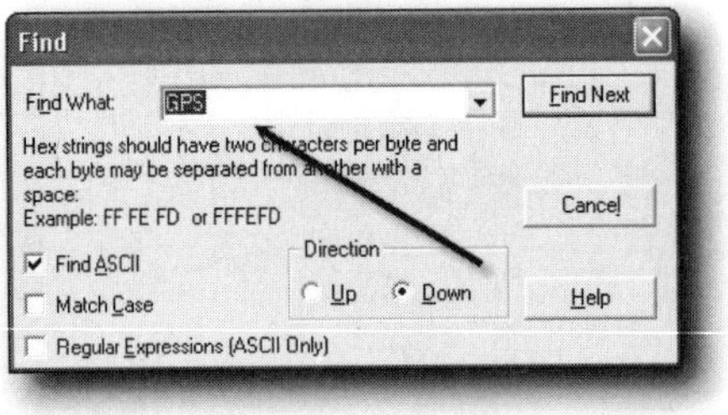

FIGURE 6-24: Entering the text to search

5. Make sure that the Find ASCII check box is checked as shown in Figure 6-25.

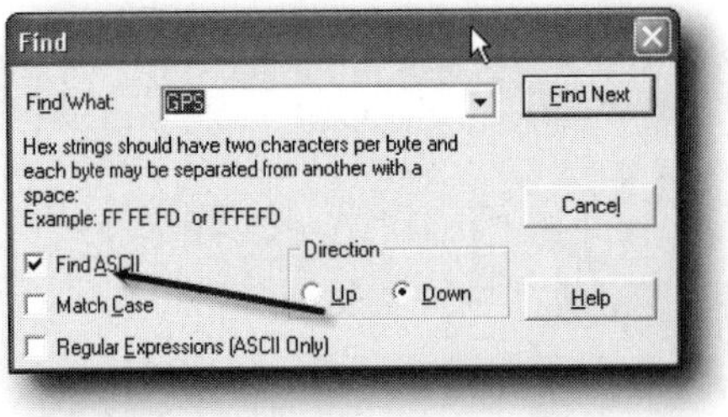

FIGURE 6-25: Make sure that the search parameters are correct.

6. Click the button labeled Find Next.

7. If you don't initially find what you are looking for, you can click the Find Next button in the dialog box (see Figure 6-26).

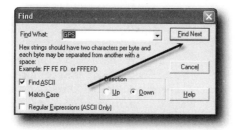

FIGURE 6-26: Use Find Next to search for the next
instance of the string in the file.

8. When you find the appropriate string that you were searching for in the file, you can then
   use the keyboard to make changes to it (see Figure 6-27). It is safer to keep the edits you
   make the same length as the original word, so if you are replacing the word "WARNING"
   (which contains seven characters) with the word "DANGER" (which contains six characters), add white space to the term to make it the same length, so " DANGER".

FIGURE 6-27: Making changes to the file

9. When you are done searching through the file and making changes, you can save the file
   (see Figure 6-28).

10. Load the firmware onto your GPS and test it out.

FIGURE 6-28: Save your changes
to the firmware.

Magellan GPS Firmware Modifications

So far, we've looked at modifying Garmin firmware. Let's look briefly at modifying the
firmware on the Magellan.

It's not as straightforward to modify the firmware on the Magellan, and as such fewer tools exist. You need tools to modify the firmware because the entire firmware is a special file, which requires you to decode it before you can work on it.

The one available product for modifying the firmware is Magellan GPS Firmware Editing Tools (GPSFET), available from `http://cnslab.mb.jhu.edu/~derrick/gpsfet/index.cgi`. To be able to run this software, you need to run it on Linux, so you will need to either install this operating system or find a system that has it. This tool contains a decoder and encoder that can read the Magellan firmware files.

The simplest thing you can do with this software tool is edit the text strings in the firmware. This could be useful and interesting for a variety of reasons:

- Add your name and details to the startup screen.

- Modify some of the text labels to make them clearer or more concise.

- Replace the English words with words in another unsupported language.

Little information exists about the editing tool for Magellan firmware so proceed cautiously and make sure you have an unaltered backup just in case things go wrong.

Recovering from a Failed Firmware Load

This section describes some steps you can take if you do run into problems when reloading firmware. Listed here are techniques for both the Garmin and Magellan units that are known to work and should help you if you get into trouble.

Garmin

Sometimes this problem will mean that you have to send your GPS unit back to the manufacturer to be fixed. However, most of the time the following procedure will get your GPS unit working again:

1. Remove the batteries from your GPS and add a set of fresh batteries or recently charged batteries.

2. Connect your GPS to the computer by the data cable, making sure that the connections are firm and secure.

3. Get your computer ready to install the new firmware.

4. Turn your GPS unit on in the usual manner. At this stage, you may or may not see anything on the screen when you do this.

5. Begin the firmware upgrade at your computer.

If this doesn't work, get in touch with the technical support representatives and see what they have to suggest. The final course of action would be to send the unit back to them for repair.

Magellan

Here are the recovery instructions for a nonfunctional Magellan Meridian or Map 330:

1. If your GPS unit is stuck in a "locked up" state, power it down by holding down MARK/GOTO and the Esc key and then press Enter. This will power down the unit.

2. Start the unit up in Software Upload Mode by holding down MARK/GOTO and the Esc key and press POWER. The GPS receiver should now power up with a "software upload mode active" message on the screen.

3. Run the update software (magup.exe). Select NO at the dialog box, click Expert, and make sure that the Expert Upload setting is checked. In addition, make sure MAP 330/Meridian is selected (not Meridian GPS) as the Unit Type and click OK.

4. Select the firmware file by clicking File ⇨ Select Code File.

5. Click Upload ⇨ OK. Make sure that Program Code and Base Map is checked. Also check Upload File.

Summary

This chapter explained how you can update the firmware on your GPS unit, thereby giving you access to bug fixes and updated features made available by the manufacturers.

You also learned several customizations that you can make to the firmware for various GPS units on the market. These customizations can be really handy because they enable you to control what happens when your GPS is switched on and what is displayed on the screen during use.

We looked at a handful of steps that you can take to reduce the chances of things going wrong during a software update. If you take care and prepare before carrying out an update, you should find that things go smoothly.

You also learned what you can do if things do go wrong — a rare event but one you should prepare for nonetheless.

Making Connections

I n this chapter, you will learn how you can connect your GPS receiver to various devices to make use of the data transfer facility. You'll first look at the different ways that receivers connect to devices, and then examine how to troubleshoot problems.

The PC — GPS Relationship

Most GPS receivers are self-contained and require no external device or data processor of any kind. The Garmin eTrex (see Figure 7-1) is a good example of a device that incorporates data processing, mapping, waypoint management, and more into a single, portable device.

Other GPS units are purely receivers that need a PC or handheld device to process the data received and to display it. Figure 7-2 shows the Bluetooth receiver from Haicom (www.haicom.tw).

These types of receiver-only GPS devices require an external device to connect to, either through a wired or wireless connection, and as such the connection methods are usually better documented than they are for other devices (although this is not always the case).

In this chapter, we will examine how GPS receivers are connected to PCs and other devices and how you can troubleshoot problems that you are likely to come across.

Note Unless you have a receiver-only GPS device, you are not required to connect the GPS to any device — but there are a lot of compelling reasons to do so.

FIGURE 7-1: Most GPS receivers incorporate a way to manage the data that they hold.

FIGURE 7-2: The Haicom HI-401 foldable GPS receiver and a Haicom Bluetooth connecting slipper

The most common device to which GPS users want to connect their device is a home PC. The following list describes some of the reasons why you should make an effort to connect your GPS receiver to a PC:

- You can transfer data (for example, waypoints) much faster than entering it into the device via the input systems offered by most GPS receivers. Figure 7-3 shows the waypoint input screen for the Garmin eTrex.

- Transferring data digitally to your GPS reduces the risk of errors and mistakes, especially in transcribing coordinates.

Note

Remember that it's always a good idea to know how to enter data manually into your GPS because you might need to do this while you're out. Read the user manual and know how to use your receiver.

- With a connection between your GPS and PC, you can take data off your device and analyze it on the PC. The most common way to do this is to download the track and overlay it on a digital map.

- Without a connection between the two devices, you won't be able to update the software on your GPS to the latest versions.

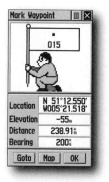

FIGURE 7-3: Waypoint input
screen on a Garmin eTrex

As you can see, there are many good reasons to take advantage of a GPS-PC connection. In Chapter 2, we looked in detail at how to make cables for a variety of GPS devices. My advice to you at this stage is if you don't have a cable, make one. If you don't want to make a cable, then get one. Either way, the benefits of having such a cable will far outweigh the time it takes to make one or the cost of purchasing one. If possible, and if you have more than one PC (a desktop and a laptop, for example) or if you have more than one GPS, you should make or get more than one cable. A good cable setup is as follows:

- A plain data cable for the desktop PC
- A combo data/power cable for laptop PC

Connection Types

There are three main ways to connect a GPS to a PC: serial (COM) port, USB, and wireless (Bluetooth). The following sections describe each of these connection methods.

Note You can also get GPS receivers that connect to the Compact Flash/PCMCIA slots on PCs and PDAs. An example of this kind of receiver is the Haicom HI-401 shown in Figure 7-2. However, each of these devices uses proprietary software and they differ a great deal from one another. If you have one of these, consult the manual.

Serial (COM) Port

The 9-pin serial port (shown in Figure 7-4) is the main way that most people connect their GPS to a PC.

Several reasons account for the popularity of the serial port:

- Most PCs, except for some of the newer ones, such as laptops, have at least one serial port to which devices (such as mice and modems) can be connected. Years ago, these ports were in great demand, and you often had to disconnect a device in order to connect a new device. Now that fewer devices need a COM port (because USB ports have superseded them), they are less in demand, and most people have the cable permanently connected to the port.

- Adding serial port support to a device is cheap, and so well established that there are rarely problems associated with it (if configured to the appropriate speed and the software is looking for the GPS on the right port).

- The data transfer to and from the GPS device does not need to be a high-speed connection, so a serial connection is ideal.

There is another hidden benefit of using a serial port connection over, say, USB. Take a look at the connector. The two thumbscrews used to hold the connector to the port secure the connection, which is usually more secure than a USB connection because of these, and they are usually more compact—USB cable connectors can extend for some distance from the port and can be more prone to damage from being knocked around than a serial port connector.

If you don't have a serial port on your system but you still want to use a serial cable, there are ways around this issue:

- Install more serial ports. Several serial port expansion cards on the market enable you to add more (or new) serial ports to your PC. This solution will work for desktop PCs that can accept expansion cards, but not with laptops.

- For systems that cannot take expansion cards, for whatever reason, you can add a USB-to-serial converter. Most of these enable you to create a new serial port on a USB port that you can connect the GPS cable to. pFranc makes one such converter, which you can see at http://pfranc.com/usb/usb.mhtml.

USB

Serial ports have slowly been replaced by the faster, more versatile, and less hassle USB (Universal Serial Bus) port (see Figure 7-5).

FIGURE 7-4: A PC serial port

FIGURE 7-5: USB ports on a laptop

A USB port can support data transfer at 12 Mbps (megabits per second), whereas serial ports can manage only 115.2 Kbps (kilobits per second). Another advantage of USB over the serial port is that it breaks the "one port, one device" rule that was pretty much absolute with a serial port. A USB port can support up to 127 devices daisy-chained to a single port.

While the USB port has gained a lot of popularity and most computers sold today have two, if not four, ports per machine, GPS manufacturers haven't been as speedy in jumping on the bandwagon. Some manufacturers (such as Garmin) make USB cables for some, but not all, of their handheld units.

Bluetooth

Wires are fine for connecting devices together, but they lack cool. For the ultimate in cool and convenience, what you need is a wireless connection. Bluetooth is a great way to achieve this. Bluetooth is a wireless communication technology that can be found on many PCs, PDAs, and cell phones. It offers many advantages over a standard wired connection:

- **Greater distance:** You can place the GPS device farther from your PC than you can with a standard wired connection (most COM cables are under a meter long).

- **Less tangle:** Cables nearly always mean tangles. Wireless connections eliminate cables and thus eliminate tangles.

- **Reduce the risk of damage:** Tangled cables can place stress on connectors that can damage the cable or the device. Wireless eliminates this problem.

- **Send the signal through walls:** If you have a GPS on a boat, for example, you might have the GPS outside and the PC inside. A wireless connection eliminates the need for holes in the wall for cables. It also makes it easier to move your GPS and PC without having to reroute cables.

- **Easier to connect:** If connections mean cables, you can find yourself needing different cables for different GPS units and PCs/handheld devices. A wireless connection eliminates this, making the process of setting up connections easier.

The only problem with wireless connections is that you need a GPS that is specifically designed for Bluetooth — it's not something you can bolt onto any GPS. GPS Bluetooth units are normally a receiver only. Figure 7-6 shows a Haicom Compact Flash GPS along with a Bluetooth "slipper" that it can be attached to, enabling the data to be transmitted to any Bluetooth receiver.

Once you have a Bluetooth device, you need a Bluetooth receiver. These are available in a variety of styles. Some devices, such as the HP iPAQ 5545 (shown in Figure 7-7), already have built-in support for Bluetooth.

PCs that don't have support for Bluetooth can have support added with a USB Bluetooth dongle, such as the one shown in Figure 7-8.

These dongles plug into a spare USB port. You install the drivers and there you have it — Bluetooth support on pretty much any PC.

FIGURE 7-6: Haicom Bluetooth GPS setup

FIGURE 7-7: The iPAQ 5545

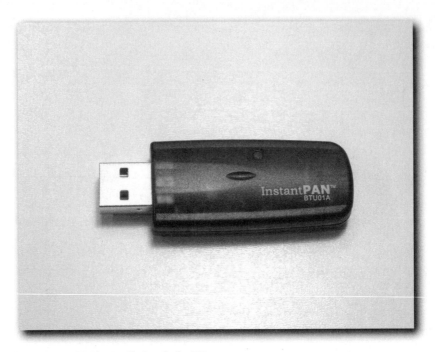

FIGURE 7-8: USB Bluetooth dongle for PCs

The range over which Bluetooth devices can work varies dramatically. The maximum range for most Bluetooth devices is 100 meters, but some have only the power to operate over distances as short as 10 meters. These are the maximum distances under ideal conditions, but several factors can dramatically reduce the range:

- **Partitions:** Walls and car and boat skins can all have an adverse effect on the range. The denser and thicker the partition, the worse the effect.

- **Trees/vegetation:** Both of these can have an adverse effect on the communication range. Tree trunks are particularly bad for the signal because they are filled with moisture, which absorbs the signal.

- **Electronic interference:** Interference from other electronic devices, and even wiring, can have an unfavorable effect on distances over which devices communicate.

- **Power consumption:** If your devices have a low-power mode, this can dramatically cut the distance over which your devices can exchange data. For the best performance, make sure low-power mode is disabled.

Bluetooth devices are in fact divided into three classes:

- Class 1 has a maximum power output of +20 dBm and a range of up to 100 meters.

- Class 2 has a maximum power output of +4 dBm and a range of up to 20 meters.

- Class 3 has a maximum power output of +0 dBm and a range of up to 10 meters.

Which Connection Is Best?

So which connection is best? It depends!

Generally, the answer depends on whether you already have a GPS or not. If you already have a GPS unit and nothing is wrong with it, you can stick with whatever connection your unit supports. If you don't have a serial port, use a USB-to-serial converter to obtain the necessary serial port for connecting. If you have a GPS that can connect to a USB port, make use of that. Be careful not to damage the connector, however, as I've found that they can be more delicate than serial port connectors.

If you are buying a new GPS, the main connection-related question that should influence your decision is whether to opt for a wired connection or a wireless connection. If you have a PC, laptop, or PDA that is or can be made Bluetooth-compatible easily (it can be quite costly for some PDAs), then a wireless connection might be your best bet.

However, remember that if you choose wireless, you will need both a GPS receiver and a data processor (such as your laptop or PDA) with you at all times. That's twice as many devices to take care of and protect from the elements and twice as many devices needing a power supply.

Generally, wireless devices make far better second GPS receivers for those already using GPS than they do GPS receivers for the first-time GPS owner.

Troubleshooting Problems

This section examines the connection problems that you might encounter when connecting your GPS receiver to another device. Fortunately, problems are few and far between, but some can be especially annoying and hard to fix.

PC Connection Trouble

The main problem that users encounter when connecting their GPS to a PC or other device is that they just can't get the two devices to communicate.

Here are some things to check if you can't get the GPS and device to communicate through a cable connection:

1. Check the cable connectors for damage. In fact, check the whole cable for any visible signs of damage. If it's a cable that you made, ensure that the connectors are sound — open them up if you suspect that there might be a problem. If you can, try the connection with a different cable. This way, you can isolate whether it is a cable problem or a settings issue on either the GPS or the PC/PDA.

2. Check the connections. If the cable seems okay, check the connections at both the GPS and the device. Undo and redo the connections and retry the connection.

3. Check the batteries on the GPS receiver. Low batteries can cause problems. Replace the batteries with known good batteries or newly recharged batteries. If possible, power the device externally.

4. Try different software. If you are having problems communicating with a particular software package, try a different software package if you have one installed. When trying different software, follow these steps carefully:

   a. Close the software involved.

   b. Switch off the GPS.

   c. Shut down the PC.

   d. After the PC is shut down, switch the GPS on and allow it to fully power on before switching on the PC.

   e. Switch the PC on and allow it to fully load.

   f. Start the software (or another GPS-capable software application) again.

5. Check connection type and speed. Many software packages can be set to a variety of communication protocols and speeds (see Figure 7-9). If you have any doubts as to how to do this, consult the software manufacturer's website. The same goes for GPS units themselves (see Figure 7-10). Garmin units can be set to either the Garmin proprietary format or the more generic NMEA protocol. Make sure that both the GPS and software are set to the same protocol and data transfer speed. For NMEA, try speeds of 4800 or 9600 bps.

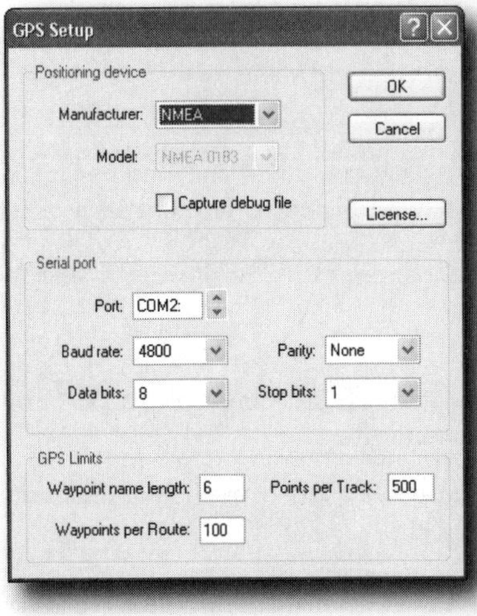

FIGURE 7-9: Port speed settings on software

6. Check the serial port with another device. This can be handy when you are having problems.

7. Try a different serial port. Another option available is to try it on a different PC if you can. This helps you isolate hardware issues.

FIGURE 7-10: Port speed settings
on the Garmin eTrex

General PDA Connection Trouble

Connecting a GPS to a PDA can be just as prone to a dead connection as can a PC-to-GPS connection. Here is the procedure for isolating and fixing a problem:

1. Check the cable connectors. Check the entire cable, including the connectors, for damage. Cables used outdoors can be subjected to damage (stretching being particularly bad for them). Check the connectors carefully for dirt or damage — dirt in the connectors can cause terrible damage to your devices, and you should take steps to protect them from the elements.

2. Check the connections. If the cable seems okay, check the connections at both the GPS and the device. Undo and redo the connections and retry the connection. Connections at the bottom of iPAQ devices are particularly prone to damage and great care needs to be taken with them. Never yank the cable from the base of a PDA and never force a connector in place — if things don't seem right, take a closer look in case you damage something further.

Note   Damaging the connector at the base of an iPAQ can result in a very expensive repair, as the whole motherboard will need replacing!

3. Check batteries. Low batteries can cause problems. Replace batteries with known good batteries or newly recharged batteries. If possible, power the device externally. Try the connection a second time, this time following these instructions:

    a. Switch off the GPS.

    b. Switch off the PDA.

    c. Disconnect the cable fully.

    d. Reattach the cable to the GPS and the PDA.

    e. Switch on the GPS and allow it to acquire a satellite lock.

    f. Soft reset the PDA (consult your manual for details as to how to do that), switch the PDA on, and run the software.

    g. See if you get a connection.

4. Check connection type and speed. As with their PC counterparts, many software packages designed for GPS use on PDAs can be set to a variety of communication protocols and speeds (see Figure 7-11). Garmin units can be set to either the Garmin proprietary format or the more generic NMEA protocol. If you have a Garmin GPS, I normally find that the connection is more stable if the Garmin protocol is used. Make sure both the GPS and software are set to the same protocol and data transfer speed. For NMEA, try speeds of 4800 or 9600 bps.

FIGURE 7-11: Pocket PC software is similar to most desktop PC software in that it will have port settings information.

General Bluetooth Connection Trouble

Bluetooth connections can sometimes be problematic to set up. Here is a guide to help you with these kinds of connections:

1. Make sure that both devices are Bluetooth-compliant. This seems obvious, but it is sometimes hard to determine which PDAs are Bluetooth-compliant.

2. Switch off all other Bluetooth devices in the vicinity.

3. Make sure that the GPS and the PDA/PC are close together and that no walls are obscuring the signal. Bring the two devices to within 1 meter of each other while troubleshooting problems.

4. Pair the devices. Most Bluetooth devices must be paired before use (for security, most Bluetooth devices have to be introduced to one another and a pin code inserted the first time they are connected to prevent unauthorized connections). Consult your manual for instructions for how to do that.

5. Check connection type and speed. Make sure that both the GPS and software are set to the same protocol and data transfer speed. For NMEA, try speeds of 4800 or 9600 bps.

Software-Specific Issues

Numerous software-specific issues can cause problems for those wishing to make use of a GPS and a PC or PDA. The following sections cover some of those issues.

Erratic Mouse Pointer after Connecting a GPS

Sometimes after you install and connect a GPS to a PC, the mouse pointer will jump around the screen in what appears to be an erratic, unpredictable fashion. As you can guess, what is happening here is that the PC is taking the signal from the GPS and interpreting it as mouse information. Use the following steps to troubleshoot this problem:

1. Restart the PC. With the GPS connected at startup, the system should detect both the mouse and the GPS and work properly.

2. If this doesn't work, download and install new drivers for your mouse from the vendor's website. This should reset the settings and cause the pointer to ignore the GPS data.

3. Unfortunately, some GPS-mouse combinations cannot be fixed directly (usually it's a bad driver issue), and these problems can generally only be fixed either by reverting to using a basic driver supplied by the operating system or by replacing the offending mouse (try to get a USB mouse, as these are less prone to problems).

4. Check for updated drivers for the GPS too. These might be helpful in solving such problems.

Windows XP Problem: Microsoft Ball Point

Here's another interesting problem: You connect the GPS to your PC, and Windows XP or 2000 identifies it as a "Microsoft Serial Ball Point." This prevents the GPS from working as a GPS because the system thinks that it is a mouse. The solution is fortunately quite simple: Disable the fictitious mouse and the GPS will then work just fine.

Here are the steps to follow:

1. Boot the computer with the GPS receiver attached. The cursor might be behaving erratically and jumping around the screen, or all sorts of other unwanted behavior may be observed.

2. Disconnect the GPS. The computer will quickly return to normal.

3. Click Start → Control Panel. If your mouse pointer isn't working, you can use the Windows button on the keyboard to bring up the Start menu. Navigate using the cursor keys and press Enter for a mouse click. If you are running Windows XP, you will need to click Performance and Maintenance before clicking System, followed by the Hardware tab and then Device Manager. If you are running Windows 2000, you won't see Performance and Maintenance and will proceed straight to System.

4. Click the plus sign (+) next to Mice and Other Pointing Devices (or navigate to it using the cursor keys and press Enter), as shown in Figure 7-12.

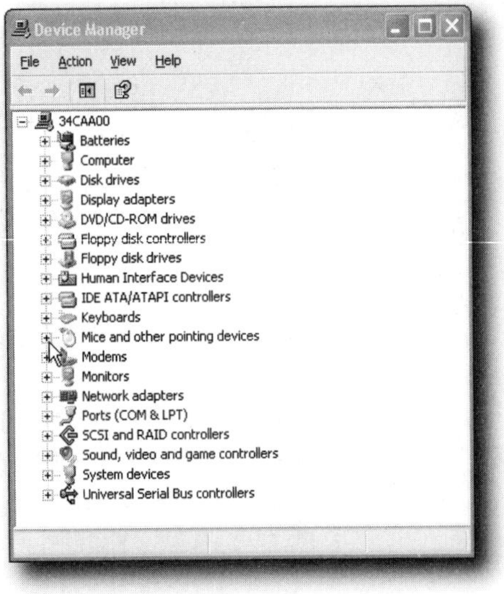

FIGURE 7-12: Pointing devices

5. Click Microsoft Serial Ball Point. This is what Windows XP thinks that your GPS receiver is.

6. Select Actions → Disable.

7. Click OK to close each window.

8. Reboot the computer with the GPS attached. The problem should now be fixed!

Microsoft MapPoint Troubleshooting

Microsoft's popular MapPoint application is used to plot GPS positions in real time on maps. Three common problems with this software can be easily fixed as follows.

If you receive error messages when using the software, follow these steps to resolve the problem:

1. Ensure that the cables are properly connected and working properly.

2. Make sure that the GPS is turned on and powered up properly.

3. Ensure that the input/output format (interface) on your GPS receiver is set to support the NMEA protocol (usually, if given a choice, use NMEA 0183 version 2.0 or later).

4. Make sure the COM serial port is set to the same speed as the GPS unit. For most devices, 4800 bps is the appropriate speed to use.

5. Ensure that the COM port that was selected during configuration is the same port to which your GPS receiver is actually connected. On the Tools menu in MapPoint, click GPS, click Configure GPS Receiver, and then select a different COM port from the list if necessary.

6. Exit or change the settings for other programs or applications that use the same COM port you have configured for the GPS receiver.

7. Make sure that your GPS device does not require a specific mapping program to work properly. Although it is rare, some GPS receivers can only be used with specific software packages. For example, some TomTom units are locked to the software and cannot be used with other software packages.

8. MapPoint cannot detect GPS receivers that connect to the PCMCIA slot in your computer (these are common on laptops).

9. A GPS for use with MapPoint must be configured to use a COM port with a number below 20. COM ports above 20 will not be recognized as being a GPS device by the software.

If your GPS receiver cannot find satellites, follow these steps:

1. Make sure you have properly installed your GPS receiver, and that you are using both the correct COM port and a functional cable.

2. Make sure your GPS receiver has been turned on, is connected to your computer, and is running for several minutes in a location where it has a clear view of the sky. Check to see if the GPS itself is tracking satellites.

3. Make sure the COM serial port is set to the same speed as the GPS unit. For most devices, 4800 bps is the appropriate speed to use.

4. Make sure the COM port that was selected during configuration is the same port to which your GPS receiver is actually connected. On the Tools menu in MapPoint, click GPS, click Configure GPS Receiver, and then select a different COM port from the list if necessary.

5. Exit or change the settings for other programs or applications that use the same COM port you have configured for the GPS receiver.

6. Make sure your GPS device does not require a specific mapping program to work properly. Although it is rare, some GPS receivers can only be used with specific software packages.

You may also find a positional error. Positional errors are likely caused by GPS errors or communication errors. Try these steps to resolve the problem:

1. Ensure that the cable is properly connected at both ends. Problems here can cause data corruption and a degradation of signal quality.

2. Verify that the GPS has a clear view of the sky and is receiving a good signal.

USB-to-Serial Converters

If you are using a USB-to-serial converter, you might encounter a few problems specific to your setup.

For example, you might find that the number assigned to the port creates changes occasionally, and you might have to reconfigure any software you are using if this has happens.

Another problem is that a USB-to-serial converter can assign ports from COM 1 to COM 255. However, some software packages can only use ports 1 to 4. Most modern applications allow you to choose any active port for GPS communication, but if you use an older software package you might be limited to ports 1, 2, 3, or 4.

Only versions 4.0 and later of the Garmin MapSource mapping program will interface with a GPS through a USB-to-serial connector. Any previous versions will fail to work.

USB-to-serial converters are not supported in Windows 95, even the OSR 2.1 version that included USB support. You will need a minimum of Windows 98.

Summary

This chapter looked at problems you might encounter when transferring data between the GPS and a PC or handheld device. As I've said a few times, you don't have to have a connection in place, but it makes life a lot easier and enables you to process and display data in a much more versatile and customizable way than is possible with most GPS units.

If you are unfortunate enough to have problems with your connection, following either the generic or specific instructions in this chapter should help you fix the problem and get your system working again.

Data Hacking

part

GPS Data

This chapter is all about data.

As you walk, drive, sail, or otherwise move around with your GPS, you are gathering a great deal of data. In this chapter, you will learn what you can do with this data while in the field and when you get back to base. You'll see how to create and edit your own waypoints and routes and how to upload these to your GPS. Then, you'll learn how you can download, modify, and upload data that you captured while using the GPS. You'll also look at various applications into which you can export your data for managing it and storage.

This chapter also describes how you can add GPS information to digital photographs, plot lightning strikes, and go wardriving. For any programmers that might be reading this, we will also be looking at some websites and applications that might be of use to you if you're interested in writing your own GPS applications.

Finally, you'll learn how you can create your own data for upload to your GPS.

GPS Data Collection

As you move around with your GPS, it is continuously gathering data and storing it so that you can access it later. The newer and more expensive the GPS, the more information it can hold. For example, the Garmin eTrex basic version can hold the following:

- 500 waypoints
- 1 route
- 50 waypoints per route
- 1,536 tracklog points

At the top to the range, the Garmin Vista has greater capacity in all areas:

- 1,000 waypoints
- 20 routes
- 125 waypoints per route
- 10,000 tracklog points

Put simply, this means you can move around longer with a Garmin Vista than you can with a basic eTrex without overwriting existing data.

Let's take a look at the different types of information your GPS collects and stores.

Position, Velocity, Time

Position, Velocity, Time (PVT) data is at the core of GPS. These three data categories cover where you are, what time it is, and how fast you are moving in relation to your last known position. This information is what GPS is pretty much all about. Let's take a look at the three parts of this data.

Position

Position data is information about where on the Earth's surface the GPS actually is. You can think of this as a spot reading taken at a point in time.

Position information consists of two parts:

- **Latitude:** These are lines that form concentric circles around the globe. The equator is the longest line of latitude, and they shrink in size until they become a point at the north and south poles (see Figure 8-1). They are measured in degrees. The equator is 0°, the north pole is +90° and the south pole is -90°.

- **Longitude:** Lines of longitude extend from the poles (see Figure 8-2). There are 360° in a full circle, but longitude is measured 0° to 180° east and 0° to 180° west, with 0° passing through Greenwich in London and 180° passing through the Pacific Ocean.

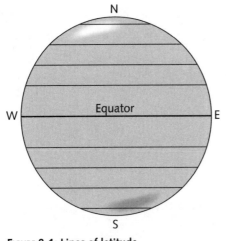

FIGURE 8-1: Lines of latitude

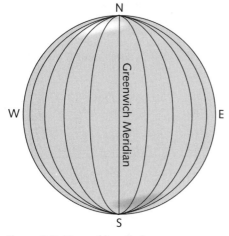

FIGURE 8-2: Lines of longitude

You can take a measurement of latitude and longitude (although the convention is to use longitude followed by latitude) and combine them to get a fixed point of the Earth's surface. This is similar to the grid system used in games such as Battleship in which by specifying how many squares to move along and up, you get to the square in question.

For example, 0° longitude, 0° latitude (written as 0°, 0°) is a point in the Atlantic Ocean off the coast of Africa, while 180° east (or west, for that matter) longitude, 0° latitude is still on the equator, but this time on the other side of the world completely, in the Pacific Ocean, off the coast of Fiji.

Degrees are a good start to plotting coordinates, but they aren't as precise as possible. What you now need to do is further divide the degrees into minutes. Each degree consists of 60 minutes:

12° 12' N 04° 08' W

In addition to minutes, you can add even greater precision by adding decimal parts of a minute:

12° 12.255' N 04° 08.345' W

Note Instead of using decimal minutes, you can also subdivide minutes into seconds (where one minute has 60 seconds). However, decimal minutes are the general coordinate format used with the WGS84 datum system that we are going to use here, and they are the default units shown on GPS receivers.

No matter what coordinate format you choose, the actual location represented on the planet is the same. The numbers may be different, but the location is the same. For example, the following three sets of coordinates represent the same spot on the globe:

N 38 deg 26 min 48.517 sec, W 76 deg 5 min 38.192 sec

N 38 deg 26.80862 min, W 76 deg 5.63653 min

-76.0939423, 38.4468104

This coordinate system gives us the ability to pinpoint locations. 51° 30.075 North, 0° 08.545 West is the location of Buckingham Palace in London, England. If you enter this into your GPS (see Figure 8-3), you will get information about how to get there.

As you move, the GPS will plot your position in relation to where you want to go, so you always know exactly where you are.

FIGURE 8-3: Coordinates entered into the GPS

Velocity

Velocity isn't the same thing as speed. Speed is a measure of how fast you are going in any direction. Velocity is more specific than that. Velocity measures how fast you are going *and* in what direction you are going. In a GPS, this is normally computed as a *track angle* (the direction of travel with respect to True North).

A GPS solution for velocity enables it to calculate whether you are moving toward or away from a particular point, and from this information a number of calculations can be computed, such as the following:

- Distance to waypoint

- Information about whether you are on course or not

- Real-time plotting on a map of your direction of travel

- Estimated arrival time

- Estimated journey time

Different units display this information differently. Figure 8-4 is a screen capture from a Garmin eTrex Vista.

FIGURE 8-4: Waypoint information
on a Garmin eTrex

How Does GPS Calculate Velocity?

Many people wonder how the GPS can accurately determine velocity from the positional information it captures for a snapshot period of time.

This is a good question. In fact, the way that GPS calculates your speed is very clever, yet at the same time quite simple. It remembers where you were the last time it locked your position and uses this information to calculate your speed.

Most GPS receivers update your position information once a second. For example, if you moved 30 meters since the last update, it calculates your speed as 30 meters per second (see Figure 8-5).

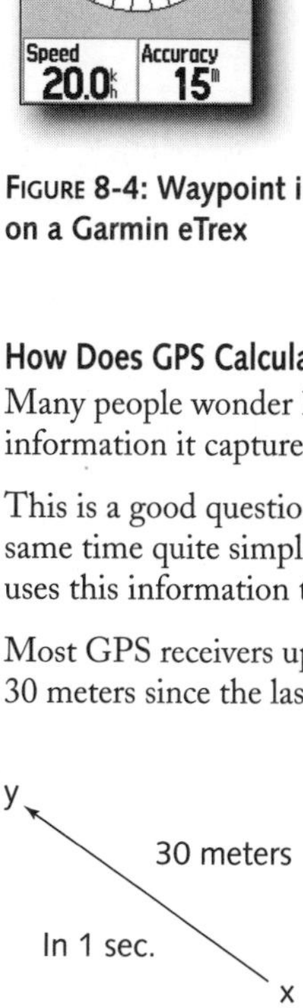

y

30 meters

In 1 sec.

x

FIGURE 8-5: Speed calculated
from distance moved

Is Direction Calculated in the Same Way?

Yes and no. Most GPS receivers use only the signal from the GPS to plot your direction of travel, which means that the only frame of reference it has with regard to your direction is where you were the last time it looked and where you are now. So in that respect, yes, it uses that information to calculate your direction (see Figure 8-6).

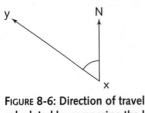

FIGURE 8-6: Direction of travel
calculated by comparing the last
location to the current location

However, some newer, more expensive receivers contain an electronic compass that works just like any other compass, detecting the Earth's magnetic field. This information can be combined with the data from the GPS satellites to provide you with even greater accuracy in plotting your direction of travel (see Figure 8-7).

FIGURE 8-7: Electronic
compass in action

Note   The lack of a compass is why some GPS receivers, depending on type, can't actually tell you which way to go to get to a certain point unless you are moving. Without a compass, it can't determine the receiver's direction from only the GPS satellite signal.

This can be a real problem at times, and the pointer on some receivers will spin wildly when the unit is stationary. An electronic compass eliminates this behavior (see Figure 8-8).

Remember, however, that built-in digital compasses are subject to the same problems as standard compasses (such as being affected by close proximity to metal and other magnets).

Time

Thanks to the four atomic clocks on board each GPS satellite, you can be pretty confident of getting a good time signal from the satellites. Local time zone information can be inputted into the GPS (see Figure 8-8) along with daylight saving information (see Figure 8-9).

FIGURE 8-8: Time zone
information

FIGURE 8-9: Daylight saving
information

Some GPS receivers, either when you buy them or when they have had exhausted batteries in them for some period of time, will ask you to input the time and date manually — this helps the receiver get a lock on the satellites, and the time will be corrected when the almanac has been downloaded.

Waypoints

A *waypoint* is a spot on the surface of the Earth as defined by coordinates that are inputted into the GPS and stored, usually along with an icon, a descriptive name, and some text.

There are two types of waypoint:

- Manual waypoints
- On-the-spot waypoints

Manual Waypointing

A manual waypoint is one that you enter into the GPS for a location that you are not currently at. For example, before you leave home, you might enter the waypoint of the parking lot at your destination or perhaps the geocache that you are looking for (see Figure 8-10).

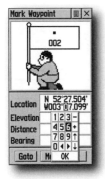

FIGURE 8-10: Manual
waypointing

To enter a manual waypoint, you need to know the coordinates of the location to which you are heading. For this you need a map of some kind or some other repository of coordinates (a map, geocache listing, points of interest, etc.).

Note Be very careful when manually entering waypoint information into your GPS because a small numerical error can translate into a massive error on the ground! In addition, make sure that you're using the appropriate datum for the coordinate system being used (for degrees/minutes/seconds, degrees/minutes, and decimal degrees, use WGS84). Using the incorrect datum can cause inaccuracies of several hundred meters.

Coordinates form the fundamental aspect of navigating with a GPS other than using dead reckoning (where you follow a path and a bearing for a certain distance over a certain amount of time), and getting comfortable with using them is the first step to really using GPS properly.

On-the-Spot Waypointing

With on-the-spot waypointing, you travel to a place and waypoint that particular location, storing the waypoint in your GPS. This stores the location that is displayed by the GPS into the memory of the device. You can then navigate back to this spot later. For example, you could waypoint the location of your car before going off in search of a geocache so that you are sure to find it on the way back).

Routes

Routes are path data that is stored in the GPS. A route is a series of waypoints contained in the GPS that form a path of travel, similar to the connect-the-dots activity found in children's activity and puzzle books.

Different types of GPS receivers enable you to store varying numbers of routes, with each route made up of a different number of waypoints (see Figure 8-11).

Once a route has been tracked by the GPS, it can be reversed so that you can backtrack and return to where you began.

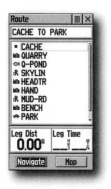

FIGURE 8-11: Routes stored in a GPS

Working with the Data

As you can see, a considerable amount of data is stored in a GPS, which means that you need to be able to access it and work with it. Two principal tasks come into play here:

- Working with the data you have already collected with the GPS
- Creating new data for upload

Before you can work with existing data, you have to get it off the GPS. Most tools that enable you to download data from a GPS also enable you to edit the data and work with it at a fundamental level, editing every aspect of the data. Some purists think that editing any data gathered by your GPS is not appropriate and prefer to keep it unedited, but others believe that because it is their data, they can do what they wish with it. There is merit in that opinion — perhaps you made a mistake when creating a waypoint, took a wrong turn in your journey when you were recording a route, or missed a few points along the way that you want to add after the fact. Another good reason to download data from your GPS is that it frees up memory on the device, enabling you to collect more data.

Everything about the data is editable. Just because you created a route or waypoint while on the move doesn't mean that you can't edit that data later.

At this point, you might be wondering why you have to download the data. Can't you just edit the data while it is still on the GPS? You can, but the problem is that you have to input numbers and data using an input system that is generally prone to error. Furthermore, remember that when you enter and edit data on a PC, you will normally have the capability to undo any changes you make, a handy feature not present in the GPS interface.

The great thing about tools that can retrieve data off your GPS is that they also enable you to create new data for upload to the GPS. This is invaluable for planning trips. For example, it is much easier to create a route as of a set of waypoints on the PC than using the interface provided by most GPS receivers. In addition, your PC provides you with access to more information (digital maps perhaps, or Internet resources) to make planning easier. You can generally accomplish more in an hour of waypoint and route management on a PC than you can with several hours using the GPS. The more data you have to work with, the more vital the PC or handheld device becomes. Errors are dramatically reduced too, which means that your trip will be a safer one. Remember that when you are creating data, you need access to reasonably accurate information on the coordinates of items, for which you will need access to maps — either paper maps or, better still, digital mapping applications.

One of the easiest ways to get this information is to use free applications. Many are available, but we will examine two of the best:

- EasyGPS
- G7toWin

EasyGPS

EasyGPS (shown in Figure 8-12) is a free software tool that enables you to work with data stored in Garmin, Magellan, and Lowrance GPS units. EasyGPS is one of the easiest ways to work with the data on your GPS receiver. You can download the latest copy of EasyGPS from www.easygps.com.

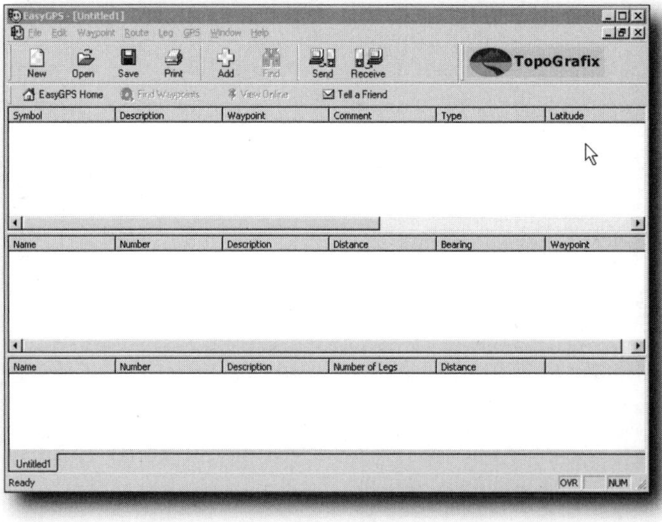

FIGURE 8-12: EasyGPS

After you have downloaded and installed the application, you are ready to work with the data:

1. Set up EasyGPS so that it can detect your GPS receiver. Click File ⇨ Preferences to bring up the Setup dialog box (see Figure 8-13).

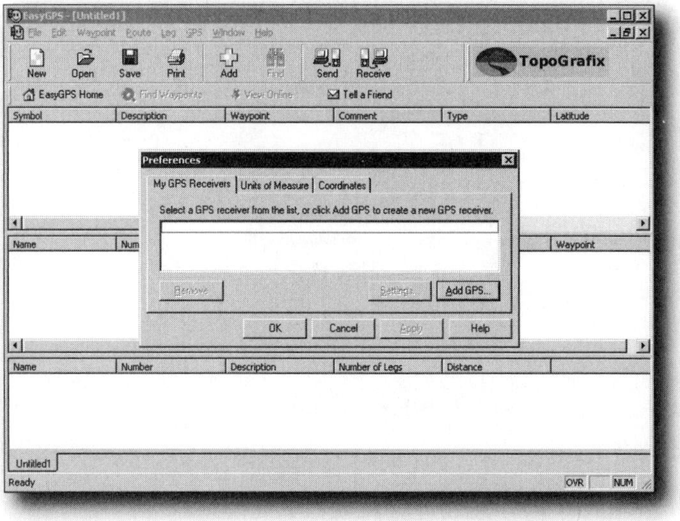

FIGURE 8-13: Setup screen on EasyGPS

2. Click Add GPS. This brings up the dialog box shown in Figure 8-14.

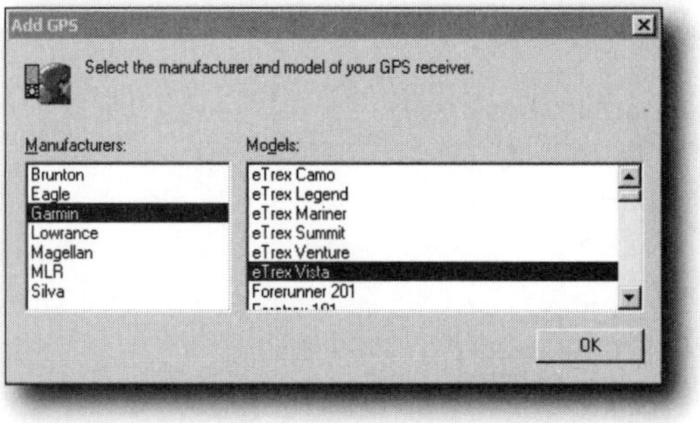

FIGURE 8-14: Selecting the appropriate GPS receiver

3. Select the GPS that you have and click OK.

4. The GPS Settings dialog box appears. Select the serial port to which the GPS unit is connected (see Figure 8-15). Click OK twice.

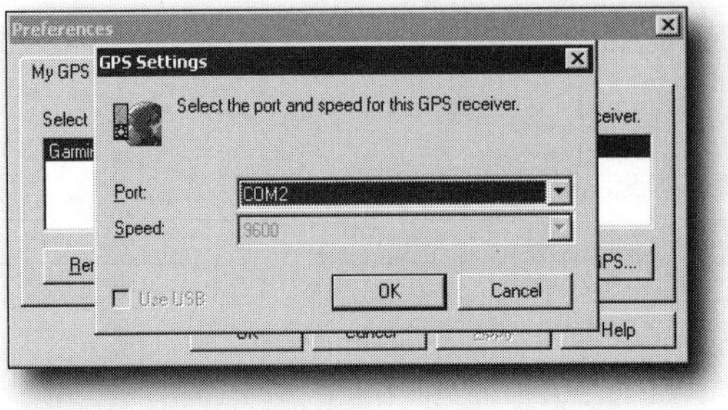

FIGURE 8-15: Selecting the serial port

5. To test your settings, click GPS ⇨ Test Serial Connection. The dialog box shown in Figure 8-16 appears. Click OK to begin the test.

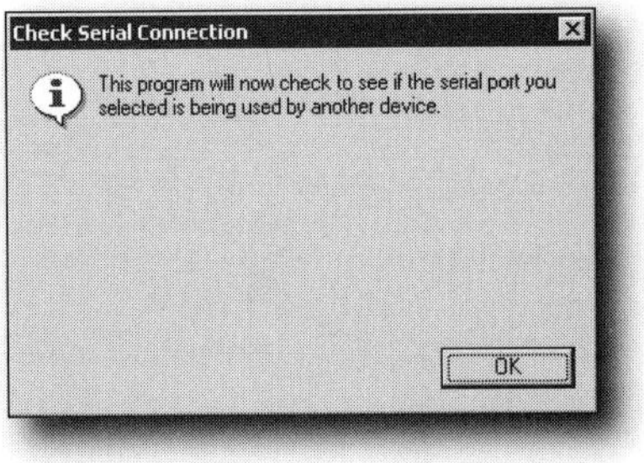

FIGURE 8-16: Testing the connection. This attempts to communicate with the GPS using the connection settings specified.

6. EasyGPS will detect the serial port. If the GPS is switched on and has satellite lock, it will detect the GPS type and version numbers (see Figure 8-17).

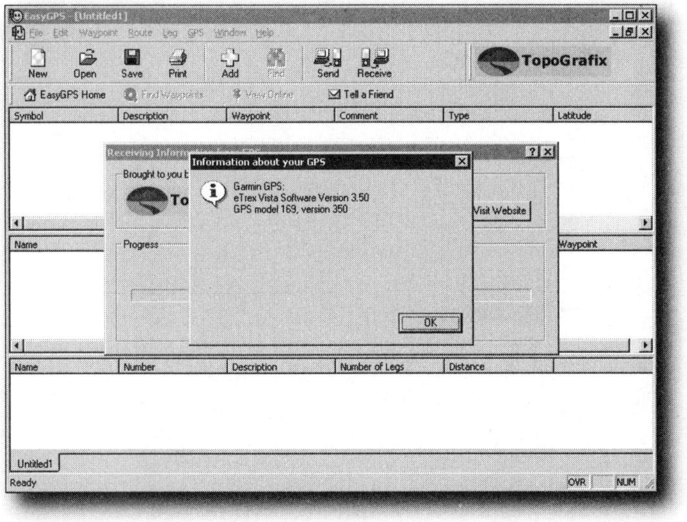

FIGURE 8-17: EasyGPS detecting the GPS

Now you can use the application to send and receive files from the GPS.

1. Click File ⇨ Open. Navigate to the folder in which EasyGPS is installed and open the sample files included.

2. This loads the data into the application, as shown in Figure 8-18.

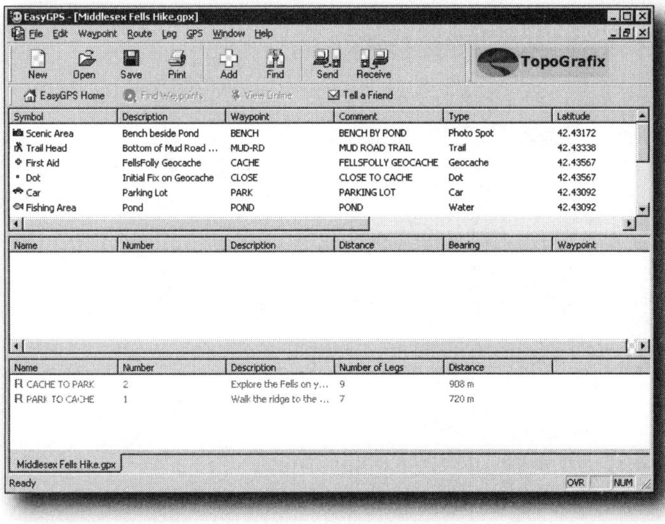

FIGURE 8-18: EasyGPS sample file data displayed

3. Now you can upload the data to the GPS. Click the Send button. EasyGPS will ask you to confirm what you want to send to the GPS (waypoints and routes) and the GPS to which it is being sent (see Figure 8-19).

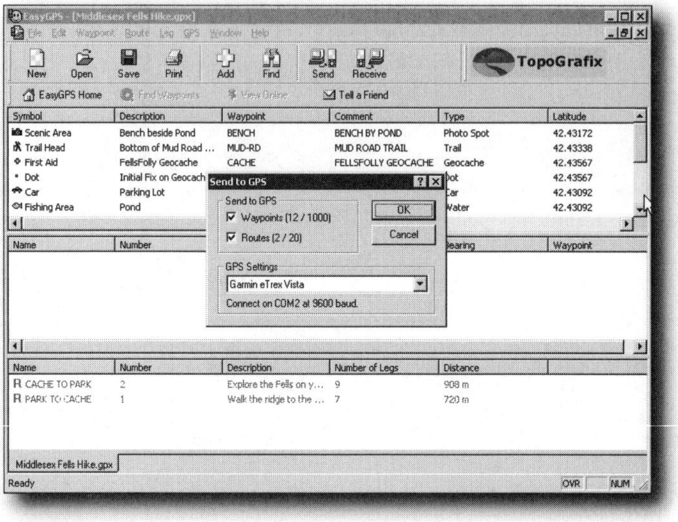

FIGURE 8-19: Sending data to the GPS

4. Click OK for the process to begin. A progress dialog box will appear, as shown in Figure 8-20.

FIGURE 8-20: Data transfer in process

5. Now you can check the GPS to determine whether the waypoints (see Figure 8-21) and routes (see Figure 8-22) have been sent to the unit.

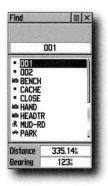

FIGURE 8-21: Waypoints
transferred to the GPS

FIGURE 8-22: Routes
transferred to the GPS

6. Now click the New button (see Figure 8-23). This will bring up a blank window, although you can still change to the previous window by clicking the tab at the bottom of the screen (see Figure 8-24).

FIGURE 8-23: Opening a new, blank
window in EasyGPS

FIGURE 8-24: Navigating between
data windows

7. Click the Receive button to download the data on the GPS into the application.

8. You will be asked what you want to download (see Figure 8-25).

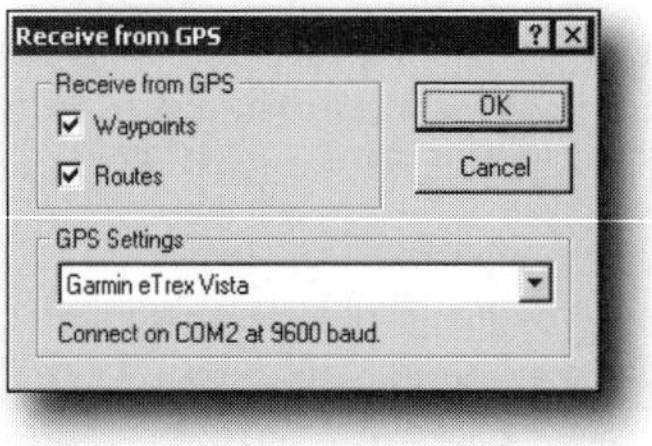

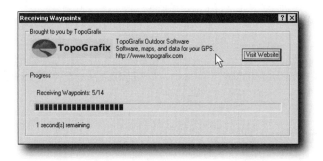

FIGURE 8-25: Selecting the data to download

9. Click OK to begin the download process (see Figure 8-26).

FIGURE 8-26: Starting the download process

After you have the data downloaded from the GPS, you can set to work editing the data. A waypoint is a convenient way of packaging all the data relating to a positional fix. This data includes the following:

- Coordinates

- Date and time of waypoint marking

- An icon to represent the waypoint

- Height data

Different manufacturers store different information in a waypoint. For example, Garmin units enable you to specify an icon to represent your waypoint from a gallery of icons (that range from urban markers such as libraries and gas stations to rural ones for places such as fishing spots, cabins, and camps). These icons are often common to a manufacturer, a range of units, or maybe even a few brands.

As mentioned earlier, there are many reasons why you would want to edit a waypoint—perhaps you marked the wrong spot, gave it the wrong name, or just want to add more information to it after the fact. Whatever the reason, and no matter what you want to change, it can be changed later quickly and easily on the PC.

The following list describes the items you can change:

- **Description of waypoint:** This is a short description of what the waypoint actually is. Only some GPS receivers store and display this data field. If your receiver does, then it's a good idea to use it because waypoints can be hard to keep track of and knowing which is which in the field based on a short title is tricky. The downside of this data field is that the more text you put here, the more memory the device consumes (which is why some units don't store this data at all).

- **Waypoint:** This is the name you give to the waypoint. Ten characters is the maximum allowed by EasyGPS, but I suggest that you try to keep the name under eight characters long, as some units will truncate it down to this.

- **Comment:** This field enables you to enter comments to augment the description. Some GPS receivers and software use this to store date and time information about the waypoint, while others ignore it.

- **Type and Symbol:** These two items are interrelated. The icon is a visual marker used by the GPS to represent the type of waypoint, either displayed on a map or as a list. Choose the icon that most closely matches the type of waypoint you are describing, as this makes finding the right waypoint a lot easier.

- **Latitude, Longitude, and Elevation:** This is the core information that forms the basis of the waypoint.

1. To edit a waypoint, right-click on the waypoint and choose Edit Waypoint (see Figure 8-27).

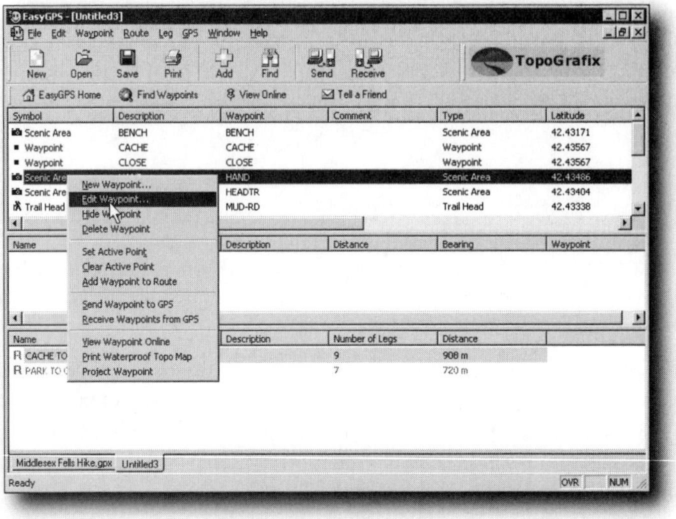

FIGURE 8-27: Bringing up the Edit Waypoint dialog box

2. This brings up an Edit Waypoint dialog box (see Figure 8-28).

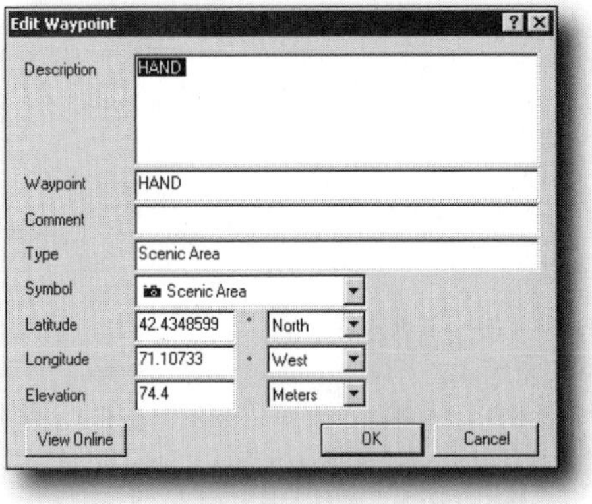

FIGURE 8-28: Edit Waypoint dialog box

3. This dialog box is the powerhouse for editing waypoints. Here you can change everything that there is to change about the waypoint (see Figure 8-29).

4. You can also create new waypoints by right-clicking in the waypoint area of the screen and choosing New Waypoint. This brings up the dialog box shown in Figure 8-30. After

you create a new waypoint, you can enter any information relating to this waypoint. Of course, the most important information are the coordinates (latitude and longitude), which you can read off of a map. Chances are good, however, that you won't be able to get a set of coordinates that are as accurate as those that you could get from being at the actual location, but it should be enough to get you there, especially if you choose an obvious landmark (visit www.maptools.com for transparent overlays for paper maps that make getting an accurate coordinate possible). With digital maps, the coordinates of the location at the cursor are normally given to a high degree of accuracy. If you choose a good landmark that's easily visible, then the actual coordinates can be off by several hundred feet and not make a difference because once you are in the vicinity you can navigate by sight.

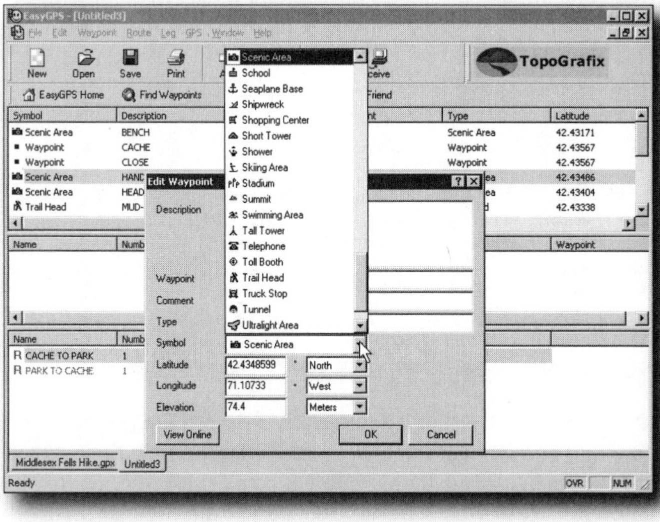

FIGURE 8-29: Changing waypoint information is easy, but take care in case you accidentally change information such as the coordinates of the waypoint!

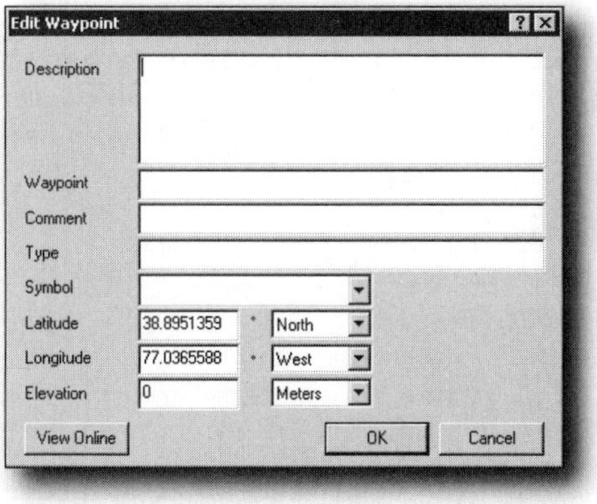

FIGURE 8-30: Creating a new waypoint

When you have finished editing the waypoints, you can either send the updated data to the GPS or save the file. You can save the information in two different file formats (see Figure 8-31):

- TopoGrafix Data file (.loc)
- GPS Exchange file (.gpx)

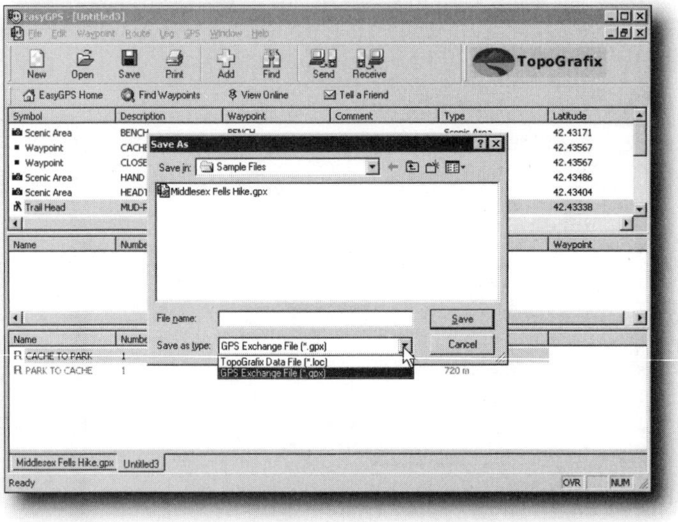

FIGURE 8-31: You can save the stored information in EasyGPS in two different file formats, which can be later opened either in EasyGPS or another compatible tool.

These two files are fundamentally different. The .loc files are binary files (see Figure 8-32), and while they can be opened in a text or hex editor, they cannot realistically be edited without using either EasyGPS or another application that can edit .loc files. For more information on the TopoGrafixs file format and editing applications, visit www.topografix.com.

The .gpx output file is a different matter. This file isn't a binary file but a text file that is laid out in a format known as XML (eXtensible Markup Language). If you have experience with creating web pages or XML in general, this will already be familiar to you. The great thing about these files is that they can be edited directly with nothing more than a text editor, which is a real bonus if you are in the field when you want to edit them.

Here is part of the contents of a typical .gpx file:

```
<?xml version="1.0" encoding="ISO-8859-1" standalone="yes"?>
<gpx
 version="1.1"
 creator="EasyGPS 1.3.7 - http://www.topografix.com"
 xmlns:xsi="http://www.w3.org/2001/XMLSchema-instance"
 xmlns="http://www.topografix.com/GPX/1/1"
 xsi:schemaLocation="http://www.topografix.com/GPX/1/1
http://www.topografix.com/GPX/1/1/gpx.xsd">
```

```
<metadata>
<time>2004-11-18T15:59:12Z</time>
<bounds minlat="42.430910" minlon="-71.107900" maxlat="42.435720"
maxlon="-71.104360"/>
</metadata>
<wpt lat="42.431709938" lon="-71.107839939">
 <ele>39.058960</ele><time>2004-11-18T15:48:31Z</time>
 <name>BENCH</name>
 <desc>BENCH</desc>
 <sym>Scenic Area</sym>
 <type>Scenic Area</type>
</wpt>
<wpt lat="42.435669968" lon="-71.104429930">
 <ele>76.550171</ele><time>2004-11-18T15:48:31Z</time>
 <name>CACHE</name>
 <desc>CACHE</desc>
 <sym>Waypoint</sym>
 <type>Waypoint</type>
</wpt>
<extensions>
</extensions>
</gpx>
```

This file contains a lot of editable information, and provides you with easy access to the heart of the data. Let's walk through some of the data the file contains:

```
<?xml version="1.0" encoding="ISO-8859-1" standalone="yes"?>
<gpx
 version="1.1"
 creator="EasyGPS 1.3.7 - http://www.topografix.com"
 xmlns:xsi="http://www.w3.org/2001/XMLSchema-instance"
 xmlns="http://www.topografix.com/GPX/1/1"
 xsi:schemaLocation="http://www.topografix.com/GPX/1/1
http://www.topografix.com/GPX/1/1/gpx.xsd">
```

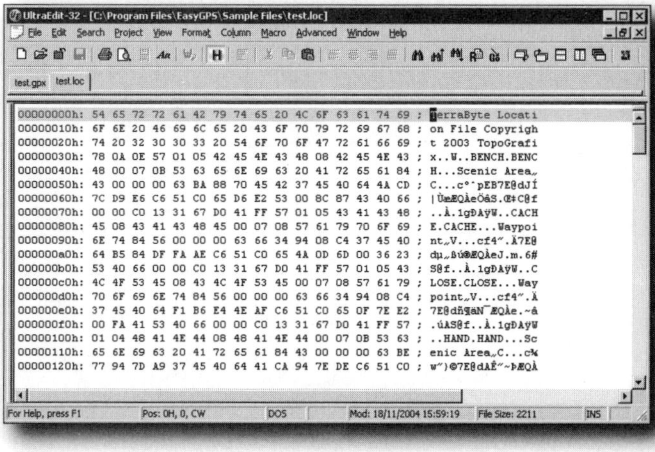

FIGURE 8-32: Binary format of the .loc files

The data at the top of the file is called the *header data* and contains information about the what the file is, what created it, and where the layout of the file is stored (the TopoGrafix website). Leave this information alone, as making changes to it can cause the file to be unreadable by EasyGPS:

```
<metadata>
<time>2004-11-18T15:59:12Z</time>
<bounds minlat="42.430910" minlon="-71.107900" maxlat="42.435720"
maxlon="-71.104360"/>
</metadata>
```

The next section of the file contains information relating to the range of data held by the file. The terms minlon and minlat stand for minimum longitude and minimum latitude, respectively, while maxlon and maxlat stand for maximum longitude and maximum latitude, respectively. This is used by the file to speed up the sorting of the data by latitude and longitude:

```
<wpt lat="42.431709938" lon="-71.107839939">
 <ele>39.058960</ele><time>2004-11-18T15:48:31Z</time>
 <name>BENCH</name>
 <desc>BENCH</desc>
 <sym>Scenic Area</sym>
 <type>Scenic Area</type>
</wpt>
```

Next you come to the data relating to the waypoints themselves. The data is quite straightforward to read and edit. Latitude and longitude (lat and lon) are stored in degrees and decimal degrees, with – used to signify southern latitudes and eastern longitudes. The + symbol is not required for northern latitudes and western longitudes. All the coordinates used are relative to WGS84. Time is stored in Universal Coordinated Time (UTC) format and not local time. Name and description are text fields and symbol specifies the type of symbol used; type enables you to enter a text description for the symbol. Symbols are device-dependant and I recommend that you only edit these with the appropriate software. Elevation (ele) information is in meters.

You can edit these values with any text editor to whatever value that you want. For example, let's say that when you look at the map, you find that the elevation at the site for the coordinates is 55 meters instead of the 39.058960 (a measurement that is accurate to a fraction of a millimeter and totally unrealistic for a GPS), you simply change the value. While you are at it, change the time too:

```
<wpt lat="42.431709938" lon="-71.107839939">
 <ele>55.000000</ele><time>2004-11-22T12:31:00Z</time>
 <name>BENCH</name>
 <desc>BENCH</desc>
 <sym>Scenic Area</sym>
 <type>Scenic Area</type>
</wpt>
```

Using the format laid out, you can also use the file to create new waypoints. The basic skeleton that holds the data is as follows:

```
<wpt lat="xx.xxxxxxxxx" lon="xx.xxxxxxxxx">
 <ele>xx.xxxxxx</ele><time>YYYY-MM-DDTHH:MM:SSZ</time>
 <name> </name>
 <desc> </desc>
 <sym> </sym>
 <type> </type>
</wpt>
```

You can add the data to this framework. You have to do it by hand, so care is needed to avoid errors. In the following example, I have added latitude and longitude information, elevation data, date and time information, along with name, a description, a symbol, and a type.

Notice that the latitude and longitude information is entered between the quotes (lat=" " and lon=" "), while the rest of the data is placed between the appropriate element's opening and closing tag (an example of an opening tag is <ele>, while the corresponding closing tag is </ele>):

```
<wpt lat="42.432232311" lon="-71.108355658">
 <ele>50.000000</ele><time>2004-11-22T12:32:00Z</time>
 <name>PLAQUE</name>
 <desc>Marker</desc>
 <sym>Scenic Area</sym>
 <type>Scenic Area</type>
</wpt>
```

Shown below is a full template that you can use to put waypoint information into the TopoGrafix file format:

```
<?xml version="1.0" encoding="ISO-8859-1" standalone="yes"?>
<gpx
 version="1.1"
 creator="EasyGPS 1.3.7 - http://www.topografix.com"
 xmlns:xsi="http://www.w3.org/2001/XMLSchema-instance"
 xmlns="http://www.topografix.com/GPX/1/1"
 xsi:schemaLocation="http://www.topografix.com/GPX/1/1
http://www.topografix.com/GPX/1/1/gpx.xsd">
<metadata>
<time>YYYY-MM-DDTHH:MM:SSZ</time>
<bounds minlat="xx.xxxxxx" minlon="xx.xxxxxx" maxlat="xx.xxxxxx"
maxlon="xx.xxxxxx"/>
</metadata>
<wpt lat="xx.xxxxxxxxx" lon="xx.xxxxxxxxx">
 <ele>xx.xxxxxx</ele><time>YYYY-MM-DDTHH:MM:SSZ</time>
 <name></name>
 <desc></desc>
 <sym></sym>
 <type></type>
</wpt>
<extensions>
</extensions>
</gpx>
```

For a detailed description of the contents of the file and for the latest changes, visit www.topografix.com/GPX/1/1/gpx.xsd.

If you don't like the units that EasyGPS uses, click File ⇨ Preferences to bring up the Setup dialog box. Here, you can change the units of measure used (see Figure 8-33) and the coordinate style (see Figure 8-34).

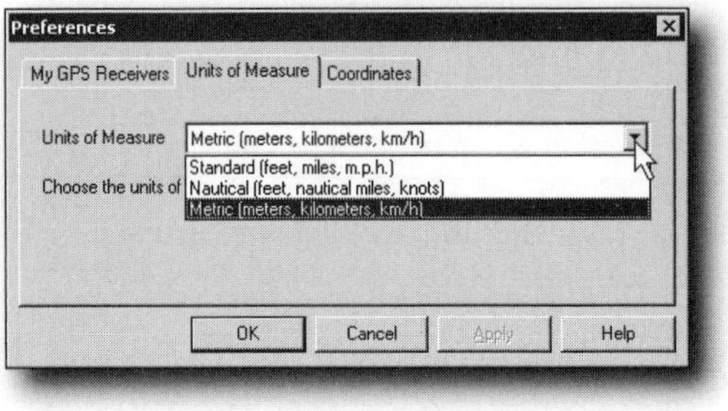

FIGURE 8-33: Changing units of measure

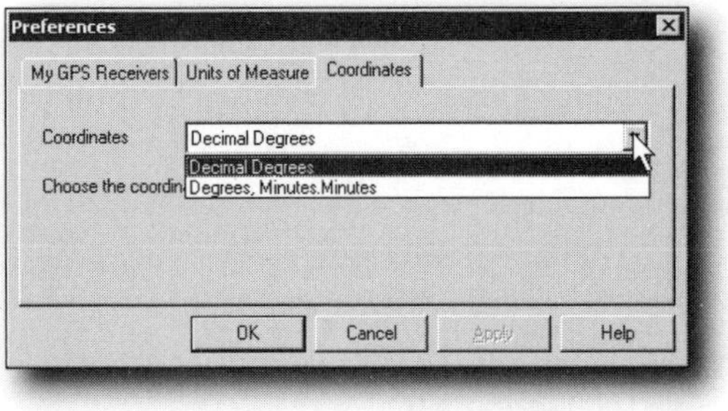

FIGURE 8-34: Changing the coordinate style

G7toWin

G7toWin also enables you to work with the data from your GPS. This is an application that you'll encounter again in Chapter 10 when we look at how to take screenshots from your GPS. G7toWin is trickier to use than EasyGPS, but it does have an advantage that we'll come to shortly.

You can download G7toWin from www.gpsinformation.org/ronh/. Even if you already downloaded the application previously, take a look for an updated version — they are released regularly.

After you have downloaded the application, you can extract it. This program has no setup applications and can be run from the folder to which you've extracted it.

As normal, connect your GPS to the PC and then you are ready to set up the application to communicate with the GPS. If your GPS is connected to serial port 1 and is a Garmin unit, the application is ready to go and will automatically detect your GPS receiver; if not, click File ⇨ Configuration and configure the GPS type and the serial port used.

After everything is hooked up, download the waypoints by clicking on GPS from the menu, select Download from GPS and then choose what you want downloaded (All, Waypoints, Routes, etc.)

After you have downloaded the waypoints (see Figure 8-35), you can then do some useful things with them, such as removing duplicate waypoints and ones with duplicate filenames, as well as removing all that have names longer than six characters (see Figure 8-36).

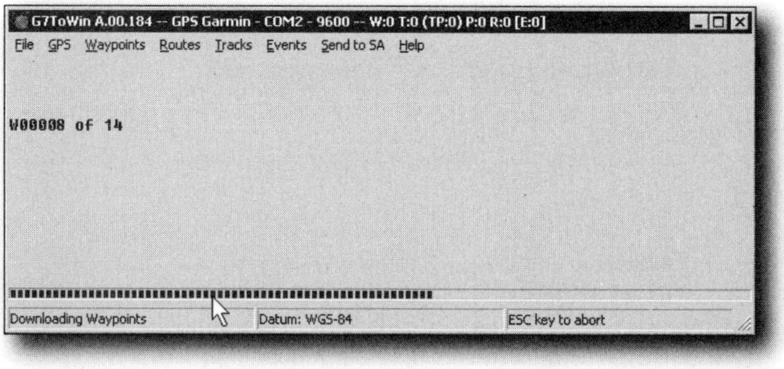

FIGURE 8-35: Downloaded waypoints

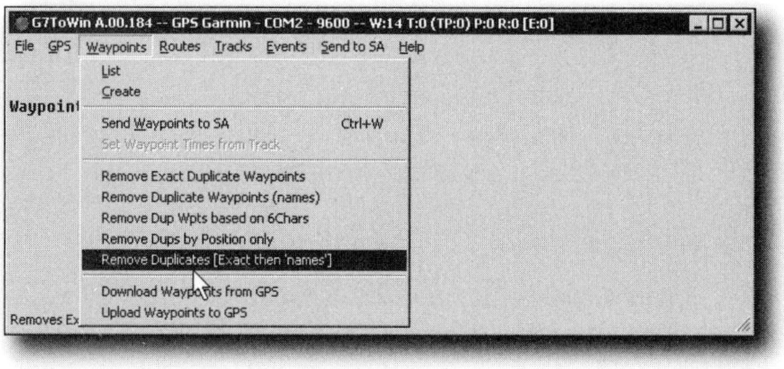

FIGURE 8-36: Working with waypoints

Want to create waypoints instead of working with existing ones? No problem. To create a new waypoint, click Waypoint ⇨ Create. This brings up a dialog box for creating the waypoint. This dialog box not only enables you to enter waypoint information such as name, coordinates, elevation, and icon details, it also enables you to choose icons that relate to GPS models and manufacturers, giving you greater flexibility. You can also easily specify the format for the coordinates you enter.

The other great thing that G7toWin enables you to do is create dummy routes (see Figure 8-37). To create a dummy route, click Routes ⇨ Create Dummy Route.

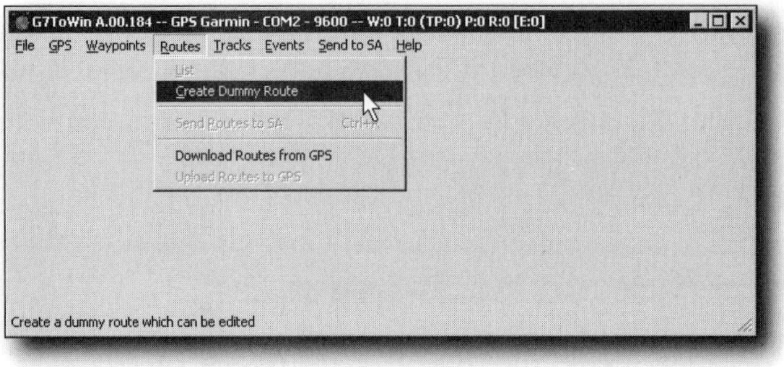

FIGURE 8-37: Creating a dummy route

After you have created the dummy route, you can then populate it with data. Double-click on the newly created route to bring up the Route Editing dialog box. This now allows you to add the waypoints you have downloaded to the route before uploading it to the GPS. This can be really handy because it allows you to experiment with the GPS by creating routes that use fake data. You can then experiment with your GPS interface and gain experience on how it functions.

Creative Uses of GPS Data

Data is data is data, as they say, so let's now move away from looking at the raw data and take a look at some creative uses of GPS data, such as how to add it to digital images, how to plot WiFi signals, and how to write your own code to use GPS data.

Sharing Waypoints

After you have collected waypoints, you might feel that you want to share them. There are a variety of ways that you can do this:

- Store them on a floppy disk or CD and pass them around
- Distribute them on paper
- Make them available on the Internet

If you choose the Internet route, then you can either make the waypoints available on your own personal homepage (the TopoGrafix format is a good format to choose for this) or you can upload them to a website dedicated to waypoints. One such website is www.waypoint. org. This is a waypoint registry where you can find waypoints for many countries around the world. To make navigation easier, these waypoints are categorized. Other such sites include the following:

- `www.waypoints.de`
- `www.swopnet.com/waypoints`
- `www.travelbygps.com`
- `www.pickatrail.com`

Adding GPS Information to Digital Photos

Hooking your digital camera to your GPS is going to cost you a lot of money and it can only be done with certain combinations of cameras and GPS units. For example, you can find kits to connect Kodak digital cameras, such as the DC 260, to a GPS receiver, but the adapter alone, excluding the camera and GPS receiver, costs over $300. A cheaper way to do this is to add GPS information to your digital photos on your PC.

The process is simple — after you have taken a picture at a location, use your GPS to create a waypoint at that spot. This will store the coordinates along with data and time information, and then you can add the waypoint information to the image file afterwards.

In order to do this, you need special software — called RoboGEO (see Figure 8-38).

RoboGEO is shareware software; it currently costs $22.95, but you can download an evaluation (trial) version from `www.robogeo.com`.

RoboGEO takes the information from waypoints you specify on your GPS and enables you to add the waypoint information to the EXIF information on the digital photo.

EXIF stands for Exchangeable Image File Format. This data storage format allows for the storage of non-image data (such as date, time, camera settings, and, in this case, latitude and longitude) within the actual image file. Virtually all modern digital cameras produce images that can store EXIF information within the file (usually only for JPG/JPEG format). This means that you don't have to add text overlays to your image that show the data. Instead, the data is stored in such as way that it can be viewed using Windows XP or another digital photograph application that uses the EXIF standard. An excellent application for viewing EXIF information is Exifer for Windows (`www.friedemann-schmidt.com/software/exifer`). This is a *postcardware application* (the only payment that the author asks for is a postcard) that enables you to view and edit this information.

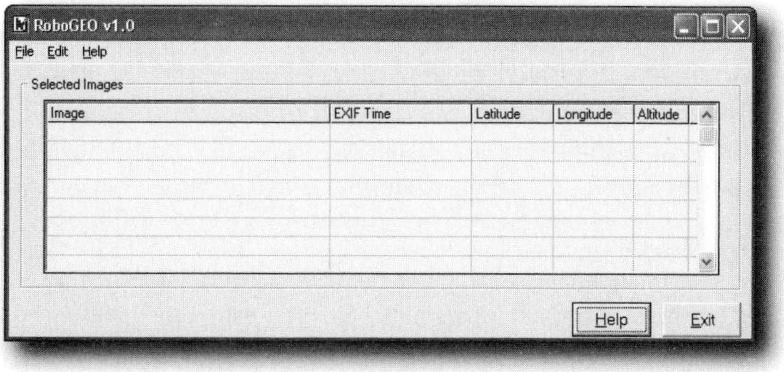

FIGURE 8-38: RoboGEO

RoboGEO is really clever because it can use the time-stamp information on your digital photos (applied by the camera) to sort out which waypoints belong to which image. This means that you should ensure that the time on your camera is correct (set it to the time shown on the GPS — unfortunately, you'll have to do this manually).

Now, information about where you took your image, along with when and how, will be stored along with the image so that you can view the information or even use it as search criteria for photographs.

Lightning Detector and Plotter

If you are at sea or in the air, then having information about lightning storms is invaluable. By combining your GPS with a lightning detector, you can do just that. There aren't many low-cost lightning detection systems (about $700) on the market, but one of the best has to be the LD-250 Lightning Detector setup. Okay, $700 seems like a lot to spend for a device that detects lightning, but if you sail or fly, then accurate, up-to-date storm information can mean the difference between life and death. On a less dramatic front, businesses find accurate weather information critical to many key decisions they make, so for up-to-the-second information, $700 is cheap.

This hardware plugs into your desktop or laptop via a serial port and it has a port for input from a GPS receiver. On the PC, you need to load software that communicates with the detector and plots the lightning storms on a map that is displayed. An antenna also forms part of the setup. This is placed outside, of course, and detects the lightning and feeds the information to the device, which processes it before sending that to the PC.

Once set up, it is ready to detect lightning storms. As soon as the external antenna picks up the electromagnetic pulse from a lightning bolt (within milliseconds after it occurs), its position is displayed onscreen.

Background maps are available of the United States and other locations worldwide. With a setup like this connected to a laptop (currently, there is no version for mobile devices such as the Pocket PC but they are planned), you have a mobile system that can warn you of bad weather as soon as it happens. By plotting the movement of the storm, you are in a position to take action to avoid it, whether on land, sea, or in the air.

For more information, visit www.geneq.com/catalog/en/ld_ld250.html.

Wardriving

Another activity that GPS plays a key role in nowadays is *wardriving*. Wardriving is the name given to the activity in which individuals drive around with a PC or Pocket PC set up to detect WiFi networks that are broadcasting signals.

There are many variations on wardriving — warwalking, warriding (bike or motorbike), and even warflying, which uses light aircraft or helicopters. The idea is to find wireless network spots, log the location, and then find another. As the popularity of WiFi grew, so did the popularity of wardriving. If you go wardriving to pick up active hotspots, the addition of a GPS to the system will enable you to store pinpoint location information about the hotspots that you discover; so rather than manually storing information such as street names and building numbers, all of which is prone to change or susceptible to input errors, the software picks up the location from the GPS automatically, eliminating errors and simplifying the process.

The most popular software used for wardriving is called NetStumbler (and its PocketPC counterpart MiniStumbler). Both are equipped to pick up and log hotspot coordinates (see Figure 8-39).

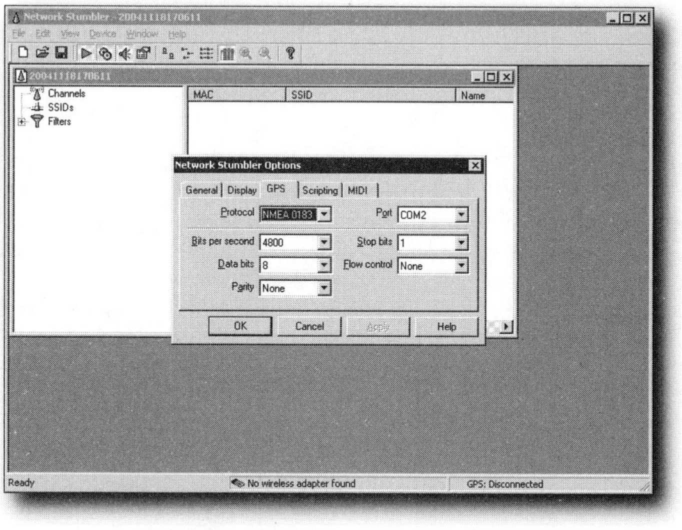

FIGURE 8-39: NetStumbler in action

Logging the access points that you discover enables you to plot them on a map or store the data or upload it to the web for exchange with others.

For more information on wardriving, visit the following websites:

- www.netstumbler.com
- www.wardriving.com

GPS in Programming

If you are a programmer, then you will no doubt want to put your programming skills to use on GPS. If this is something that interests you, then in order to interface with your GPS, you can either write code completely from scratch (tedious work, I can tell you) or you can use a drop-in GPS module that does all the hard work for you.

One such component is the GPS Toolkit.NET by Scientific Components (www.scientific component.com/gps_toolkit_net.htm).

GPS Toolkit.NET enables you to quickly and easily add GPS support to any Visual Basic .NET, C#, or C++ project. With one simple component, you gain the capability to drop into your application a whole host of GPS features easily.

This software isn't cheap ($179), but if you are serious about developing an application using GPS, this is money well spent.

In addition, if you are interested in programming GPS applications, you should go right to the source for good information: www.ngs.noaa.gov/gps-toolbox/.

This site has some fantastic algorithms and code samples to help you make the most of the GPS data that will flow into your applications.

Summary

This chapter has covered what you need to know about data, including how to use and store the data on your GPS. The data can either be data that you've collected while using the GPS outdoors or data that you've created using applications for uploading to your GPS before you set off on your journey. You looked at two applications that you can use to download the data, examine it, edit it, and upload it to your GPS. You also looked at how you can create new data for upload. These applications also give you the capability to download the data from your GPS for storage on your PC, enabling you to free the memory on your GPS for more data collection.

You also learned about some other possible uses for the data that your GPS outputs, how you can add waypoint information to digital photographs, how to plot lightning strikes, as well as applications that you can use to program GPS-enabled applications of your own.

No matter what form your interest in GPS takes, this chapter will have something of interest to you.

Examining the Data

When you connect a GPS to another device (such as a PC or an iPAQ) or to a software application, it is quite probable that the communication protocol used by this connection will be based on a standard known as NMEA. NMEA is crucial to this communication, and by understanding the format that NMEA takes and how the data is structured, you are in a position to directly examine the data stream. If you can read NMEA, you can troubleshoot GPS problems, directly examine the data retrieved, and also check for corrupted data.

In this chapter, we are going to take a close look at the NMEA protocol and the format in which the data is output by a GPS receiver. By the end of this chapter, you will be familiar with the following topics:

- Communicating with other devices
- Software applications that enable you to capture and store NMEA data
- Troubleshooting

The more you know about and understand the data, the more you can do with it.

NMEA

NMEA is the protocol most used by GPS receivers to communicate with other devices — either for data transfer to and from the unit, or for communication with other devices. The fact that this standard is used for GPS betrays its marine roots.

NMEA stands for National Marine Electronics Association, which is the body that sets and defines the standard. The full name of the standard most commonly used by GPS receivers is NMEA 0183. This standard covers not only GPS receivers but a variety of other electronic devices.

Most computer programs that provide real-time position information are capable of understanding the NMEA format. Some can only understand the NMEA plaintext format, while others use a variety of different data formats.

NMEA data sent from a GPS contains full PVT (Position, Velocity, and Time) data calculated by the GPS unit.

NMEA Sentences

The concept behind NMEA is to send data one line at a time. Each line of data (called a *sentence*) is completely standalone — self-contained and independent from other sentences. There are two kinds of sentences:

- Standard sentences for each device category
- Proprietary sentences for use by the individual devices and manufacturers

All of the standard sentences have a two-letter prefix defining the device that uses that sentence type. For GPS receivers, the prefix is always GP — most sentences that a GPS receiver understands are prefixed by these two letters. They are followed by a three-letter sequence that defines what the sentence contains.

As I've already mentioned, the NMEA standard permits hardware manufacturers to define and use their own proprietary sentences for any purpose they see fit. The only prerequisite is that all proprietary sentences must begin with the letter P, and are followed with three letters that identify the manufacturer controlling that sentence. For example, Garmin sentences start with "PGRM," while Magellan sentences begin with "PMGN."

Note

Proprietary sentences vary from receiver to receiver and over time and are not covered here. Proprietary sentences contain more, and more specific, information than NMEA does, which is considered the lowest common denominator.

NMEA Sentence Structure

Each NMEA sentence begins with a dollar sign ($) and ends with a carriage return/line feed sequence. Most sentences can be no longer than 80 characters. All the data is contained inside this single line, and data items are separated by commas. The data itself is in the form of ASCII text, and the data can, especially if it's complex, be spread over many separate NMEA sentences, but it is normally fully contained in just one sentence.

The precision of different sentences varies depending on the data. For example, time information might be given in seconds correct to one decimal place, while positional information might be given to three or even four digits after the decimal place. NMEA uses commas to separate individual fields of data. If the field doesn't contain data, it's left blank, but a comma is still required.

To improve accuracy, there is a provision to include a checksum at the end of each sentence, which may or may not be checked by the unit that reads the data. The checksum field consists of an * and two hex digits representing the exclusive OR of all characters between, but not including, the $ and *. The checksum is used to validate the contents of the sentence.

Note

A checksum is required on some sentences, and optional on others.

A Closer Look at NMEA Sentences

No detailed study of GPS is complete without a study of the most commonly used protocol for communication between the GPS and other devices. Even if you have no intentions of writing applications that process or work with GPS data, and instead plan on using only readymade applications, a basic knowledge of NMEA is very handy when it comes to diagnosing GPS problems and understanding what goes on between the GPS and the device with which it is communicating.

Here is a list of the current NMEA sentences relating to GPS receivers along with a description of what they do:

String Type	Description
$GPAAM	Waypoint Arrival Alarm
$GPALM	GPS Almanac Data
$GPBEC	Bearing & Distance to Waypoint, Dead Reckoning
$GPBOD	Bearing, Origin to Destination
$GPBWC	Bearing & Distance to Waypoint, Great Circle
$GPFSI	Frequency Set Information
$GPGGA	*Global Positioning System Fix Data (Time, Position, Elevation)
$GPGLC	Geographic Position, Loran-C
$GPGLL	*Geographic Position, Latitude/Longitude
$GPGRS	GPS Range Residuals
$GPGSA	*GPS DoP (Dilution of Precision) and Active Satellites
$GPGSV	*GPS Satellites in View
$GPHDG	Heading, Deviation & Variation
$GPHDT	Heading, True
$GPHSC	Heading Steering Command
$GPMWV	Wind Speed and Angle
$GPRMC	*Recommended Minimum Specific GNSS GPS/TRANSIT Data (Time, Position, Velocity)
$GPROT	Rate of Turn
$GPRPM	Revolutions
$GPRTE	Routes

Continued

String Type	Description
$GPSTN	Multiple Data ID
$GPTRF	Transit Fix Data
$GPVBW	Dual Ground/Water Speed
$GPVDR	Set and Drift
$GPVLW	Distance Traveled through the Water
$GPVPW	Speed, Measured Parallel to Wind
$GPVTG	*Track Made Good and Ground Speed (Course over ground and ground speed)
$GPWCV	Waypoint Closure Velocity
$GPWNC	Distance, Waypoint to Waypoint
$GPWPL	Waypoint Location
$GPXTE	Cross-Track Error, Measured
$GPXTR	Cross-Track Error, Dead Reckoning
$GPZDA	UTC Date/Time and Local Time Zone Offset
$GPZFO	UTC & Time from Origin Waypoint
$GPZTG	UTC & Time to Destination Waypoint

NMEA consists of sentences; and for each of these sentences. the first word, called a *data type*, defines how the rest of the sentence is interpreted. Each data has its own unique interpretation, as defined by the NMEA standard.

For example, take the GGA sentence shown here:

```
$GPGGA,180432.00,4027.027912,N,08704.857070, W,2,07,1.0,212.15,M,-
33.81,M,4.2,0555*73
```

This NMEA sentence shows an example that provides fix data information.

Sentences vary in the information they contain. Some sentences will repeat some of the information already provided, while others provide new data. Devices attached to the GPS can look for the NMEA sentence they want and choose to ignore others.

Normally, there are very few ways to control which NMEA sentences are sent from a GPS and which aren't. The usual state of affairs is that each GPS receiver simply transmits all of the data and lets the attached device pick and choose what to read and what to ignore. Some receivers can be set to send only certain types of sentences, but there is little benefit to doing this. There is no way for the receiving device to acknowledge receipt of the data or to request that the data be retransmitted because it was lost or garbled — if the receiving unit checks the checksum on a sentence and finds it is corrupted, the receiver must wait until the next time a similar NMEA sentence is transmitted.

Examining NMEA Sentences

Many applications enable you to look at, examine, and even save NMEA sentences from your GPS because this is the closest, purest way to work with the GPS data. However, most people don't give them much thought because the sentences themselves seem to complex. Little information is provided as to what they contain and how the data is structured.

This is a real shame — with a bit of information and a little practice, reading NMEA can become quite easy as you learn what to look for and where to look for it.

The following sections examine some of the common NMEA sentences that you will come across if you view NMEA data. There are the main sentences, the ones that relate to navigation and signal quality.

RMB (Recommended Minimum Navigation Information)

RMB is the "recommended minimum navigation" sentence, and it is sent whenever a route or a goto (such as going to a waypoint) is set as active. Some systems are set to transmit this all the time, transmitting null data if no goto is selected, while others only send it when required.

$GPRMB,A,x.x,a,c--c,d--d,llll.ll,e,yyyyy.yy,f,g.g,h.h,i.i,j*kk

A	Data status (A = OK, V = Void)
x.x	Crosstrack error (measured in nautical miles, maximum 9.99)
a	Direction to steer to correct crosstrack error (L = left, R = Right)
c--c	Origin waypoint ID#
d--d	Destination waypoint ID#
llll.ll	Destination waypoint latitude
e	N or S (for latitude)
yyyyy.yy	Destination waypoint longitude
f	E or W (for longitude)
g.g	Range to destination (measured in nautical miles, maximum 999.9)
h.h	Bearing to destination, True degrees
i.i	Velocity towards destination (measured in nautical miles)
j	Arrival status (A = arrived, V = not arrived)
*kk	Checksum

RMC (Recommended Minimum Specific GPS/TRANSIT Data)

This is the NMEA equivalent of PVT (Position, Velocity, Time) data.

$GPRMC,hhmmss.ss,A,llll.ll,e,yyyyy.yy,f,x.x,y.y,ddmmyy,z.z,a*hh

`hhmmss.ss`	UTC of position fix (time)
`A`	Data status (A = OK, V = Void)
`1111.11`	Destination waypoint latitude
`e`	N or S (for latitude)
`yyyyy.yy`	Destination waypoint longitude
`f`	E or W (for longitude)
`x.x`	Speed over ground made good (measured in nautical miles)
`y.y`	Track made good (measured in degrees True)
`ddmmyy`	UT date
`z.z`	Magnetic variation (easterly variation is subtracted from True course)
`a`	E or W (for magnetic variation)
`*hh`	Checksum

GGA (Global Positioning System Fix Data)

This sentence provides 3D location and accuracy data.

```
$GPGGA,hhmmss.ss,1111.11,e,yyyyy.yy,f,a,bb,x.x,y.y,M,z.z,M,s.s,
####*hh
```

`hhmmss.ss`	UTC of position fix (time)
`1111.11`	Destination waypoint latitude
`e`	N or S (for latitude)
`yyyyy.yy`	Destination waypoint longitude
`f`	E or W (for longitude)
`a`	Fix quality: 0 = Invalid 1 = GPS fix (SPS) 2 = DGPS fix 3 = PPS fix 4 = Real Time Kinematic 5 = Float RTK 6 = Estimated (dead reckoning) 7 = Manual input mode 8 = Simulation mode
`bb`	Number of satellites in use
`x.x`	Horizontal error (dilution or precision)
`y.y,M`	Antenna height in meters
`z.z,M`	Height of geoid (mean sea level) in meters

s.s	Time in seconds since last update
####	DGPS station ID
*hh	Checksum

VTG (Actual Track Made Good and Speed Over Ground)

This sentence provides the velocity made good information.

`$GPVTG,t,T,?,??,s.ss,N,S.SS,K*hh`

t	Track made good
T	Fixed text T indicates that track made good is relative to true north
?	Not used
??	Not used
s.ss	Speed over ground (measured in nautical miles)
N	Fixed text N indicates that speed over ground is in knots
S.SS	Speed over ground (measured in kilometers/hour)
K	Fixed text K indicates that speed over ground is in kilometers/hour
*hh	Checksum

RMA (Navigation Data from Present Position)

This sentence provides navigational data based on current position.

`$GPRMA,A,llll.ll,e,yyyyy.yy,f,?,??,ss.s,ccc,zz.z,a*hh`

A	Data status (A = OK, V = Void)
llll.ll	Destination waypoint latitude
e	N or S (for latitude)
yyyyy.yy	Destination waypoint longitude
f	E or W (for longitude)
?	Not used
??	Not used
s.ss	Speed over ground (measured in nautical miles)
ccc	Course over ground
z.z	Magnetic variation (easterly variation is subtracted from True course)
a	E or W (for magnetic variation)
*hh	Checksum

GSA (GPS DoP and Active Satellites)

This sentence provides detailed information on the satellite fix. It includes the numbers of the satellites being used in the current solution and the dilution of precision (DoP). DoP is an indication of the effect of satellite geometry on the accuracy of the fix. DoP has no units of measure — it is a case of smaller is better.

```
$GPGSA,A,B,x1,x2,x3,x4,x5,x6,x6,x8,x9,x10,x11,x12,x,y,z*hh
```

A	Fix mode: M = Manual (where the receiver is forced to work in 2D or 3D) A = Automatic
B	Fix mode: 1 = Fix not possible 2 = 2D 3 = 3D
x1 - x12	IDs of satellites (SVs) used for position fix
z	Positional dilution of precision
y	Horizontal dilution of precision
z	Vertical dilution of precision
*hh	Checksum

GSV (Satellites in View Data)

This is a very interesting and informative NMEA sentence. Satellites in view shows data about the satellites that the unit might be able to find based on its viewing mask and almanac data. It also shows the unit's current ability to track this data.

Note One GSV sentence can provide data for up to four satellites, so three sentences may be needed for the full information. The GSV for all satellite sentences do not need to appear in sequence.

```
$GPGSV,A,B,C,D1,E1,Az1,SNR1,D2,E2,Az2,SNR2,D3,E3,Az3,SNR3,D4,E4,
Az4,SNR4*hh
```

A	Number of messages required to hold data on all SVs in view
B	Message number
C	Total number of satellites in view
D1-D4	Satellite PRN number
E1-E4	Elevation in degrees (90 maximum)
Az1-Az4	Azimuth (measured in degrees from True north, 000 to 359)
SNR1-SNR4	Signal-to-noise ratio (the higher the number the better the signal)
*hh	Checksum

WPL (Waypoint Location)

When a route is active, this NMEA sentence is sent once for each waypoint that the route contains, in sequence. When all waypoints have been sent, GPR00 is sent in the next data set to indicate the end.

In any block of NMEA sentences, only one WPL or GPR00 sentence will be sent.

$GPWPL,llll.ll,e,yyyyy.yy,f,####*hh

llll.ll	Destination waypoint latitude
e	N or S (for latitude)
yyyyy.yy	Destination waypoint longitude
f	E or W (for longitude)
####	Waypoint ID
*hh	Checksum

ZDA (Date and Time)

This sentence provides date and time information.

$GPZDA,hhmmss.ss,dd,mm,yyyy,xx,yy*hh

hhmmss	UTC time
dd	Day
mm	Month
yyyy	Year
xx	Local zone hours (-13 to 13)
yy	Local zone minutes (00 to 59)
*hh	Checksum

ALM (GPS Almanac Data)

The GPS almanac data sentence contains GPS week number, satellite health, and complete almanac data for one satellite. Multiple satellites mean that multiple messages may be transmitted, one for each satellite in the GPS constellation (up to a maximum of 32 messages).

Note This sentence breaks the 80-character rule.

$GPALM,A,B,C.D,E,F,G,H,J,K,L,M,T1,T2,*hh

A	Total number of messages
B	Current message number
C	Satellite PRN number (01 to 32)
D	GPS week ID (0 to 1023)
E	Satellite health
F	Orbital eccentricity
G	Almanac reference time
H	Sigma – Inclination angle
I	OmegaDOT – Rate of right ascension
J	Square root of semi-major axis
K	Omega – Argument perigee
L	Longitude of ascension node
M	Mean anomaly
T1	Clock parameter
T2	Clock parameter
*hh	Checksum

BOD (Bearing: Origin to Destination)

This NMEA sentence shows the bearing angle of a line calculated at the origin waypoint and extending to the destination waypoint for the active navigation leg of the journey.

`$GPBOD,xxx,T,yyy,M,DESTID,STARTID*hh`

xxx	Bearing (True, from origin to destination)
T	True
yyy	Bearing (Magnetic, from origin to destination)
M	Magnetic
DESTID	Destination ID
STARTID	Origin ID
*hh	Checksum

BWC (Bearing and Distance to Waypoint Using a Great Circle Route)

This represents time, distance, bearing to, and location of a specified waypoint from the present position calculated along the great circle path. The *great circle path* means along the surface of the earth as opposed to a straight-line path.

`$GPBWC,hhmmss,llll.ll,e,yyyyy.yy,f,xxx,T,yyy,M,zzz,N,###*hh`

hhmmss	UTC time
llll.ll	Destination waypoint latitude
e	N or S (for latitude)
yyyyy.yy	Destination waypoint longitude
f	E or W (for longitude)
xxx	Bearing to waypoint (degrees True)
T	Degrees True
yyy	Bearing to waypoint (degrees Magnetic)
M	Degrees Magnetic
zzz	Distance to waypoint (measured in nautical miles)
N	Nautical miles
###	Waypoint ID
*hh	Checksum

NMEA Checksum

You may have noticed the checksum that appears at the end of the NMEA sentences. If you are wondering what this is and how it is calculated, it's not that tricky, and it generally only applies to mathematicians and programmers.

The checksum is always a two-character hexadecimal number. It is determined by looking at all the characters that fall between the $ symbol and the * symbol, converting them to byte values and then performing an exclusive OR or XOR on the bytes and then converting the final byte checksum to hexadecimal.

You can find numerous examples of code on the web that will show you how to check this value in a variety of languages. Using your favorite search engine, enter the words "NMEA checksum" and you will find hundreds of code samples in several languages.

This might seem rather academic, but if you plan to write applications that interface with GPS receivers and work on the NMEA sentences, then checking the checksum is vital.

SiRF

Another protocol that you might hear of is the SiRF protocol. This is a protocol developed by SiRF Incorporated to work with their latest hi-tech GPS devices.

The SiRF protocol is different from NMEA sentences in several fundamental ways:

- The SiRF protocol is binary. This offers a lot of advantages over using ASCII as the medium for transmitting information.

- SiRF is faster. The NMEA protocol specifies a speed of 4800 bits per second. This is okay, but it can create a bottleneck if you want to transmit large amounts of data. SiRF supports data speeds of 38,400 bps and greater.

- SiRF can carry more data. NMEA sentences are generally limited to 80 characters. A single SiRF instruction string (called a *payload*) can be as long as 2×10^{15} bytes (actually $2 \times 10^{15} - 1$, or 2 billion gigabytes!).

- SiRF has greater information integrity. Not only does SiRF use a checksum to check for data integrity, but it also contains other message validation code.

- SiRF uses message encapsulation. The message is encapsulated by specific start and stop characters that also form part of the message validation code, meaning that sentence confusion cannot happen.

However, the SiRF protocol is more complex and harder to navigate than NMEA. Because of this, I'm not going to cover it in greater detail here, but if you want more information (free, as opposed to paying for the NMEA-0183 standard), visit www.sirf.com/reps/Technical.html. Here you will find tools, information, and utilities to help you make the most out of SiRF.

Using NMEA Sentences

Let's take a look at how you can make use of NMEA sentences directly from your GPS. All you need is a GPS connection between your GPS and your PC or PDA. In order to be able to use these applications, you need to make sure that your GPS is set to output NMEA data.

Examining the NMEA output is a great way to learn more about GPS and how it interfaces with software and other devices. It is also a great way to troubleshoot problems — you can test for incorrect output, which can lead you to solutions to your problems.

In addition, if you are a programmer, you may see something that you can do with the NMEA data that cannot currently be done — with a bit of programming and the ability to decode NMEA, you'll be able to leverage your existing skills in a completely different arena.

A lot of available software will enable you to read and log NMEA sentences from your GPS receiver. The following sections describe a few of the better applications.

GPS NMEA LOG

GPS NMEA LOG might be an unimaginative title, but the software does exactly what is says it will—enable you to see and log NMEA data from your GPS (see Figure 9-1).

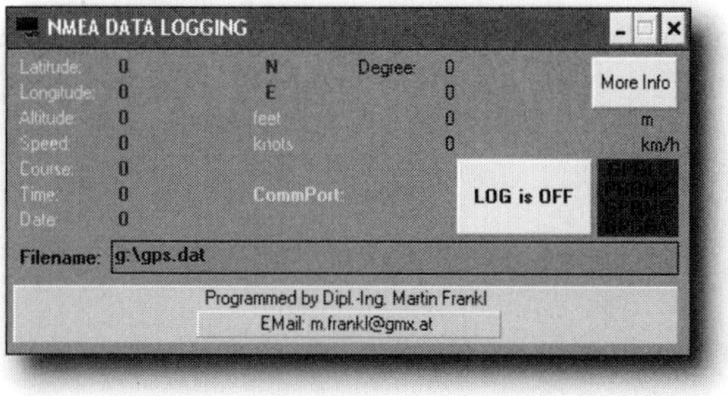

FIGURE 9-1: GPS NMEA LOG in action

This application can be downloaded from `http://frankl.comdesign.at/Geo/GPSNMEA.html`.

Note

To run this application, you might need to download the Visual Basic runtime file `VBRUN300.DLL`. This can be found on many sites on the Internet. Copy this file into the system32 subfolder where your Windows operating system is installed.

This is a simple but effective application that requires only a small amount of hard drive space and RAM, making it ideal for older systems and laptops.

GPS NMEA LOG can also display real-time information decoded from the NMEA sentences for times when you don't feel like decoding NMEA (see Figure 9-2).

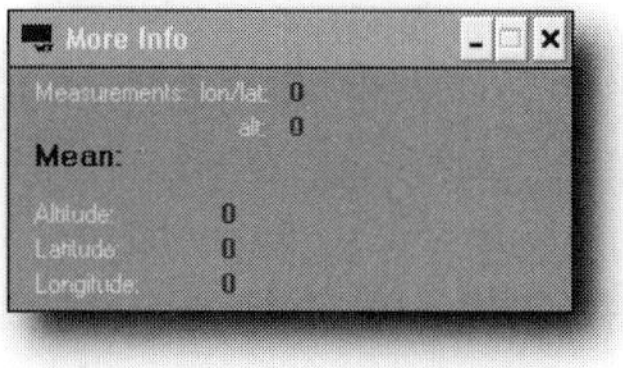

FIGURE 9-2: Decoding NMEA sentences on-the-fly

On this site you will also find another useful application—GPS data logging software. This enables you to hook your GPS to a computer and have it log data. The software comes in both Windows (WINNGPS) and DOS (NGPS) formats and can run on a variety of systems, including old, run-down PCs for which you might not have much use.

The application also comes with an effective log reader to read the files containing the NMEA data, as shown in Figure 9-3.

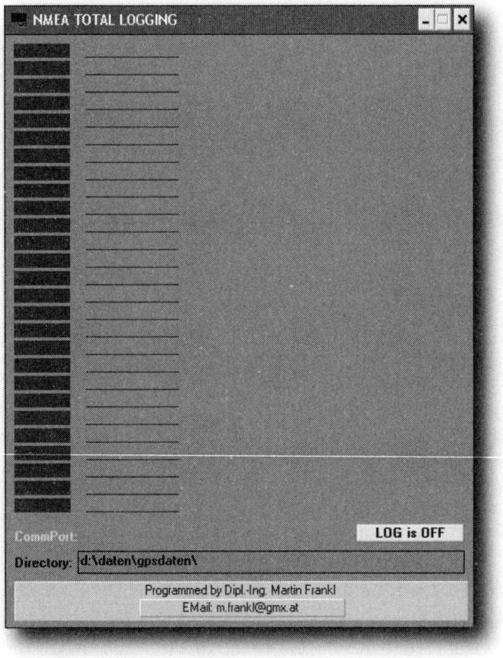

FIGURE 9-3: Reading existing logs

The log file can store the following information:

- Longitude
- Latitude
- Date
- Time
- Altitude
- Speed
- Direction
- Three accuracy indicators

GPS Diagnostic

GPS Diagnostic by CommLinx Solutions is another great tool that enables you to work at a low level with the GPS data and NMEA. GPS Diagnostics is available as a free download from www.laipac.com/gps_gpsdiag_eng.htm.

As you can see from Figure 9-4, what is different about GPS Diagnostics is that it displays interpreted data in the top half of the screen and the raw data in the bottom half.

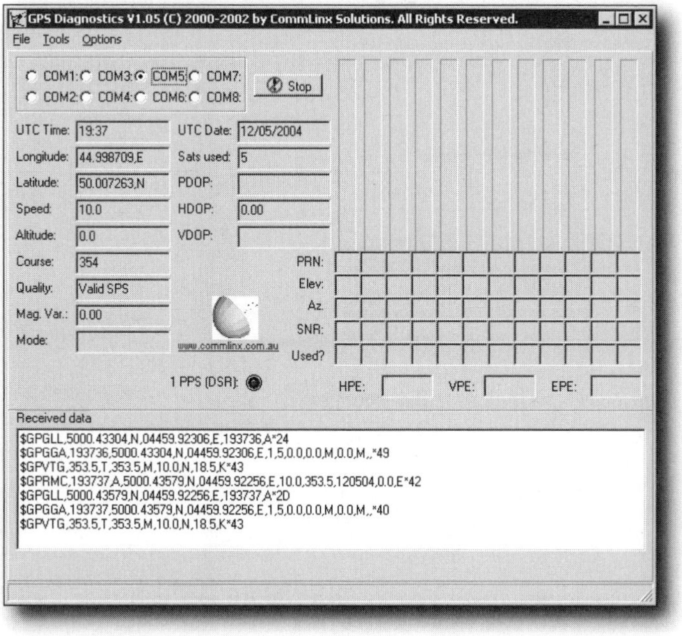

FIGURE 9-4: GPS Diagnostics

This excellent utility offers you a great deal in the way of customizations. You can choose to ignore certain NMEA sentences and select which timestamp to use (see Figure 9-5).

The software also enables you to choose customized data fields to display (see Figure 9-6).

Finally, GPS Diagnostics enables you to replay data that you've collected, and even choose the replay rate (see Figure 9-7).

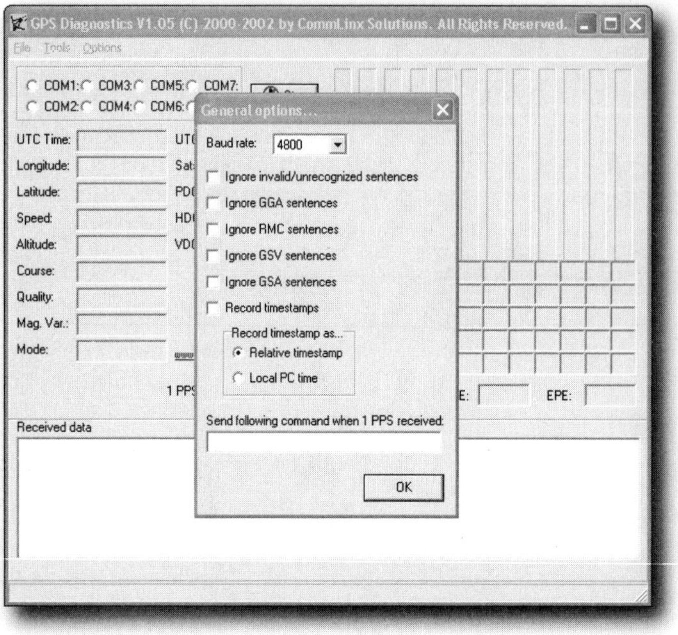

FIGURE 9-5: Ignoring some NMEA sentences makes them easier to read.

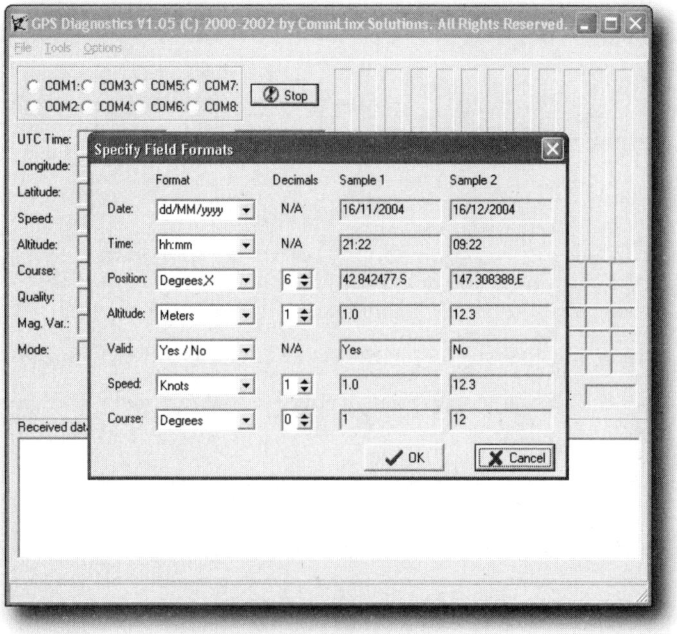

FIGURE 9-6: Choosing customized data fields

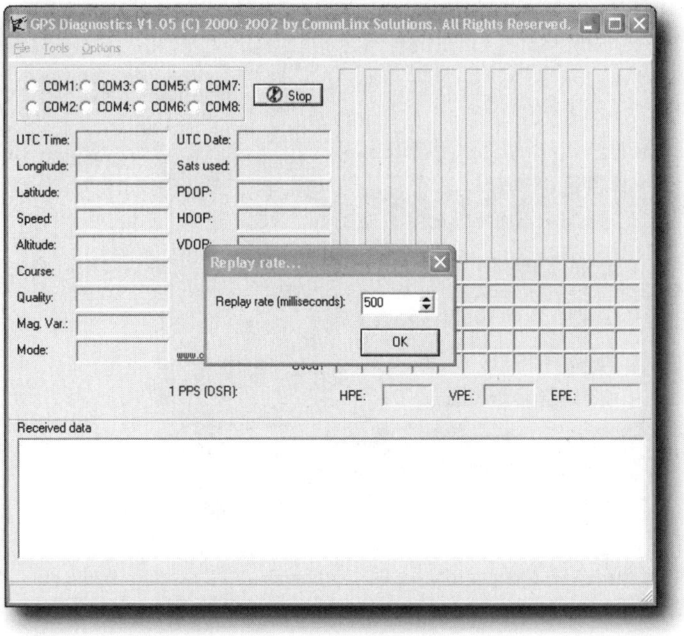

FIGURE 9-7: Playing back NMEA sentences

RECSIM III

Finally, let's take a look at some software that enables you to simulate NMEA sentences for yourself with no GPS required! This is called RECSIM III (see Figure 9-8), and an evaluation copy is available for download from www.effective-solutions.co.uk/recsim.html.

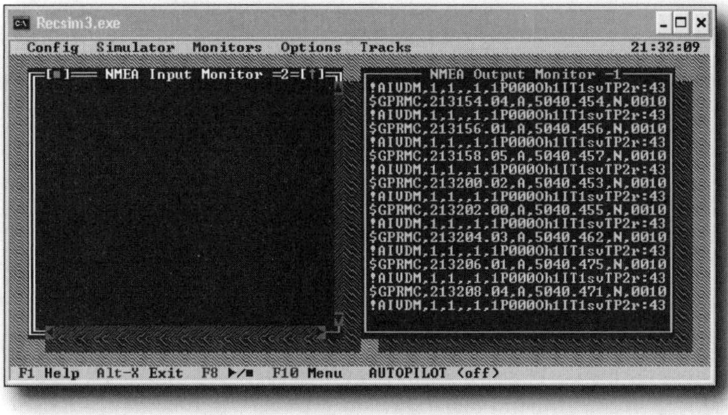

FIGURE 9-8: RECSIM III

RECSIM III is an NMEA generator that can create all sorts of GPS data for you. If you have a license, if can even send data via the serial port. Even the evaluation copy allows you to customize the type of output that the software generates (see Figure 9-9).

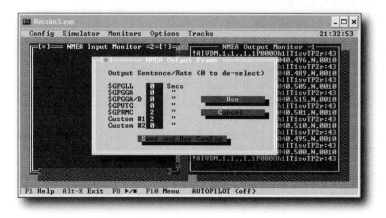

FIGURE 9-9: Customizing NMEA output

In addition to that, RECSIM III enables you to generate NMEA data based on simulated course and speed data (see Figure 9-10).

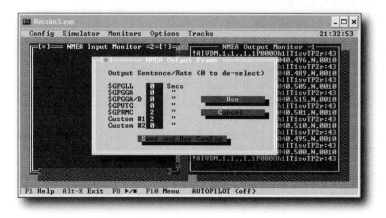

FIGURE 9-10: NMEA data simulating course and speed

Finally, to make the simulation even more realistic, you can also get RECSIM III to add an error into the NMEA sentences that it outputs, so that the course information it generates is closer to its real-world counterpart (see Figure 9-11).

FIGURE 9-11: Adding errors to the simulated GPS data

Using NMEA

But what can you actually do with NMEA? All these sentences containing information are a method of communicating the data displayed on the screen of the GPS. For what other, possibly more useful, purpose can we use NMEA?

You can do two very interesting things with NMEA data:

- You can store the NMEA output of your GPS on an electronic device and use this as a record of the journey. As you will see, there are advantages to storing the data in NMEA format that aren't immediately obvious.

- You can create your own NMEA data and store it in a file that can later be played back to other applications, which will believe that they are receiving data live from a GPS, when in fact they are receiving only fake data.

GpsGate

A variety of applications can effectively work with NMEA, but one of the best and most versatile in called GpsGate.

GpsGate is published by Franson Technology AB, and is available for download from http://franson.biz/gpsgate. GpsGate is a commercial application available in two versions: Windows, shown in Figure 9-12, and the Pocket PC, shown in Figure 9-13.

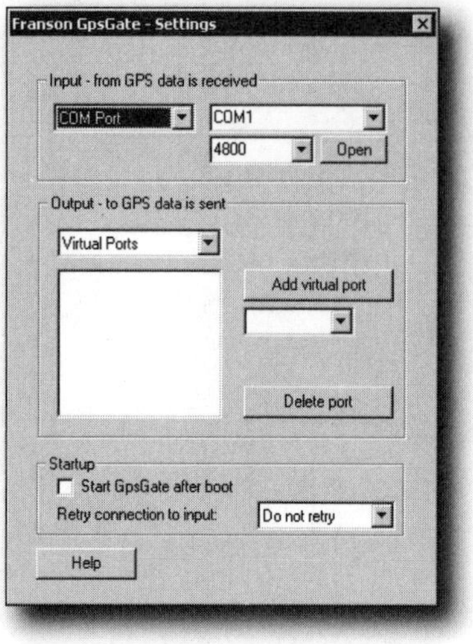

Figure 9-12: GpsGate for Windows

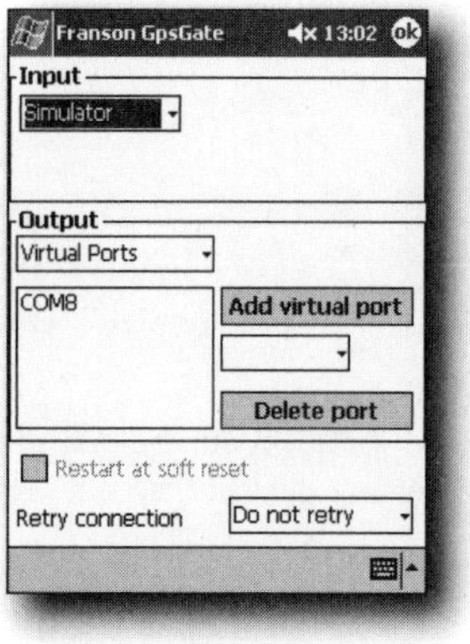

FIGURE 9-13: GpsGate for Pocket PC

A single commercial license for Windows or Pocket PC is $30, but you can download a fully functional 14-day trial version.

Installation of the Windows version is very straightforward:

1. Download the zipped package from the website.

2. Extract the setup file contained within the zip file.

3. Run the setup file. This will install the application.

Once the application is installed, it puts an icon in the Start Menu. If you choose to run the application after installation, you will notice than an icon is placed in the Windows System Tray (on the right-hand side of the taskbar).

The icon in the System Tray is the main control center for GpsGate. Right-click on this icon and you will be presented with a comprehensive menu of functions (see Figure 9-14).

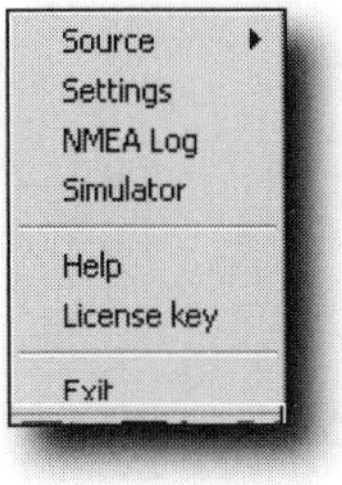

FIGURE 9-14: GpsGate menu

Click Settings and a settings window will be displayed, as shown in Figure 9-15.

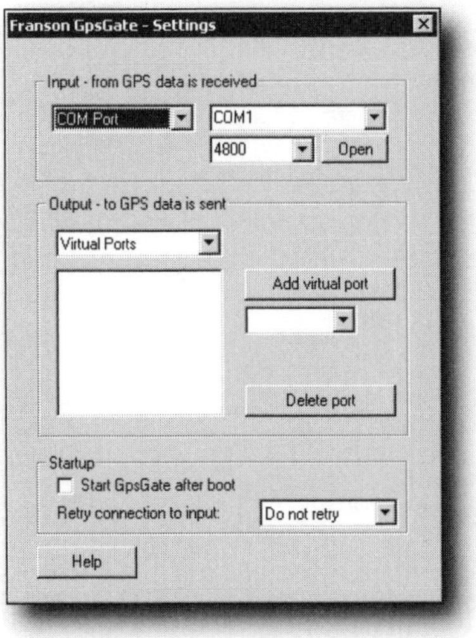

FIGURE 9-15: GpsGate settings window

In this screen, you can specify the input that the application should receive and process. Inputs include the following:

- COM port (a GPS attached to the PC)
- Gate Direct (data passed through the application directly)
- NMEA Log (this processes data from a log)
- Simulator (GpsGate can act as a virtual GPS)
- Virtual Port (processes data received from a virtual port)
- TCP/IP (data received over a network)
- UDP (data received over a network)

You can also set up virtual ports to which the data can be sent. Any virtual ports created appear in the list of ports available for most applications, and enable you to take one GPS input and send it to a number of ports. Generally, the GPS can only be accessed by one application, because applications lock a port when using it. GpsGate enables you to take one signal and send it to multiple applications on both a Windows PC and a Pocket PC device, as shown in Figure 9-16.

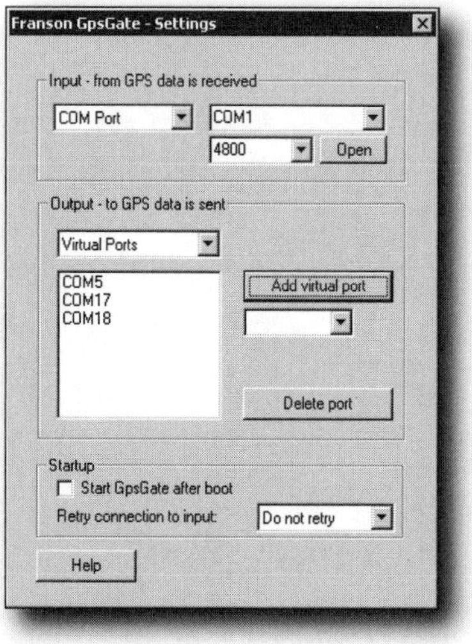

FIGURE 9-16: GpsGate can send a GPS signal to multiple virtual ports.

Recording Actual NMEA Sentences with GpsGate

If you have a GPS connected to your PC, you can use GpsGate to record the NMEA sentences from the GPS to a file on the PC. There is an advantage to storing the GPS data in an NMEA file, rather than in a proprietary format: An NMEA file can be imported into a variety of applications, whereas proprietary formats (such as TomTom or Memory-Map logfiles) require specific software.

Capturing NMEA sentences for storage in a file is easy:

1. Connect your GPS to the PC as normal.

2. Switch the GPS on.

3. In GpsGate, set the source to COM Port (see Figure 9-17).

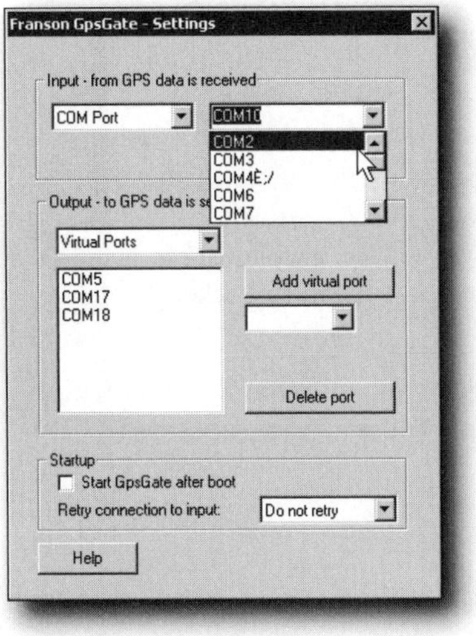

FIGURE 9-17: Setting the input to COM
Port in GpsGate

4. Right-click on the GpsGate System Tray icon and choose Settings.

5. In this window, choose the input port that matches the one to which the GPS is connected.

6. Once again, right-click on the GpsGate System Tray icon and choose NMEA Log (see Figure 9-18).

FIGURE 9-18: Choosing
NMEA Log in GpsGate

7. To record the input, click the Record button. This brings up a dialog box asking you to choose a location in which to save the NMEA output file.
8. To stop recording, click Stop.
9. Once you are done, you can examine the NMEA output file. A sample is shown in Figure 9-19.

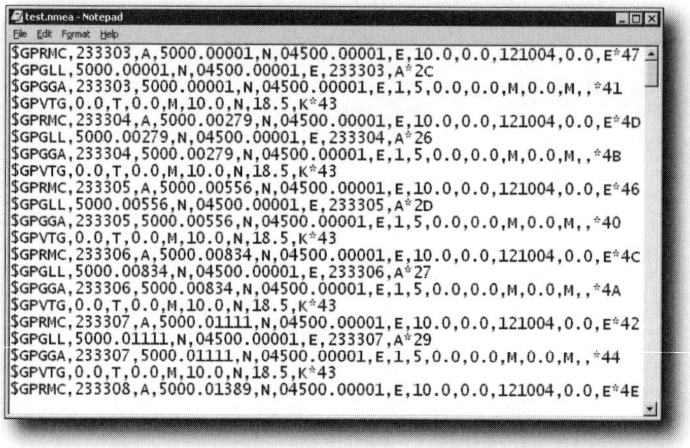
test.nmea - Notepad

File Edit Format Help

```
$GPRMC,233303,A,5000.00001,N,04500.00001,E,10.0,0.0,121004,0.0,E*47
$GPGLL,5000.00001,N,04500.00001,E,233303,A*2C
$GPGGA,233303,5000.00001,N,04500.00001,E,1,5,0.0,0.0,M,0.0,M,,*41
$GPVTG,0.0,T,0.0,M,10.0,N,18.5,K*43
$GPRMC,233304,A,5000.00279,N,04500.00001,E,10.0,0.0,121004,0.0,E*4D
$GPGLL,5000.00279,N,04500.00001,E,233304,A*26
$GPGGA,233304,5000.00279,N,04500.00001,E,1,5,0.0,0.0,M,0.0,M,,*4B
$GPVTG,0.0,T,0.0,M,10.0,N,18.5,K*43
$GPRMC,233305,A,5000.00556,N,04500.00001,E,10.0,0.0,121004,0.0,E*46
$GPGLL,5000.00556,N,04500.00001,E,233305,A*2D
$GPGGA,233305,5000.00556,N,04500.00001,E,1,5,0.0,0.0,M,0.0,M,,*40
$GPVTG,0.0,T,0.0,M,10.0,N,18.5,K*43
$GPRMC,233306,A,5000.00834,N,04500.00001,E,10.0,0.0,121004,0.0,E*4C
$GPGLL,5000.00834,N,04500.00001,E,233306,A*27
$GPGGA,233306,5000.00834,N,04500.00001,E,1,5,0.0,0.0,M,0.0,M,,*4A
$GPVTG,0.0,T,0.0,M,10.0,N,18.5,K*43
$GPRMC,233307,A,5000.01111,N,04500.00001,E,10.0,0.0,121004,0.0,E*42
$GPGLL,5000.01111,N,04500.00001,E,233307,A*29
$GPGGA,233307,5000.01111,N,04500.00001,E,1,5,0.0,0.0,M,0.0,M,,*44
$GPVTG,0.0,T,0.0,M,10.0,N,18.5,K*43
$GPRMC,233308,A,5000.01389,N,04500.00001,E,10.0,0.0,121004,0.0,E*4E
```

FIGURE 9-19: Sample NMEA output

NMEA output files are plaintext files that can be processed by a variety of GPS applications. For example, you can import a file into an application such as Memory Map and have the NMEA data translated into a route that appears on the map as an overlay. However, unlike a real-time signal from a GPS, the file can be replayed without requiring a clear view of the sky.

In theory, this enables you to separate the tracking and mapping elements of recording the data. This would enable you to create a simple yet effective tracking system (for, say, a car). All you need is a GPS and a Pocket PC device running GpsGate.

Connect the GPS to the Pocket PC and set up GpsGate to log the NMEA (the software is the same as the Windows version). This will create a log file that you can later examine. Because each NMEA sentence contains a checksum, tampering with the actual log is unlikely (hide the system well and no one need know it was fitted to the vehicle!).

Recording Simulated NMEA Using GpsGate

As a GPS user and someone who uses a lot of mapping software, there have been times when I wished that I could create an NMEA file quickly and without the fuss of hooking up a GPS to the PC. Well, using GpsGate, this is possible:

1. Right-click on the GpsGate icon in the System Tray and choose Source ⇨ Simulator.

2. Now right-click the icon again and choose Simulator. This brings up the screen shown in Figure 9-20.

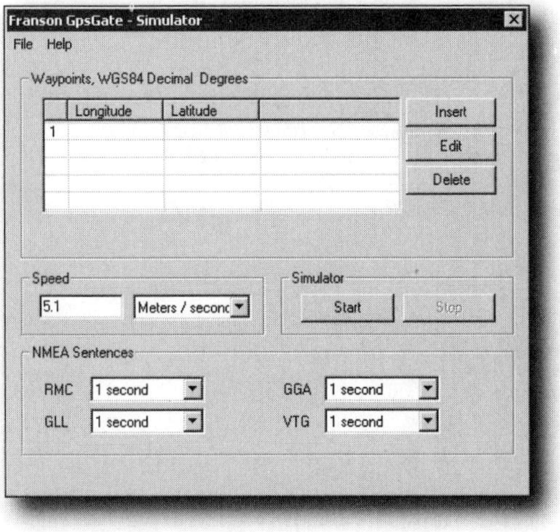

FIGURE 9-20: GpsGate simulator window

3. The window that is displayed controls the parameters of the simulated NMEA output. It enables you to enter waypoints along which the simulator will travel, as well as the speed of the simulated travel and what NMEA sentences are output, along with their frequency of appearance of the sentences.

4. Choose the settings that are appropriate to you (I suggest outputting each NMEA sentence once a second, which will provide quite a genuine output).

5. Click the Start button.

6. Once again, right-click on the GpsGate System Tray icon and choose NMEA Log.

7. To record the input, click the Record button. This brings up a dialog box asking you to choose a location in which to save the NMEA output file.

8. To stop recording, click Stop.

9. Once you are done, you can examine the NMEA output file.

The file created will contain NMEA data similar to the output from a GPS, but this data is simulated and has not been generated by a GPS.

Data Playback

Now that you have the NMEA files, you can output the data. While some applications will accept NMEA directly, with GpsGate, as long as the application can take the data and output it to a virtual port from which the application can take the data, the application will treat the data as though it's coming directly from a GPS, when it fact it's coming from a log file.

To set this up, follow these steps:

1. Choose the output virtual port for the data by right-clicking on the GpsGate icon in the System Tray and choosing Settings.

2. Fire up the application you want to send the data to and choose the virtual port and the incoming GPS data port (how you do this will vary from application to application, so consult your manual for details).

3. Right-click on the GpsGate icon and choose Source ⇨ NMEA Log. This will bring up the window shown in Figure 9-21.

FIGURE 9-21: GpsGate NMEA Log playback window

You can now control the playback of the log using the Play, Stop, Pause, Rewind, and Forward buttons. Clicking Play will output the NMEA log to the application listening to the virtual port.

Why Bother with NMEA?

You might be wondering why so many applications enable you to examine and record the NMEA sentences that come from a GPS. Are all these software programs and utilities driven purely by curiosity?

Well, partly, yes! However, there is a serious side to examining NMEA. Let's look at two aspects now.

Ensuring That Your GPS Works

A GPS, like all other electronic gadgets, is prone to failures. If, one day, you are unable to switch on your GPS even after you change the batteries for fresh ones, then you know it's dead. But electronic devices are just as prone to erratic problems as a result of failures.

A good way to determine whether your GPS (or antenna) is picking up satellites properly is to hook the device up to a PC or portable device and look at the NMEA being produced. Does what you see look like valid NMEA? Do all the sentences look okay or do you find that there are blank lines being displayed onscreen?

If your GPS is outputting valid NMEA that contains accurate positional information, then the GPS is working (even if other components of the GPS, such as the screen or input buttons, aren't). I've seen GPS receivers with broken screens or nonfucntioning buttons put to excellent use when connected to another device.

If your NMEA sentences seem wrong or cut off or include blank lines, before you condemn your GPS to the trash can (or recycling depot), check all the cables and connections. Follow the instructions in the cable chapters to test your cables (remember that heat and vibration can affect cables, so test them under these conditions if possible). If possible, try a different cable to see if the problem persists.

Avoiding Data Corruption

When you have a GPS connected to a PC or portable device for navigating with (in-car especially), you'll likely notice that most of the track information for your journey is smooth and accurate and follows the road closely. However, you might also find that occasionally you get what are known as *spikes* in the data. Spikes are when you appear to have moved a great distance very fast indeed. Sometimes the jumps can be very small (a few hundred meters), while at other times the spikes can be huge, momentarily propelling you hundreds, if not thousands, of miles off course before bringing you back to where you are supposed to be.

These can be irritating and make you lose faith in your system, and it's a good idea to try to pinpoint the cause of the problem.

This kind of problem usually indicates one of two root causes:

- A problem with the GPS
- A problem with the device to which the GPS is connected

If the problem is with the actual GPS itself, then the way to test it is simple: First make a log of the NMEA sentences. Then, when you see a problem with the tracklog produced, look through the NMEA sentences for data that corresponds to the glitch. You can save yourself a lot of time by only looking at the $GPGGA sentences that contain the position, velocity, and time data.

With practice, just a cursory look through the listing will highlight problems. Generally, the numbers represeting coordinates and velocity change gradually over time, and sudden changes are usually a result of either the systyem being switched off and back on again, the GPS reaquiring satellite lock after losing it, or an intermittant problem with the receiver. Here is an example (the last part of the sentences is omitted for clarity):

```
$GPGGA,182129.04,5040.642,N,00102.255,W,
$GPGGA,182130.03,5040.643,N,00102.256,W,
$GPGGA,182131.02,5040.644,N,00102.258,W,
$GPGGA,182132.01,5040.645,N,00102.259,W,
$GPGGA,182133.05,5040.646,N,00102.261,W,
$GPGGA,182134.04,5040.647,N,00104.339,W,
$GPGGA,182135.03,5040.648,N,00102.264,W,
$GPGGA,182136.02,5040.649,N,00102.266,W,
$GPGGA,182137.00,5040.650,N,00102.267,W,
```

Take a look at line 5. Notice how the longitude reading jumps from 102.261 degrees west to 102.261 degrees west before returning back to normal? That's the kind or error you are looking for, and it stands out clearly when you learn how to read NMEA.

However, you might find nothing wrong with the NMEA sentences and that the spike isn't present in the actual data received from the GPS. If this is the case, then switch your focus to look for applications that might be interfering with the mapping software. Shut down any unwanted applications. In addition, check for electrical interference from other devices, especially cell phones. If none of these tactics work, consider either reinstalling the software that you use or trying it on a different device.

While most applications have the capability to log NMEA received, some don't; and this can present a problem when trying to diagnose ptoblems. In this case, you should use an application such as GpsGate, described in the preceding section.

Summary

In this chapter, you looked at the two communication protocols that GPS uses with external devices: NMEA and SiRF.

You examined in detail many types of NMEA sentences that a GPS can output and looked at the structure of the sentences and what the individual parts mean.

You also looked at software that enables you to access the raw data that is output from the GPS. This can be useful for GPS diagnostics and giving you experience in decoding NMEA sentences.

Finally, you looked at software that enables you to create simulated NMEA sentences in order to practice decoding them and gain experience in troubleshooting them for a variety of situations.

More Data Tricks

In this chapter, we will examine some cool tricks you can do with your GPS, relating specifically to data. Rather than looking at purely positional data and things you can accomplish with that, this chapter takes a broader, more general look at GPS data and how you can use it.

Screenshots

You might have noticed that some web pages and manuals have screenshots of what is actually displayed on the GPS. Being able to capture actual screenshots could be very useful if you are creating a manual or a set of instructions, if you are trying to diagnose problems, or indeed for many other uses.

Generally, there is no feature that enables you to grab a screenshot from your GPS from within the GPS firmware itself or from the associated software that you get with your GPS (usually very little, if anything). However, you can find software that will let you do so.

G7toWin

G7toWin, shown in Figure 10-1, is software that can take screenshots of the screen displayed on most Garmin GPS units and import them onto your PC.

G7toWin is available for free download from www.gps information.org/ronh.

This software works for most GPS receivers by Garmin, Magellan, and Lorance/Eagle. In addition to taking screenshots, it does a lot more. G7toWin, as you might have seen in previous chapters, can also be used to transfer various kinds of data to and from your GPS:

- Routes
- Tracks
- Waypoints
- Events (Lowrance/Eagle units only)
- Satellite information (such as the almanac data)

FIGURE 10-1: G7toWin

In my experience, I've noticed that G7toWin offers very good levels of compatibility with many different kinds of GPS receiver.

The process of taking screenshots is as follows:

1. Download the software from the website (`www.gpsinformation.org/ronh`).

2. After you have downloaded the software, open the zipped file.

3. Extract the files to a convenient location on your hard drive. This software doesn't require any installation, so the place you extract it to is the place from which you will need to run it.

4. Connect your GPS receiver to the PC and switch it on.

5. Run the main executable file (`g7towin.exe`).

6. Running the application brings up a blank screen.

7. Make sure the software is looking for your GPS on the appropriate serial or USB port (or even a Bluetooth connection) and is using the right settings. To check on and change these setting, click File ⇨ Configuration. The Options Setup screen that appears is displayed in Figure 10-2.

8. This screen looks quite complex, but there are a few key areas for you to look at.

    a. First, make sure that the right GPS is selected (see Figure 10-3).

    b. Choose the appropriate port, along with the port speed (see Figure 10-4). Here you can also choose whether the GPS is connected via USB.

    c. After you are done with that, click the Save Configuration button (see Figure 10-5). You will only need to go through this process once unless you have multiple GPS receivers.

9. With the settings specified, you are now ready to capture screenshots (if you have the appropriate receiver).

10. To do this, click GPS ⇨ Commands ⇨ Get and Show Bitmap.

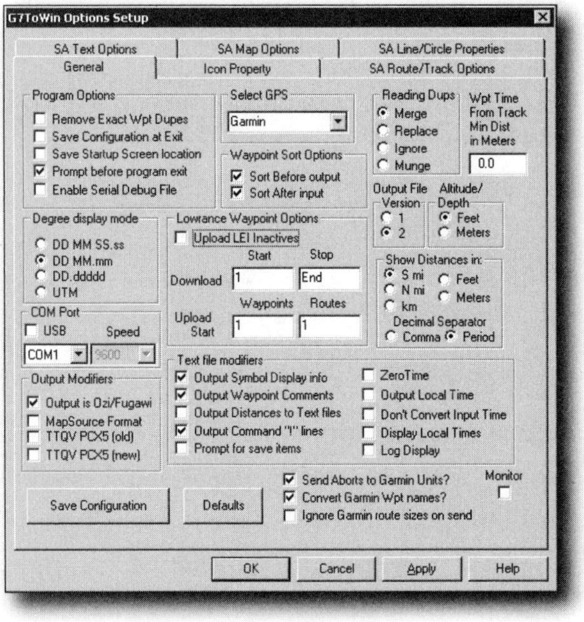

FIGURE 10-2: G7toWin configuration screen

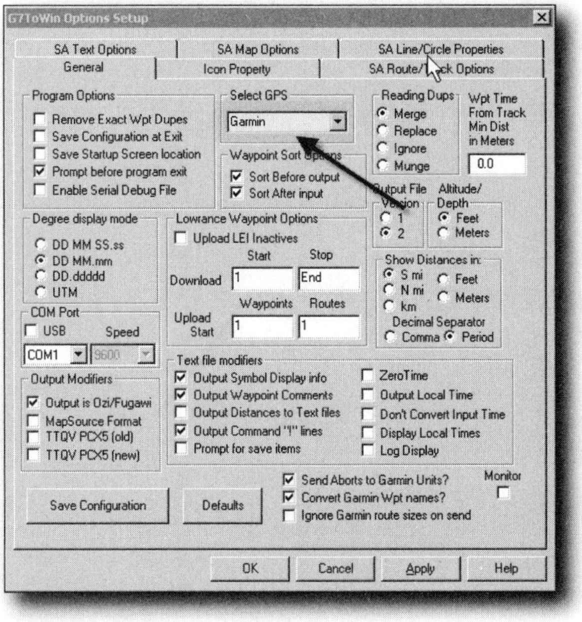

FIGURE 10-3: Select the correct GPS receiver.

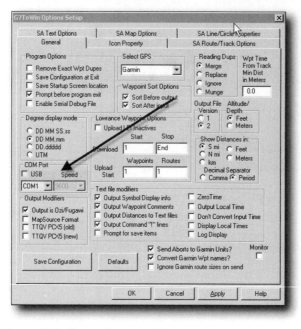

FIGURE 10-4: Choose the appropriate port.

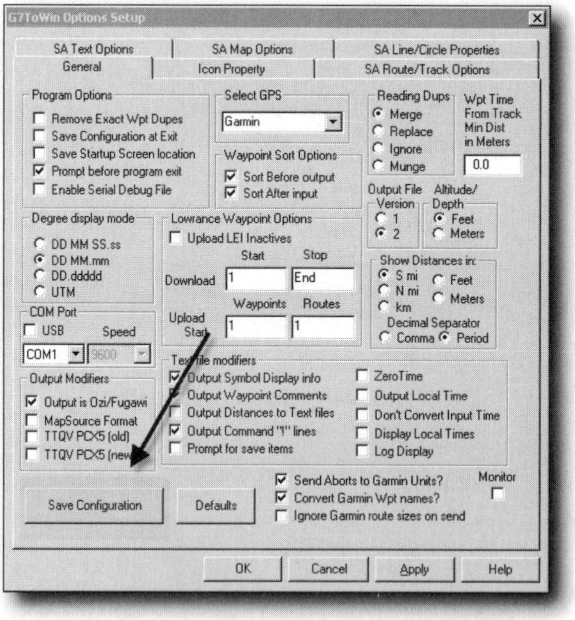

FIGURE 10-5: Save the configurations for the software.

Note The term *bitmap* is used not to indicate that the screen display is a static display but because what is displayed on your GPS consists of a bitmap of black and gray or colored dots. This information is what is downloaded from the GPS to the PC.

11. The screen displayed on the GPS will be transmitted to the PC over the connection and displayed onscreen (see Figure 10-6).

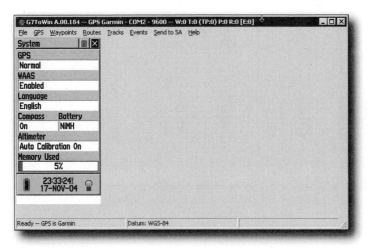

FIGURE 10-6: Transferring the screenshot bitmap to the PC

Once the bitmap display is loaded onto the PC, it is available to you to manipulate:

- The bitmap can be rotated left (see Figure 10-7).

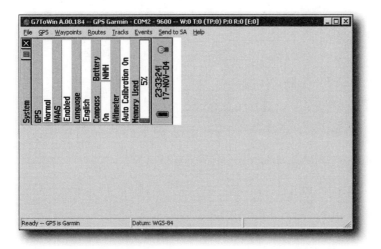

FIGURE 10-7: Rotating the bitmap

- The bitmap can be stretched (see Figure 10-8).

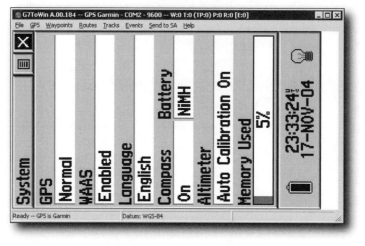

FIGURE **10-8: Stretching the bitmap to fit the screen**

- The bitmap can be copied to the clipboard (see Figure 10-9).

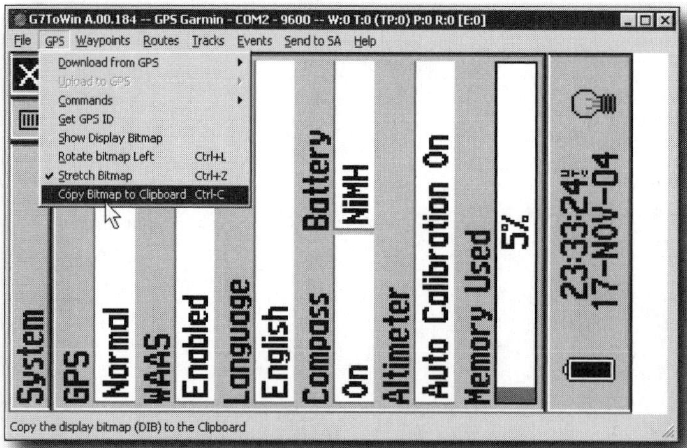

FIGURE **10-9: Copying the bitmap to the clipboard**

- Once copied to the clipboard, the screenshot can be pasted into a graphics package such as Windows Paint (see Figure 10-10).

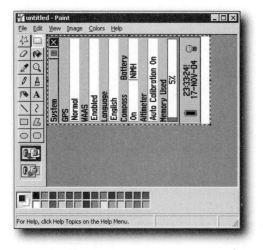

FIGURE 10-10: Pasting the bitmap into Windows Paint

There is only one problem with using your PC to take screenshots of your GPS: Your GPS has to be hooked to your PC, and PCs aren't easy to carry about — even laptops, which are portable, don't really stand up well to use in the field.

It would be far better to be able to be out and about.

G7toCE

G7toCE is a version of G7toWin that will run on Windows CE and Pocket PC versions of the Windows operating system. There aren't many CE devices about these days, but Pocket PC devices, such as iPAQs, are common.

In fact, several different versions of G7toCE are available. The versions for portable devices are as follows:

- Pocket PC 2003
    - ARMV4 version
- Pocket PC 2002
    - ARM version
- Pocket PC
    - SH3
    - ARM
    - MIPS

- H/PC 2000
    - ARM
    - MIPS
- H/PC 2.11
    - SH4
    - SH3
    - ARM
    - MIPS

The different versions are for different processors running the handheld devices. To find the processor that your device contains, refer to the manual or consult the "About" screen, accessible from somewhere in the operating system. The screen shown in Figure 10-11 is from an iPAQ 3950.

FIGURE 10-11: G7toCE in action

The good thing about G7toCE is that all the different versions are virtually identical in the way they work and look.

Before you can start to use G7toCE, you will need to install it on your handheld device. First you have to download the appropriate file for your hardware and operating system from www. gpsinformation.org/ronh. People who have problems installing this software normally do so because they have downloaded the incorrect file for their combination of hardware and operating system. Currently, there is no single "install" file that covers all possibilities, so you have to choose carefully.

For this example, we are installing it onto a Pocket PC 2002 machine, so we need to download the appropriate file for that. This file is called g7toce_PPC_2002_arm.zip.

After you have downloaded the package (a zipped, or compressed, file), you can open it using a utility such as WinZip. This file contains four program files (see Figure 10-12):

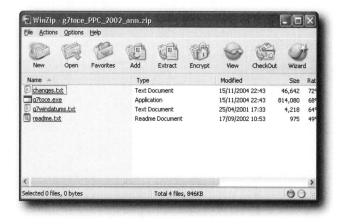

FIGURE 10-12: Contents of the downloaded file

- **g7toce.exe:** The main program file.

- **G7windatums.txt:** This file is used to control how coordinate datum conversions are carried out and can be ignored.

- **changes.txt:** A file listing the changes to the application.

- **readme.txt:** The installation instruction file.

There is no installation program; you have to carry out the installation manually. The procedure is as follows:

1. Copy the file g7toce.exe to the Windows\Start Menu folder on the handheld device (see Figure 10-13).

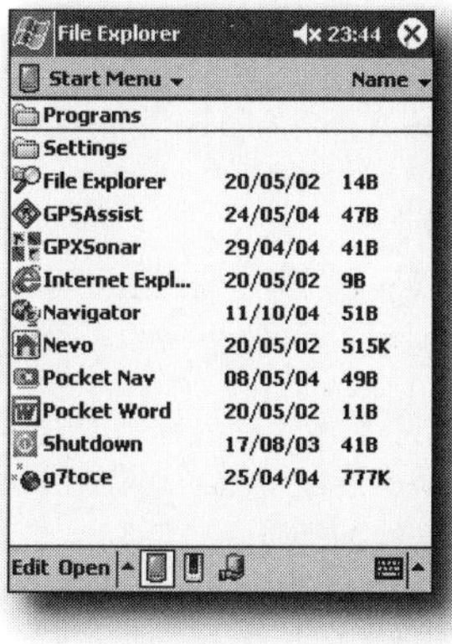

FIGURE 10-13: Copy the executable to the Pocket PC.

2. Create a folder called G7ToCE under the My Documents folder. Into that folder copy the `g7windatums.txt` file (see Figure 10-14).

FIGURE **10-14: Create the appropriate folder for the application.**

3. Run G7ToCE. When you do this for the first time, an error message regarding a file called `g7toce.ini` will be displayed (see Figure 10-15). This is normal.

FIGURE **10-15: Initial error message displayed**

4. You'll fix this error now. Select File ➪ Configuration (see Figure 10-16).

5. Select the DMS tab (see Figure 10-17).

6. Select Save Configuration at Exit (see Figure 10-18). You may also change other parameters at this stage if you want.

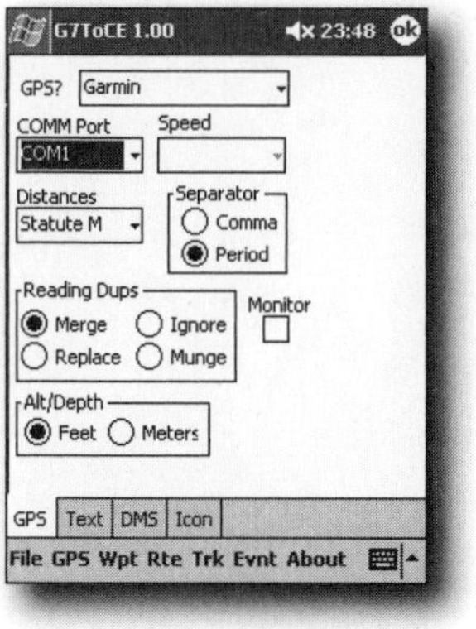

FIGURE 10-16: The G7toCE
configuration screen

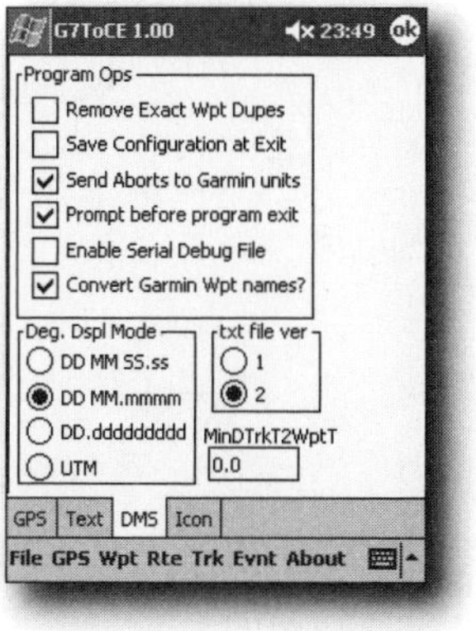

FIGURE 10-17: The DMS screen

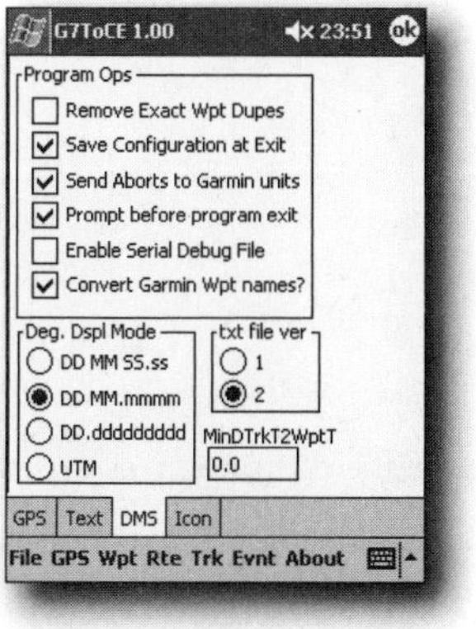

FIGURE 10-18: There is a lot of room
for configuration in G7toCE.

7. Select any other tabs (GPS, Text, Icon) to set the startup parameters suitable to your needs (see Figure 10-19).

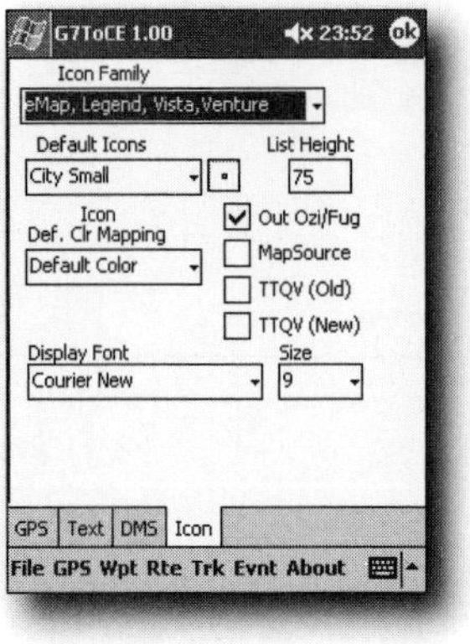

FIGURE 10-19: Set your startup parameters.

8. Click OK (see Figure 10-20).

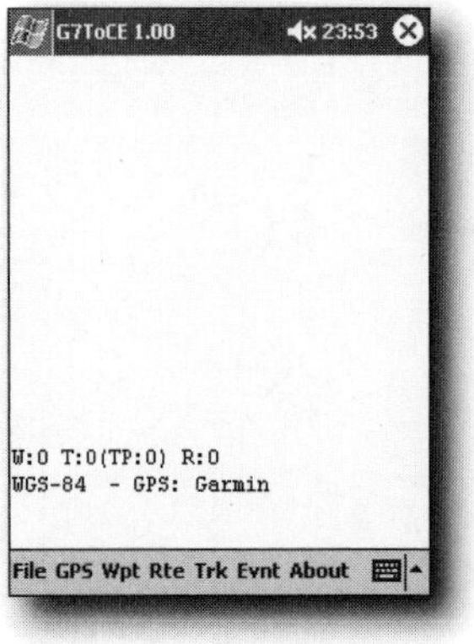

FIGURE 10-20: Save the configuration file.

9. Exit the application.

10. Check the folder My Documents\G7ToCE for the file g7toce.ini to ensure that it has been created properly.

11. Now you are ready to use the application.

Now you need to connect the GPS to the device. To do this via a cable connection, follow these steps:

1. Turn off the device.

2. Connect the cable between the device and the GPS receiver.

3. Switch the GPS on and let it start up fully (it should be ready to acquire satellites but need not have locked on to them).

4. Start the handheld device and start up G7toCE.

You've now got the application set up well enough for you to take screenshots from Garmin units. To do this, click GPS ⇨ Get Display Bitmap (see Figure 10-21).

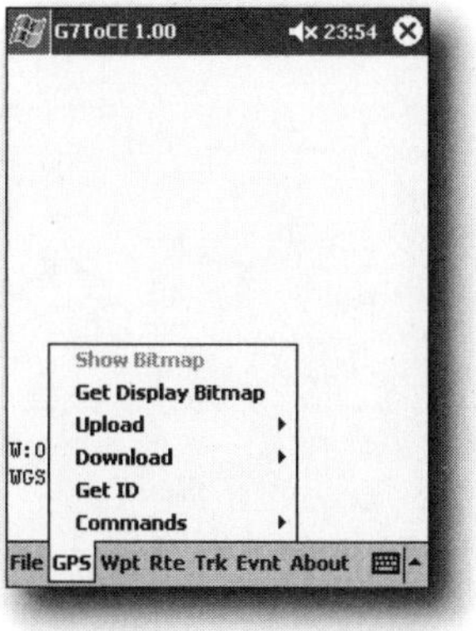

FIGURE 10-21: Retrieving the bitmap display

G7toCE will now download the display on the screen of the GPS to your handheld device. After the bitmap of the display has been transferred to the handheld device, you can display the image by clicking GPS ⇨ Display Bitmap (see Figure 10-22).

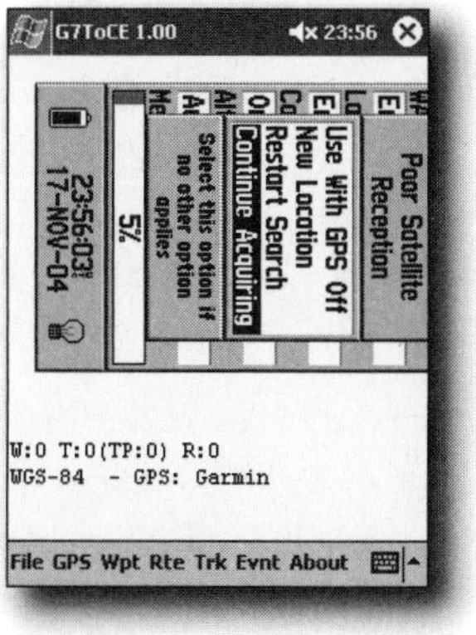

FIGURE 10-22: Bitmap displayed in the application

Turning Your PC into a High-Precision Atomic Clock

For many people, having accurate time is important, and some people go to great lengths to ensure that the time on their PC is as accurate as possible.

For the ultimate in accurate timing, you need access to an *atomic clock*. This will give you undisputed accuracy, but it comes with a huge price tag. Another option is to synchronize your PC clock with a time server on the Internet.

Many of these use National Institute of Standards and Technology (NIST) time, but there are many others around the world.

Here is a list of the U.S.-based NIST time servers:

Name	IP Address	Location
time-a.nist.gov	129.6.15.28	NIST, Gaithersburg, Maryland
time-b.nist.gov	129.6.15.29	NIST, Gaithersburg, Maryland
time-a.timefreq.bldrdoc.gov	132.163.4.101	NIST, Boulder, Colorado
time-b.timefreq.bldrdoc.gov	132.163.4.102	NIST, Boulder, Colorado
time-c.timefreq.bldrdoc.gov	132.163.4.103	NIST, Boulder, Colorado
utcnist.colorado.edu	128.138.140.44	University of Colorado, Boulder
time.nist.gov	192.43.244.18	NCAR, Boulder, Colorado
time-nw.nist.gov	131.107.1.10	Microsoft, Redmond, Washington
nist1.symmetricom.com	69.25.96.13	Symmetricom, San Jose, California
nist1-dc.glassey.com	216.200.93.8	Abovenet, Virginia
nist1-ny.glassey.com	216.200.93.9	Abovenet, New York City
nist1-sj.glassey.com	207.126.98.204	Abovenet, San Jose, California
nist1.aol-ca.truetime.com	207.200.81.113	TrueTime, AOL facility, Sunnyvale, California
nist1.aol-va.truetime.com	64.236.96.53	TrueTime, AOL facility, Virginia

These time servers offer you a way to quickly and regularly update your clock to ensure that it is as accurate as possible. Of course, it does require a connection to the Internet, and high traffic on the Internet or your connection can cause problems with the accuracy.

Note

If you are using time servers located on the Internet to adjust your PC clock, make sure that you are using the most accurate stratum 1 time servers.

If you are interested in setting your clock over the Internet, rather than GPS, and you want control over the time server used, you can't do much better than to use a piece of shareware called Sync-It with Atom, available from www.tolvanen.com/syncit.

One of the best ways that I have found to synchronize a PC with an atomic clock is to use the GPS signal. This offers several advantages over using the Internet:

- You don't need a connection to the Internet. You do, however, need a clear view of the sky.

- Each GPS satellite carries with it four atomic clocks. This means that the time signal you will be getting is very accurate indeed.

- In addition to the four atomic clocks, you can also take advantage of the capability to average the time from three or more satellites, giving you access to between 12 and 24 four atomic clocks.

All you need to take advantage of this useful access to atomic clocks is a GPS and some software that enables you to make use of it.

The best software I've found to carry out this task is called NMEATime by VisualGPS. This software is shareware and it costs $20 to register. NMEATime is available for download from the Visual GPS website at www.visualgps.net/NMEATime/default.htm. If you want to just try it out before committing to buy (always a wise idea), a 30-day trial period is available.

Note NMEA is an abbreviation for National Marine Electronics Association. It defines the standard that specifies how receivers communicate with each other and other devices (although there are manufacturer specific protocols too). NMEATime can also be used to synchronize a PC's clock with Internet time servers.

Setting Up the Software

Before you can do anything, you need to set up the software:

1. Download NMEATime from the VisualGPS website.

2. Locate the download and run the executable file.

3. Follow the installation instructions. After NMEATime is installed, you can run the application.

The best thing about NMEATime is its versatility. To get to the configuration screen of the application, right-click on the clock and choose Properties.

Note You can also gain access to the application by right-clicking the icon in the system tray and choosing Properties.

Doing this brings up a Properties window filled with settings, as shown in Figure 10-23.

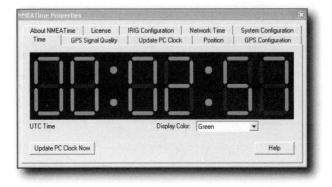

FIGURE 10-23: The NMEATime Properties window

There are several settings on the GPS Configuration tab that will be of interest to you. The first is Comm Settings (see Figure 10-24). Clicking this brings up the Communication Settings dialog box, from which you can select the appropriate Comm port and baud rate, or communication speed (as shown in Figure 10-25). The standard speed for NMEA communication is 4800 bps.

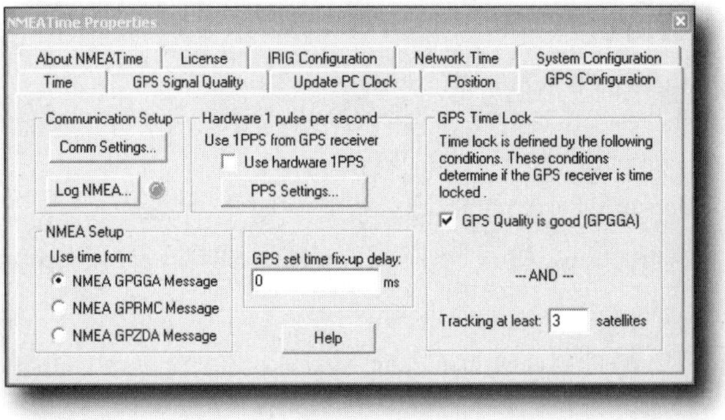

FIGURE 10-24: NMEATime port settings

You can also choose which part of the protocol (or more accurately, which NMEA message contained within the NMEA sentence) is used to get the time information (see Figure 10-26). Of the three NMEA messages to choose from, I recommend that you use the first or second to ensure compatibility:

- **GPGGA:** Provides accurate timing information and is commonly output by GPS receivers

- **GPRMC:** Also provides accurate timing information and is commonly output by GPS receivers

- **GPZDA:** Provides both time and date information but is not usually output by many GPS receivers

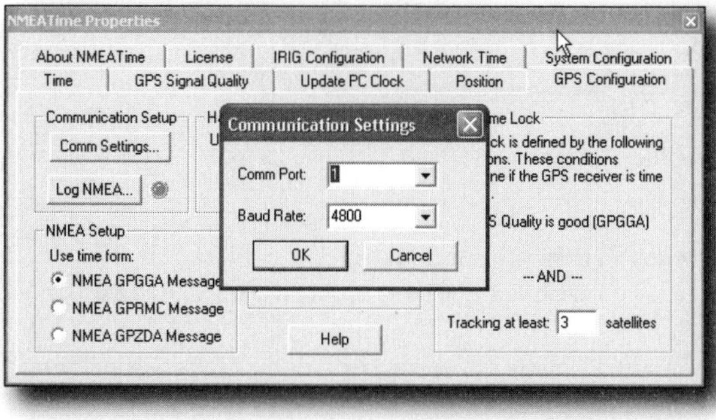

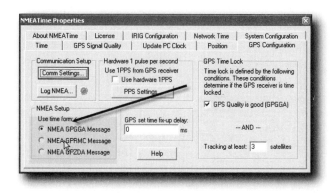

FIGURE **10-25: Choosing the appropriate port settings**

FIGURE **10-26: NMEA sentence options**

There is also the "Hardware 1 pulse per second" setting to consider (see Figure 10-27). When this check box is selected, NMEATime waits for the RS-232 DSR (Data Set Ready) or CTS (Clear To Send) line to change state before setting the PC clock. If the GPS receiver outputs a 1PPS signal, this signal can then be fed back to the DSR or CTS line to maximize synchronization accuracy.

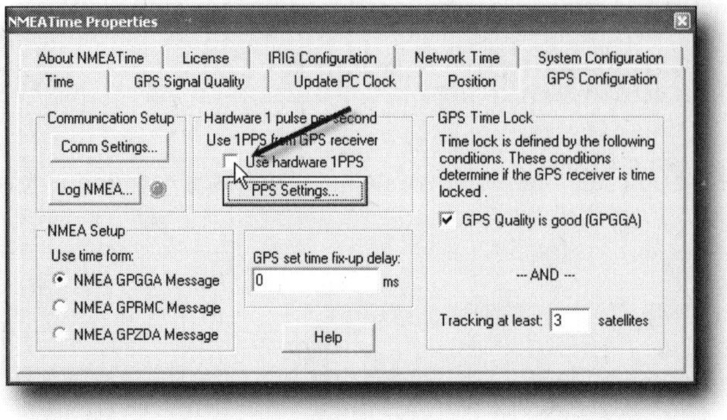

FIGURE 10-27: Hardware pulse option

Clicking the PPS Settings button also uncovers useful settings (see Figure 10-28). Use the PPS Settings dialog box to select the hardware line to be used as the 1PPS input (DSR or CTS). You can also set the trigger polarity:

- **Trigger on High to Low Transition:** Causes the time to be set on a high to low transition of the 1PPS input

- **Trigger on Low to High Transition:** Causes the time to be set on a low to high transition of the 1PPS input

- **Trigger on Any Transition:** Causes the time to be set on any transition

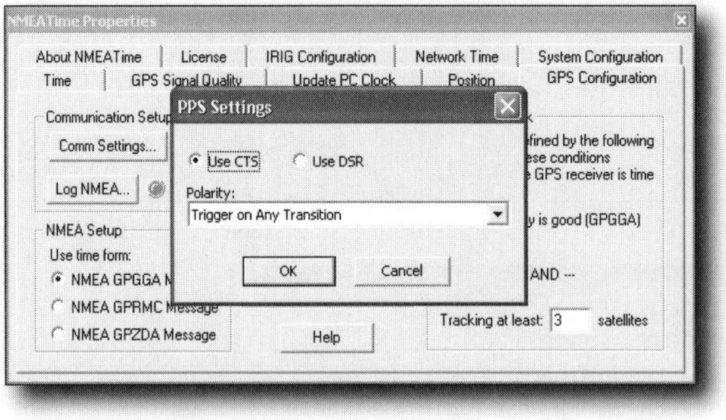

FIGURE 10-28: PPS Settings dialog box

Sometimes, there may be a slight delay between the time a GPS receiver sends its timing information to the computer and the time the computer receives it. Back in the Properties dialog box, you can factor in this delay using the GPS Time Fix-up Delay value, adjusting the time ahead or behind in milliseconds when setting the system time. The allowable values are from –999ms to 999ms, set as follows:

- If the GPS time is early, then a negative value is used.

- If the GPS time is late, then a positive value is used.

- The GPS Time Fix-up Delay should be set to 0 if the Use Hardware 1PPS option is enabled.

The final set of features on the Time tab is GPS Time Lock. NMEATime enables you to change the criteria that the software considers for a good GPS signal lock. There are two customizable parameters:

- The GPS Quality is good (GPGGA) option is directly related to the GPGGA NMEA message. If the GPS Quality indicator from the GPGGA sentence contains any information (that is, it is nonzero), it is considered to be good. If the GPS receiver does not support the GPGGA sentence, then this check box should be unchecked.

- Tracking multiple satellites can also be very important. In locations such as urban areas where sky visibility is low because of large buildings blocking the sky, it might be a good idea to have the GPS receiver track multiple satellites before considering the signal, and thus the time, before accepting a signal. For a good, reliable time signal, I recommend that you consider three satellites as the minimum for a good signal lock.

Other settings come into play within the Properties dialog box too. Click the System Configuration tab (see Figure 10-29) and make sure that Set PC Clock Using GPS is checked.

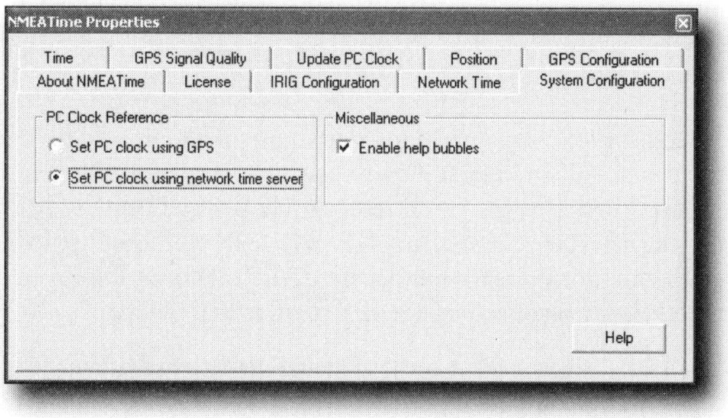

FIGURE 10-29: NMEATime system configuration options

Now click the Update PC Clock tab (see Figure 10-30). Here you can set the update interval for the PC clock. For systems on which you want very accurate time information, you might want to update the clock every 1–10 minutes, whereas for lower accuracy needs you could drop that to twice a day (an interval of 720 minutes). The maximum possible interval is 31 days (44,640 minutes).

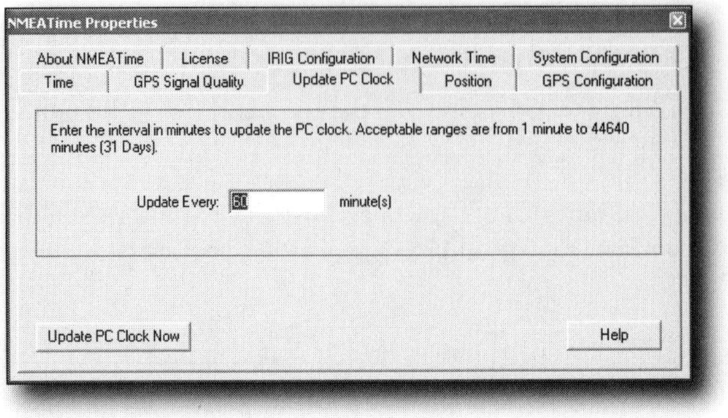

FIGURE **10-30: Choosing how often to update the PC clock**

With the software set up, it's now time to set up the hardware that you will need.

Setting Up the Hardware

To set up the required hardware, you will need the following:

- A GPS
- A cable/wireless connection
- A long-term power supply (a wall adapter is ideal — choose one with the appropriate input and output voltages, depending on your location and equipment) for the GPS (batteries aren't going to last long if the GPS is on 24/7)

The type of GPS you use is important. I consider the long-term use of a handheld GPS such as the Garmin eTrex to be a bit wasteful; and depending on location, it might be vulnerable to loss, theft, or damage. I recommend investing in a small receiver such as the Leadtek GPS Smart Antenna GPS 9532 (www.leadtek.com/gps/gps9532/9532.htm). These are low-cost receiver-only setups and are designed for long-term exposure to the elements. However, if you only need to set up the time occasionally, your existing GPS receiver will suffice.

Power is important — for long-term use, you don't want to change batteries regularly. The Leadtek receiver mentioned in the preceding paragraph draws power from the 5/12 volt supply and contains an internal backup battery in case of power failure.

Choosing a good position for your receiver is vital. The best position for the receiver is the tallest, least obstructed spot, away from trees and not overshadowed by other buildings. Figure 10-31 shows some good locations for the antenna, while Figure 10-32 indicates some bad locations for a receiver.

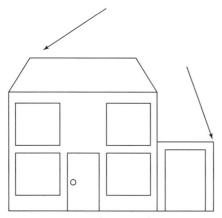

FIGURE 10-31: Good antenna locations

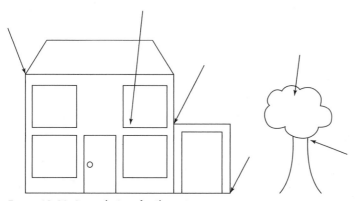

FIGURE 10-32: Poor choices for the antenna

Hooking Up Hardware to Software

Now all that is left to do is create the interface between the hardware and the software:

1. Make sure that the GPS is connected to the PC properly.

2. Switch the GPS on and make sure that it is getting an adequate signal (remember that a spot that provides you with good signal at one time might not do so later as the satellites move — check on it).

3. Run the NMEATime application.

4. From the NMEATime Properties screen, click the GPS Signal Quality tab (see Figure 10-33). Use this to check the signal quality being received by the software.

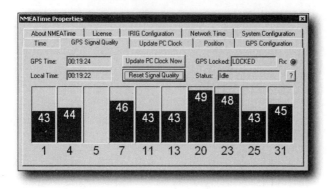

FIGURE 10-33: GPS signal quality displayed

5. That's it! Check the signal quality periodically to ensure that you've chosen a good location for the receiver. If the signal quality becomes poor, you might need to reconsider the placement of the receiver.

The accuracy you get from using GPS to synchronize your PC clock is truly amazing. Furthermore, you can access the signal 24/7 and it requires no connection to the Internet. It's fast, reliable, and very, very geeky!

Bringing a GPS Signal Indoors

This atomic clock system relies on an antenna located outdoors, using this to bring the signal indoors. The signal is usually routed indoors via cable because wireless technologies such as Bluetooth don't offer the range needed, especially when signals have to work through walls, roofs, and ceilings. In addition, leaving a GPS antenna outdoors 24/7 not only exposes it to the elements, but also to theft and damage.

Much better than leaving a GPS outdoors is to use only an antenna to bring the GPS signal indoors. The cheapest way to do with is to use what's called a *reradiating antenna*. A typical reradiating antenna is shown in Figure 10-34.

These antennas consist of the following:

- A power supply (usually 12V, DC)
- An active antenna (that is, a powered antenna)
- A transmitting antenna (this is, the antenna that retransmits, or reradiates, the GPS signal)
- Connecting cables

As you can see, the active antenna is the antenna that receives the signals from the GPS satellites. After the signal is received, it is transmitted along a coaxial cable to the transmitting, reradiating antenna. This antenna, also powered by the 12-volt DC supply, transmits the signal received by the active antenna. The transmitted signal is then picked up normally by the GPS receiver.

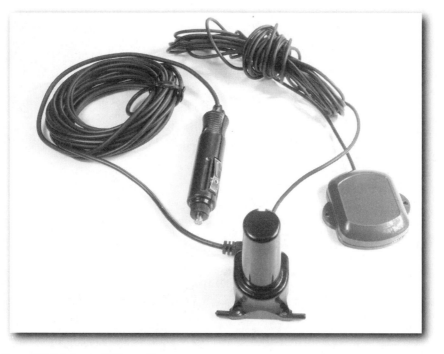

FIGURE 10-34: A reradiating antenna

The same rules of placement regarding the GPS receiver apply to the antenna. Because it is an active antenna and has more power at its disposal, active antennas on reradiating kits are normally better at getting a decent signal in less than ideal conditions.

Here are some tips to help you with your reradiating set up:

- Site the antenna well, firmly attaching it — if possible, use either the magnetic base on the antenna or screws.

- Remember that the antenna needs power. Even though it is only drawing 12V DC, take care to waterproof all connections and joints in the cables. Do this properly and don't rely on taped up connections. Short circuits can cause fires and damage your gear.

- Be aware that the longer the cable you put between your receiving antenna and transmitting antenna, the more signal you lose through attenuation. If you need to use a cable longer than the one provided with the antenna kit, consider using cables that are low-loss and shielded. This kind of cable can be expensive, but so is buying poorer quality cable and finding it won't work because of signal loss.

- Finally, it's vital to carefully consider placement of the transmitting antenna. If you place the transmitting antenna and the receiving GPS in a place where you can still pick up a signal directly from the GPS satellites, this can result in what is known as *multi-path error* (see Figure 10-35), whereby the GPS picks up a signal from the antenna and the satellites directly. This can cause quite a substantial error in position. The error in time is quite small, however, so unless you require atomic clock precision, you should be okay.

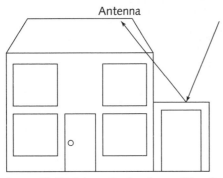

Antenna

FIGURE 10-35: Schematic showing multi-path errors

Other Uses for GPS Data

What you can do with GPS data really depends on the software you're using. While you were at the website from which you downloaded NMEATime (www.visualgps.net), you might have also come across software called VisualGPS. VisualGPS comes in two flavors:

■ VisualGPS: A standard free version (see Figure 10-36).

■ VisualGPSXP: A full-featured version of VisualGPS (see Figure 10-37). This software is not free (currently a license costs $25 and a 30-day trial is available).

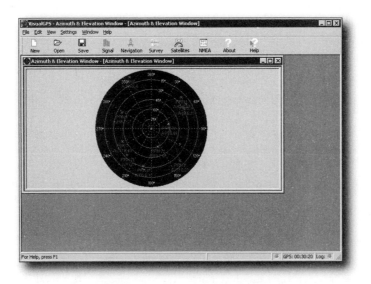

FIGURE 10-36: VisualGPS

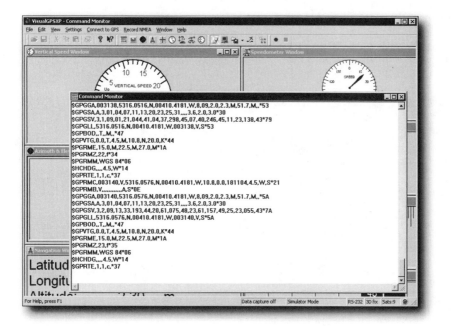

FIGURE 10-37: VisualGPSXP

There is also a version for Pocket PC 2002 devices (only for those using the ARM processor). This is called VisualGPSce (see Figure 10-38) and is currently considered a beta/experimental program; it is currently free. I've used this program and have found it to be useful and stable.

VisualGPS is very useful software because it enables you to work with the data that the GPS outputs at a very low level. The following sections outline some of the features of VisualGPS.

FIGURE 10-38: VisualGPSce

Azimuth and Elevation Graphs

This window (see Figure 10-39) enables you to view any satellites that are in view from your current location (or, more accurately, from the location of the GPS receiver).

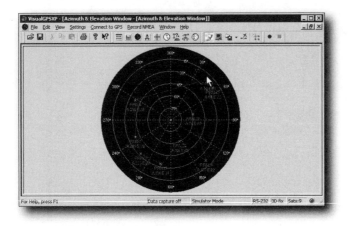

FIGURE 10-39: Satellites currently visible

Each satellite is identified by its pseudo-random number (PRN), its azimuth (denoted by the letter A), and its elevation (denoted by the letter B). This window also enables you to do something else that is interesting: plot and print the physical mask angle. When you are using your GPS in a stationary or static application (such as to get the signal for synchronizing your PC clock), it is important that you place the antenna where it can get a clear view of the sky. However, sometimes obstructions block the signal from the GPS to the antenna. Knowing the effect of these obstructions on the tracking of satellites can be essential because there may be times when the obstruction is adversely affecting reception.

The Azimuth and Elevation window can graphically demonstrate the elevation mask angle. The mask angle is represented by a blue, jagged line that is built by using satellite information. The mask angle is, in effect, the "horizon" for the GPS antenna at that point. Using the information from the SNR (signal to noise ratio) and satellite status, a graphical representation of the mask angle is created (as shown in Figure 10-40).

| Note | It can take up to 24 hours of continuous tracking of satellites to gather all the information needed to build an accurate mask angle. |

| Note | If you want more details about satellite availability, along with details about how obstructions will affect your reception, I suggest you visit www.trimble.com/planningsoftware.html. Here you can download free software that enables you to calculate satellite availability, create sky plots of availability, and get information on visible satellites. |

FIGURE 10-40: Mask angle displayed for the current location

Surveying

The Survey window displays both position and xDOP (x Dilution of Precision). HDOP represents horizontal dilution of precision, or inaccuracy in the position displayed, while VDOP represents vertical dilution of precision, or height/altitude inaccuracies (see Figure 10-41).

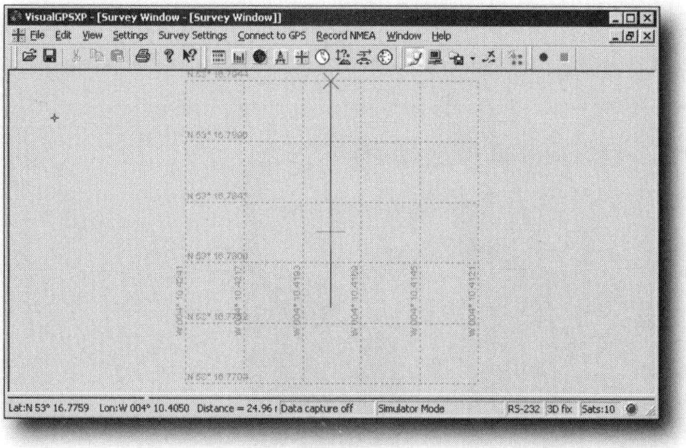

FIGURE 10-41: The Survey window

If you are using a stationary antenna, this window can provide very accurate measurements of position and elevation.

You can also print this information.

Navigation

VisualGPS also provides detailed navigational information for when you are using it on the move (see Figure 10-42). This information includes latitude, longitude, and altitude.

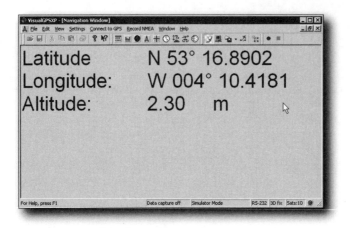

FIGURE 10-42: Navigation window

Signal Quality/SNR Window

The Signal Quality window enables you to monitor satellite signal-to-noise ratios and see them graphically on the screen (see Figure 10-43).

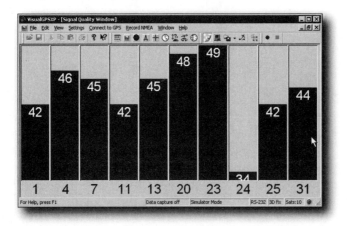

FIGURE 10-43: Signal-to-noise ratio display

This window is dynamic and the signal quality bars increase and decrease according to the current SNR. The window will expand and contract to accommodate the number of satellites in view at any one time.

NMEA Command Monitor

This window enables you to see NMEA sentences as they are being received (see Figure 10-44).

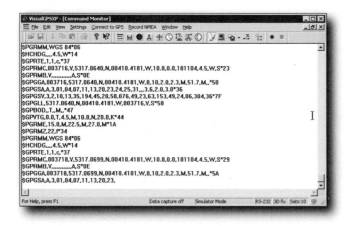

FIGURE 10-44: The NMEA Command Monitor window enables you to see NMEA commands output by the GPS.

Experiment for Yourself

If you have programming experience, you might be wondering whether you can put your existing skills to use in the GPS field. You can, but I've found that good examples are usually few and far between.

However, I have found one place that does make code examples and information available — and freely available at that. Again, this is on the VisualGPS website and the project is called NMEAParser. Details and code are available at www.visualgps.net/Papers/NMEAParser/default.htm.

Another site that you might find useful in helping you to program your own GPS software tools and utilities is www.adelpha.com/~davidco/FarStar/nmea083.htm, where you will find more information and tools.

The NMEA standard itself is published by the NMEA. Unfortunately, full details of the standard costs over $200. Fortunately, you can find resources available on the Internet. One of the best I've come across is http://vancouver-webpages.com/peter/nmeafaq.txt.

For more information on NMEA, also see Chapter 9.

Summary

This chapter described how you can play with the data that comes out of your GPS and use it to do interesting things, some of which have nothing to do with navigation!

Now it's up to you to get out your GPS, hook it up to a PC or handheld device, and start experimenting!

Playtime

Hacking Geocaching

If a gadget or device penetrates the consumer market well enough, it will eventually be incorporated into some sort of game activity. GPS is no different, and because GPS can be used to pinpoint locations, making a game out of getting to locations marked by others was an obvious evolution. Before any games could spawn from GPS, however, accuracy had to increase. This chapter examines geocaching, after a little history of the accuracy of GPS.

GPS Accuracy

For years, GPS wasn't available to the likes of you and me; it was purely military-only equipment. Back then, GPS receivers were too expensive for most people. The price eventually dropped, but GPS still had limited appeal, and its main users were sailors and hikers. What GPS needed to become popular was an injection of accuracy, and this is exactly what happened on May 1, 2000, when former President Bill Clinton removed the deliberate error contained in the GPS signal up until then.

This error, known as Selective Availability (SA), degraded the signal that consumer units could pick up. Selective Availability meant that 95percent of the time the position shown on a GPS receiver was supposed to be off by 100 yards or less, while for the other 5 percent of the time the error might be even greater, or there might not be any error at all! You never knew. Basically, the 100-yard error meant that you could only reliably plot your position within a circle 200 yards in diameter, as shown in Figure 11-1.

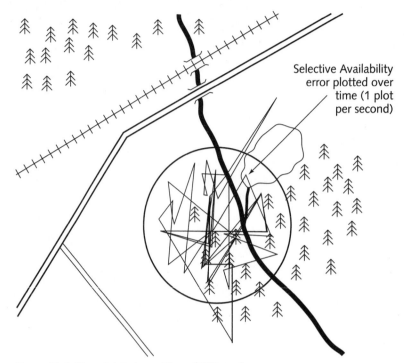

Selective Availability error plotted over time (1 plot per second)

FIGURE 11-1: Uncertainty in position of 200 yards

This really wasn't the level of accuracy demanded by the consumer and it only appealed to people to whom navigation was important. With the SA signal degradation removed, accuracy instantly increased, and you could now plot your position reliably within a circle 20 yards across or less, as shown in Figure 11-2.

Because this massive improvement in accuracy was signal-related, it didn't require users to buy new receivers in order to benefit — most users had receivers capable of handling the more accurate coordinates. (Some units, however, did have a feature that rounded down the accuracy internally to reduce the effects of SA, and these units did this with data from the non-SA signal too, meaning that these units were still as inaccurate as before.)

With increased accuracy, GPS now took almost all the guesswork out of navigating. As long as you had a GPS, a clear view of the sky, and an unlimited supply of batteries, you could get an accurate fix on your position anywhere in the world, accurate to within a few yards.

The modern era of GPS gaming was born.

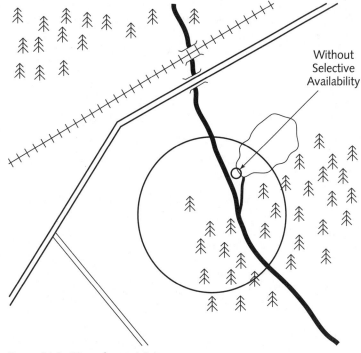

FIGURE 11-2: 20-yard uncertainty

The Birth of Geocaching

On May 3, 2000, someone placed a container filled with treasure (well, not really "treasure" in the true sense of the word—more like a few cheap trinkets) just outside of Portland, Oregon, to celebrate the removal of SA. Within three days, the "cache" had been visited twice.

The first to find the container was a chap named Mike Teague, and he decided to create a website to document and publish the location of these containers filled with goodies. These locations were also posted on the `sci.geo.satellite-nav` newsgroup.

But the sport still didn't have a proper, catchy title. This had to wait for someone else to get involved. In July of 2000, Jeremy Irish came across Teague's website and became hooked on the sport. Irish approached Teague with ideas for the redesign of the website, along with ideas of logging the finds online, mapping the finds, and creating an easier way for newcomers to the sport to find and place these containers. Irish also came up with a new name for the sport, and so the term *geocaching* was born. The treasure-filled containers were renamed *geocaches,* the participants were called *geocachers,* and all of a sudden a lot of people became interested.

This new site (www.geocaching.com) enabled the sport of geocaching to grow fast and spread quickly to what it is today (nearly 121,000 geocaches in 210 countries as of Sept 2004). The appeal of geocaching is easy to understand — it makes real our childhood dreams and fantasies of treasure hunting and combines that with hi-tech yet affordable gadgets, a massive online community, and the great outdoors.

Geocaching Made Simple

Before we look at geocaching-specific hacks and software that might be of benefit to you, this section explains a little bit about geocaching in case you aren't sure what it is. If you are already familiar with geocaching, you might want to skip this section.

For more specific information on geocaching, visit one of the following websites:

- www.geocaching.com
- www.navicache.com
- www.brillig.com
- http://geocaching.gpsgames.org

What Is Geocaching?

In its simplest form, geocaching is a modern-day treasure hunt. There are no sailing ships or pirates, and instead of using an old map with an X to mark the spot, you use the Internet and your GPS. Instead of a treasure chest filled with gold and jewels, the treasure is a plastic lunch box or an ammo box (or maybe even something much smaller) filled with small trinkets and a log book. (Who knows? You might be lucky and find a treasure chest that's bursting at the seams with riches. I've never come across one, but if some kind geocacher wants to hide one, I'll sure have a go at finding it!) The object of the game is simple: find the cache.

Note There can be more to it than that — some geocachers like to be the first to find a new cache (finding a new, unlogged cache is called an *FTF*), while others might attempt to find a certain number in a day or a year, whereas others just enjoy it for the sense of adventure and the new places they discover. These are all variations on the same theme. What always matters is finding the cache!

So, what's the process involved? The following section explains geocaching, compressed into a few simple steps!

Geocaching from Beginning to End

Here is what geocaching is all about, from beginning to end:

1. Someone has to prepare a cache and hide it somewhere. This person is called the *cache owner* or *cache hider*.

2. Different listing sites have different rules, but there are a few commonsense rules that anyone placing a cache should follow. To avoid disappointment, make sure that your cache follows the rules of the listing site. Some of the most common rules include the following:

   - No alcohol, tobacco, firearms, or drugs in the cache. If possible, try to populate the cache with "family-friendly" items.

   - At the very least, your cache should contain a logbook and a pencil.

   - No food or drink in the cache—animals will sniff it out and at best trash your cache; at worst, they may get stuck in it or become ill as a result.

   - Get the landowner's permission before placing the cache.

   - Take care not to hide caches where many cachers coming to search for it might damage the environment. This also means no burying of caches.

   - The person placing the cache assumes responsibility for maintaining it.

3. The person placing the cache should accurately (or as accurately as possible) use a GPS to get the coordinates of the cache he or she places. The more accurate this reading is, the easier it will be to find the cache.

4. The cache hider then registers the cache with a cache listing site (basic membership of the site is free). This involves filling in a form detailing the cache location. Some people also provide a short description of the cache or a clue as to where it is hidden. The clues are normally encrypted using a simple ROT 13 system whereby A = N, B = O, C = P . . . X = K, Y = L, Z = M. Don't worry, though, you won't have to encrypt the clue manually, as the system does that.

Note   You can also have the clue decrypted automatically too, either on the website or by one of the many geocaching software aids available.

5. The cache will then be approved by the listing site (or declined with an explanation). It is at this stage that the cache details are made available for others to see.

6. Other geocachers now visit the listing site, choose the geocaches they are interested in visiting, and download the details of the cache (or print out the information).

7. The geocacher then loads the coordinates onto his or her GPS and sets off to try to find the cache. This might seem easy but trust me, geocachers can be clever when it comes to hiding.

8. If the geocacher is successful in finding the cache, he or she fills in the logbook, swaps a trinket or two, and replaces the cache.

9. When the finder comes home, he or she accesses the listing site and logs the find.

That's it! That's geocaching! There are many different kinds of geocaches and many variations on the theme, but the overall idea is the same—to find a specific object hidden somewhere on the face of the planet and log it. Only the pinpoint accuracy of the GPS enables ordinary people to achieve such a level of precision. This level of accuracy goes well beyond what anyone could expect from a map and compass.

Note One variation is the use of *travel bugs*. These are trinkets that move (with the help of other geo-cachers, of course) from geocache to geocache. Their movements are logged online and their progress monitored.

Just think about it for a moment and I think you will be impressed. I can take an average lunch-box and place it anywhere on the Earth (with a view of the sky) and give you those coordinates, and you will be able to navigate to it to within a few yards thanks to a handheld receiver, access to a constellation of satellites orbiting the Earth, and billions of dollars of hardware.

Once the GPS has taken you to within a few yards of the cache, the rest is up to you. You might need to have a good scrabble around the place before you find it. However, at least you are now looking at scouring an area a few tens of square yards (see Figure 11-3) . . .

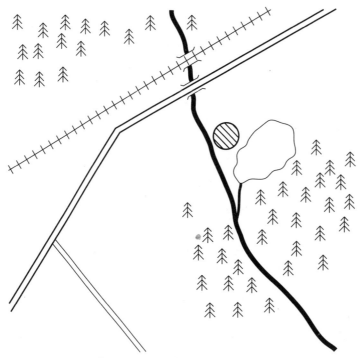

FIGURE **11-3: A smaller area to search in**

. . . rather than hundreds of square yards (see Figure 11-4)!

So how do you find the cache in the last 20 yards? Many cache listings, but not all, will provide clues as to where the cache is hidden, such as "in the roots of the rotten tree." Of course, you will often find that there are many such rotting trees in the search area. This is where your GPS skills really come into play!

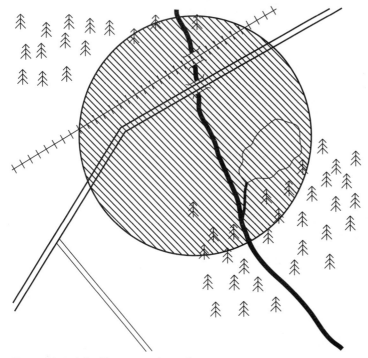

FIGURE 11-4: A far bigger search area!

The Final 20 Yards

You'd think that after getting to within 20m or so of your desired location with a GPS, the final few yards would be a walk in the park (pun intended!). After all, GPS manufacturers boast superb accuracy nowadays, so in theory you should be able to walk right up to the geocache and reach right under that log or in that bush and retrieve your prize. The truth is that, all things being equal, the final 20 yards or so can be the most difficult. Here's why:

- Your GPS isn't 100 percent accurate! It doesn't know where you are, it estimates where you are. There is a big difference. Remember that this is true of the GPS receiver or the person that set the cache, and if the conditions aren't good, the error experienced by the person setting the cache compounds any error you are experiencing.

- Playing the averages: As you travel, GPS in hand, the device is averaging your position all the way. The further you are from the cache, the less all these averaging errors matter because when you are, say, 1,000 yards from the cache (or 100 yards for that matter), the direction of travel arrow on your GPS is still going to point in the general direction you have to go.

- As you get closer to the cache there is a natural tendency to slow down. After all, the slower you go, the more accurate everything will be, yes? Well, in fact, no. Most GPS receivers rely on the GPS being in motion in order to determine the right direction to go (it uses the GPS signal as a compass, although some GPS receivers do have a built-in compass). Slowing down as you get nearer to the cache is not normally going to help you!

- Cachers usually don't hide caches in plain sight or on open ground. Look for things that stand out — a lone tree or a rocky outcrop. Usually, substantial tree cover is involved, which can interfere with the signal to your GPS receiver.

- Remember too that the cache itself has been hidden — the geocacher who placed the cache doesn't want to make your task too easy!

There are some other tricks that will help you too:

- Don't aim for the cache — aim beyond it.
- Look for signs of disturbance.
- Look for a break in the tree cover.
- Use search patterns.
- Stop and average.
- Approach it from a different direction.
- Look for the unnatural.

The following sections look at each of the preceding hints.

Aim Beyond the Cache!

This sounds like the logical thing to do. Walk and walk and walk until the distance reading reads 0 yards and then you must be there. You've been conditioned by the GPS receiver to count down the distance over however many hundreds or thousands of yards you've been walking, so it's natural to think that this is what you can expect.

A far better trick is to aim beyond the cache — the GPS is unlikely to take you much closer than, say, 5–10 yards, so use this to your advantage. Note when your GPS unit indicates that you are 10 yards away from the cache and then keep going. The direction of travel arrow will probably begin to waver and spin erratically. Keep walking in the direction you were going and eventually the arrow will settle and point behind you. Keep going until you are about 10 yards away. Now stop. Look behind you to the location where you made a mental note of being 10 yards away from the cache and halve the distance between where you are and that point. That gives you a very good starting point for your search.

Note Resist the temptation to slow down and stop when doing this 20 yard bit—this will only add to your errors! Rather than slow down, stop instead, letting your GPS receiver get a good fix before moving on.

Look for Signs of Disturbance

Chances are good that you're not the first person who has looked for and visited the cache; and even if you are the first to find it, remember that the person who placed the cache has been there already! In other words, look closely for signs that others have been there before you. Many of the popular caches are dead easy to find because the previous cachers have left a wide trail in the undergrowth leading right up to the cache. In addition to this ground disturbance, many cachers, after finding the cache, sit themselves down near the hiding place in order to fill in the log book and do their swaps. Therefore, when hunting for a cache, think about where would you sit—it might just lead you to it!

Things to look for include the following:

- Footprints
- Flattened grass
- Broken twigs
- Garbage (sadly, trash is often found near caches—why not take a bag with you and clean it up? Cache in-trash out!)
- Objects out of place
- Other disturbances, such as overturned logs or rocks

These signs can quickly give away the position of a cache from many yards away. In fact, with a little experience, you won't even need to look at the GPS when you are within 50 yards of the cache!

Look for Breaks in the Tree Cover

If the cache you are seeking is under tree cover, searching is going to be tougher. Leaves absorb the signal from the GPS satellites, which means that accuracy will suffer. Your best option here is to look for a break in the tree cover and then sit there for a few minutes until your GPS gets a good signal lock before resuming the hunt.

After you regain signal lock, start moving again, making a mental note of the direction in which your receiver is telling you to go and going that way. If you lose signal lock again, try to find a different break in the tree canopy and wait there for a few minutes again to get a good lock. Once you begin to move again, you should get a direction to the cache. If you are lucky, the direction that you are being told to go in will intersect with your previous direction—this will give you a good clue as to where the cache is.

Search Patterns

You might find it very hard to get a good fix so you will need to adopt some search patterns. There are two that can help:

- **Spiral pattern search:** Get to a position where you are quite close to the location given for the geocache (say, within 25 yards or so) and work your way around the area in a spiral pattern, checking possible hiding areas. This method gives you a good way to be methodical (see Figure 11-5).

- **Crisscross or grid search:** This is for areas where you can't get a good signal close up. Get to the general area of the cache (say, within 50 yards) and start walking up and down past the area where you think the cache might be hidden. If this doesn't reveal the cache, try again, but this time work across the area instead of up and down. Again, work methodically and take your time (see Figure 11-6).

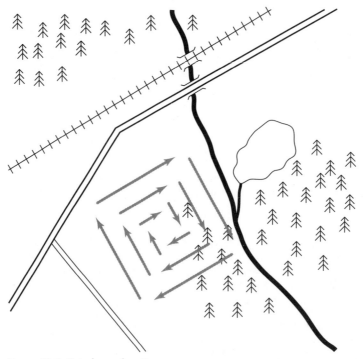

FIGURE 11-5: Spiral search pattern

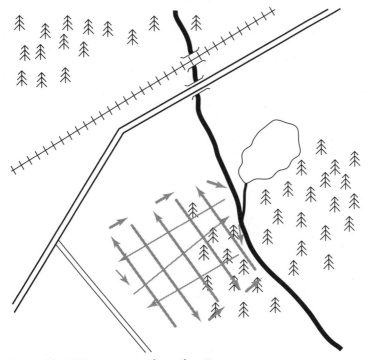

FIGURE 11-6: Crisscross or grid search pattern

Stop and Average

Some caches are just plain elusive; they may be well hidden under a log or rock, or in a massive field of logs and rocks. This can make things mega tricky. At this point, it might be a good idea to just take a break and let your GPS receiver get a good lock (a few minutes), giving you a good high-precision estimate of the distance to the cache. Then move a bit and let the GPS unit get another lock. Keep doing this until you have narrowed down the position of the cache.

This is a slow process but it does get results.

Approach It from a Different Direction

This is a simple but effective trick. Just overshoot the cache location and approach it from the opposite direction. Many caches are only well hidden from the direction in which the cacher thinks you will approach!

Look for the Unnatural

This is a common cache giveaway that most geocachers (both cache placers and finders) don't spot. When they hide a cache, most geocachers disturb the area around the cache, but this isn't all. Geocachers will use materials they find to cover the cache; rocks or tree bark are common. The thing to notice is materials that are out of place — for example, bark from a different tree (this is most noticeable when the wrong bark is used to cover a cache hidden at the base of a tree) or a rock that's different from the other rocks in the area. Of course, this advice is not going to be of much use to you if the hider is devious and has camouflaged the cache well.

Learn to spot things that are "out of place" and recognize signs of disturbance.

Geocaching Hacks

Now it's time to look at geocaching GPS hacks. These hacks are designed to get you to the cache quicker and let you spend more time geocaching and less time messing around.

The following sections outline my recommendations, in no particular order.

Go Paper-free

Nothing beats paper-free geocaching. Running around with a GPS in one hand and a sheaf of papers in the other hand not only really slows you down but is totally inefficient. In effect, you are taking data that is in digital format (on the PC) and converting that into an analog format (paper). This means that everything you do from that point on (taking waypoints and loading them onto your PC, decrypting the cache clue, copying waypoints to your GPS, etc.) involves reconverting the data into a digital format (by manually reentering it). This is time-consuming, boring, and prone to human error. Remaining digital is therefore far better.

Here's how you can do that . . .

First, you need a portable computer. There are numerous kinds incorporating all sorts of features, but they fall into two camps based on operating system:

- Microsoft Pocket PC (Windows-based)
- Palm

Which is best? Well, that's a matter of choice, but I have found that I get greater functionality and flexibility with the Pocket PC–driven devices. In addition, they accommodate a greater range of software while I'm on the move.

Once you are paper-free, you will need software to help you geocache. Several programs are available that can help you.

GPXSonar

- **License:** Free
- **Operating system:** Microsoft Pocket PC 2002 and later

GPXSonar is software written by a geocacher to help other geocachers. It goes well beyond being purely software that enables you to view static cache details (on your Pocket PC 2002 and later). Figure 11-7 shows the interface.

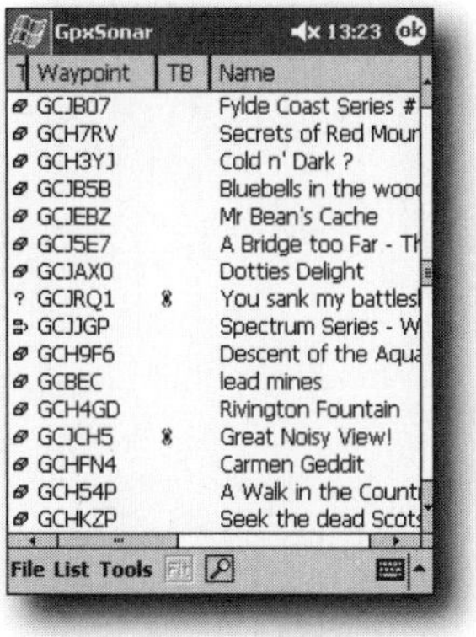

FIGURE 11-7: GPXSonar

GPXSonar is available for free download from `http://gpxsonar.homeip.net`.

GPXSonar is very useful in the field because it enables you to do so much. Here are just a few of the amazing features of this tool:

- It is compatible with files available for download from www.geocaching.com, which means that there is no need to print out web pages before going geocaching!

- The application generates dynamic HTML pages containing cache details.

- GPXSonar enables you to carry out text searches and apply custom filters (for example, cache type, difficulty, and terrain) to find only the caches in which you are interested.

- Hints and clues can be decrypted automatically. This single feature alone is a savior when it's cold and wet and you are not in the mood to manually decrypt the clue.

- It contains a built-in field logbook, so you can electronically log your find for later transcription onto the listing site (the author of the application is currently working on a version that will log the cache automatically when the device is connected).

GPXView

- **License:** Donateware (if you like it, make a donation!)
- **Operating system:** Microsoft Pocket PC 2002 and later

GPXView is a lightweight software application that does a good job of replacing paper when geocaching. The interface is shown in Figure 11-8.

This product is available for download from `http://strandberg.org/gpxview`.

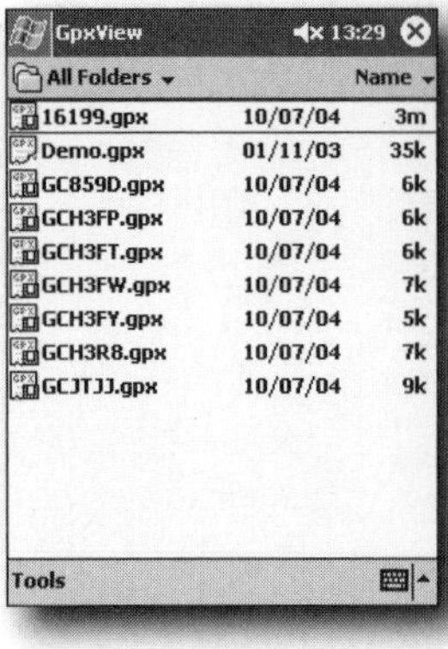

FIGURE 11-8: GPXView in action

GPXView enables you to take a listing of geocaches in your area and sorts them based on a variety of parameters (such as difficulty or distance from your current location) and displays the cache that you want (see Figure 11-9).

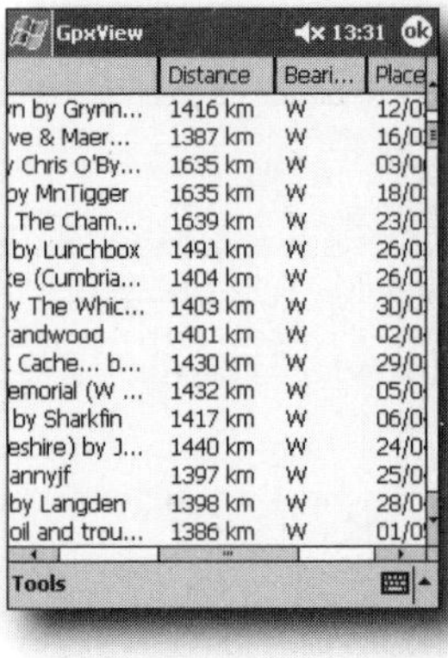

FIGURE 11-9: You can sort caches based on a number of parameters, such as distance or degree of difficulty.

iSolo

- **License:** Shareware (trial available) and limited-function free version

- **Operating system:** Palm OS and Microsoft Windows, Pocket PC, and Windows CE

iSolo is a document reader that enables you to read files that you create on your PC while on the move. You can't view geocaching files directly, so you have to use another application to create these files, which makes this system more complicated. If you want to use iSolo, you will also need GPXSpinner to create the appropriate files.

Note

GPXSpinner is available from www.gpxspinner.com.

You can download a trial version of iSolo from www.isilo.com.

Plan Before You Leave

Being paper-free while on the move is a real bonus, but don't let that fool you into thinking that you don't need to plan before you leave. There are tools that can help you do just that.

One really handy tool is the Geocaching Swiss Army Knife (GSAK), shown in Figure 11-10. This application is available as a free download (although there are benefits to registering) from http://gsak.net.

FIGURE 11-10: GSAK in action

GSAK is an amazing program that automates and simplifies a lot of the administrative tasks associated with geocaching:

- Work with and combine multiple cache databases.
- Import/export data to and from your GPS.
- Advanced sorting of geocache lists (see Figure 11-11).
- Incorporates the capability to convert geocache locations into data that can be sent to various mapping applications.
- Batch processing of important tasks.

Another stage of preparation is planning your geocaching journey, both on and off road. By using an application such as GASK, you can also plot your data using mapping software (such as Microsoft Autoroute, Garmin Mapsource, or many other mapping applications available).

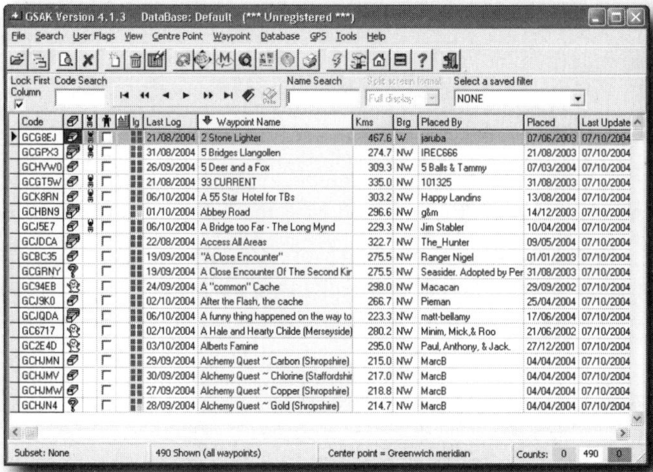

FIGURE 11-11: GSAK advanced sorting—in this case, alphabetically by geocache name

Figure 11-12 shows one of the most popular mapping tools available, Microsoft AutoRoute.

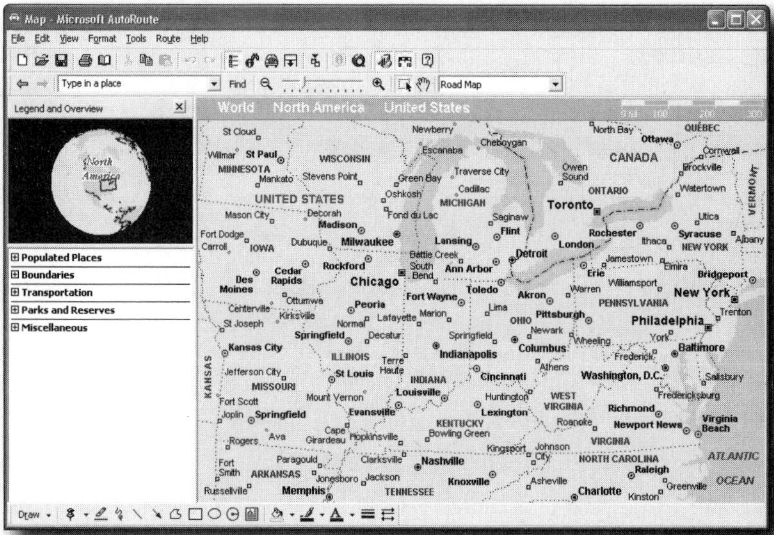

FIGURE 11-12: Microsoft AutoRoute

Of course, the GPS makers don't want to be left out. Figure 11-13 shows MapSource, the software that Garmin recommends.

FIGURE 11-13: Garmin MapSource

With these applications, you can take the data from the geocache listing sites and load them into the mapping application, planning the best route to get from your starting location, and going from geocache to geocache until you are finished.

If you have the right kit, you can plan not only while behind your PC, but also while on the move. Figure 11-14 shows TomTom Navigator, an application well suited for this purpose.

FIGURE 11-14: TomTom Navigator
on a Pocket PC

Note TomTom software offers mapping information for all of the U.S. and Europe. European countries and the American states are all available separately.

TomTom takes most of the guesswork out of road navigation, because as well as route planning, TomTom Navigator can also provide you with voice instructions to help you get where you want to go. If you get into a traffic jam or are detoured, there's no need to worry because TomTom will keep track of your location in real time via GPS and plan a new route, automatically updating the remaining distance and estimated time of arrival. It also contains some superb features such as night vision mode, which enables you to drive more easily during hours of darkness (see Figure 11-15).

FIGURE 11-15: TomTom's night vision mode

Remember too that TomTom Navigator is useful for more than just geocaching!

Note Route-planning software isn't of much use when it comes to actually finding the cache. Software for use when you are driving rarely requires the same level of accuracy and is unlikely to give you reliable distance and heading information when you are 50 yards or less from the cache. At that point, you need the precision of the GPS interface to navigate the final few yards.

Sort Out Cabling

If you are going to connect your GPS to a PDA and possibly want to power your GPS from an alternative power supply, make sure that you have all the cables you need with you. A sample is shown in Figure 11-16.

Clearly label each of your cables, as shown in Figure 11-17. This way, if you have more than one GPS or PDA, you won't get confused and take the wrong cable or damage something trying to fit the wrong connector into the socket. Make life even easier on yourself by labeling the cable at both ends, detailing what the connector fits.

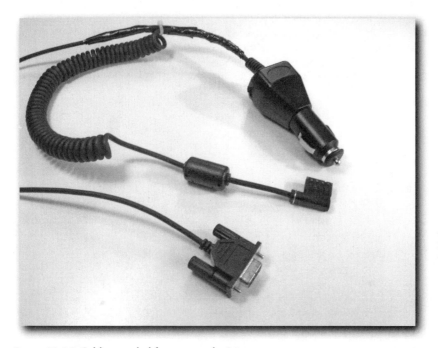

FIGURE 11-16: Cables needed for a geocache trip

FIGURE 11-17: Clearly labeled cables

In addition, because you are going to be outdoors, take care that dirt and water don't get into the cable connectors. Some connectors (such as the serial connector on an iPAQ) are quite delicate and can be easily damaged by foreign objects in the connector. A handy tip to prevent damage is to cover the ends with a small plastic bag when not in use, as shown in Figure 11-18.

FIGURE 11-18: Connector protected by a small plastic bag

Keep cables as short as required, because they can snag on branches or other items and damage equipment. Loop and tape them to keep them under control, as shown in Figure 11-19.

Power for the Trip

There is nothing worse than being out hunting geocaches and running out of juice for the GPS or PDA. We've already covered powering the GPS on the move, but let's take a quick look at issues specific to geocaching and how to keep your PDA powered while out hunting for caches.

GPS Power Considerations

The easiest way to keep a GPS powered is by keeping a good selection of batteries. Never just rely on having a full set in the GPS — they might discharge more quickly than normal, get lost or damaged, or you might be out for longer than expected. I tend to work with a full set in the GPS, and carry two spare sets for a day's geocaching. I always use rechargeable NiMH batteries, so cost beyond the initial purchase is low; and I keep them charged up with a car charger. I also have a natty, little solar charger that's really useful in summer. Figure 11-20 shows a selection of my favorite powering gear.

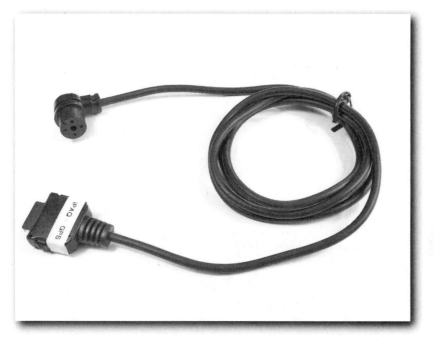

FIGURE 11-19: Keep cables under control with tape

FIGURE 11-20: My favorite GPS powering gear

To keep the PDA going, I use a combination of an expansion battery pack that gives me a few extra hours, a car cord, and an external battery pack that will power or charge the iPAQ from four AA batteries (see Figure 11-21). I find that the pack is an ideal way to carry a few spare batteries for the GPS.

FIGURE 11-21: iPAQ external battery pack

Another option to charge an iPAQ while on the move is a solar charger, as shown in Figure 11-22. If you have a car cord for your iPAQ, then using a solar charger such as the Silva Battery Saver, you can, given some sunlight, plug the car cord into it and charge the internal iPAQ battery.

 Note When using solar panel chargers, take care to protect the panels from damage. While they are quite robust, they aren't indestructible.

You could also use a portable lead-acid battery (shown in Figure 11-23) and a socket splitter, which would enable you to power both the GPS and your PDA. The drain on a lead-acid battery will be a lot less than it would be for other kinds of batteries and you can charge up the battery in your vehicle. The main disadvantage of using such a battery is the weight associated with it.

 Note To help others, some geocachers put spare batteries into geocaches as swaps. These are really good swap items and could really get someone out of a jam if their batteries are low and they need to navigate their way back to the car. Putting batteries in a cache is referred to in geocaching parlance as "leaving GPS food"!

FIGURE 11-22: A solar charger is a good option if you go geocaching during the day.

FIGURE 11-23: Portable lead-acid battery

Test all the batteries you plan on taking with you before setting off. You can use a simple battery meter (see Figure 11-24), available from photographic outlets and other electrical stores.

FIGURE 11-24: Battery tester

Better Antennas

If you don't have good satellite reception, then geocaching is a no-no. Usually, when outdoors you get pretty good reception, but if you have to travel into tree-covered areas or valleys, you may find it easier if you take steps to improve the reception of your GPS receiver. There are two things you can do.

The first is to use an external antenna, like the one shown in Figure 11-25, which is designed for the Garmin GPS III, GPS III+, and GPS V.

These antennas either replace the existing antenna or connect to a separate socket. Along with the upside of better reception, there are downsides. While they are usually much better than built-in antennas when under the cover of trees or in areas where rock faces reduce the efficiency of the factory-shipped antenna, they do draw more power from the unit than the built-in antenna. This means that having additional power sources becomes vital.

FIGURE **11-25: Lowe external antenna**

Another option is to use a reradiating antenna, shown in Figure 11-26, which is a strong antenna for capturing the signal from the GPS satellites, which then retransmits it via a transmitter. The built-in antenna then picks up this amplified signal and gets a lock from that. The great thing about this is that if you geocache in a group, you can use the one reradiating antenna to work with several GPS receivers.

To use a reradiating antenna, you will need to use an external power supply (such as a 12-volt supply, or batteries, usually AA or 9-volt batteries) because it relies on this to amplify and retransmit the signal. This kind of setup is great in locations where you might otherwise not get a good satellite lock.

The drawbacks, however, are that this kind of setup is cumbersome, needs batteries, and requires a lot of cables that you need to keep under control. Again, careful use of tape and cable ties is essential.

FIGURE 11-26: Reradiating antenna

Protecting the GPS

GPS receivers get quite a few knocks, bumps, and scrapes outdoors. They are quite robust and handle life outdoors pretty well, but you should still take a few precautions to ensure its safety. The following sections describe some steps you can take to do just that. In addition to protecting your unit from damage, you need to ensure that your GPS makes it home with you!

Protect Your GPS from Loss

"Found cache, took plastic toy, left GPS."

This isn't something that you read often in cache logs, but it does happen. The geocacher navigates to the cache paying close attention to the GPS unit on the way there. However, once they get to the cache, they lose interest in the GPS and put it down somewhere. They retrieve the cache, do a swap, fill in the logbook, and then replace the cache and leave — without the GPS.

It may seem unlikely but it isn't. Unless you're made of money, or have access to a lot of units, take steps to protect your GPS from loss. Here are some simple steps that you can take:

Tie It to Yourself

It seems simple and obvious, but this is the best way to prevent loss. Most people use a wrist lanyard, but this can become awkward. It's far better to tie it to a convenient loop on your jacket or pants. Use strong parachute cord for this job.

Hanging a GPS from a cord around your neck is not recommended, as it presents a grave danger to you if it snags on a branch while you are moving through undergrowth. If you want to hang a GPS around your neck, use a ball chain (such as those used with military dog tags) that will break away under pressure. However, remember that if the chain does break away, your GPS will end up on the ground!

Add Contact Details

Add your contact details to the startup screen of your unit, as shown in Figure 11-27. Many units enable you to do this. It doesn't prevent you from losing the GPS receiver, but many people have had their units returned to them by honest geocachers because they did this. If possible, add the same information to any case in which your gear is carried.

FIGURE 11-27: Contact details on the GPS

Make It Easier to Spot

Drop your GPS receiver onto leaf-covered ground, and I'll guarantee you that you'll have a hard time finding it. Drop it at night and it'll be even harder, if not impossible, to find. You have several simple options for making your unit easier to see.

One of the easiest things to do is add a piece of reflective tape to the lanyard, as shown in Figure 11-28.

Alternatively, you could replace the parachute cord lanyard with cord that contains a reflective strand within the cord, as shown in Figure 11-29.

Both of these work great. If you drop your GPS unit, all you need to do is shine your flashlight around and you are bound to find it. If you want a system that doesn't rely on reflective tape or cord, you can add an always-on light source to your GPS by adding a Glowring, shown in Figure 11-30.

FIGURE 11-28: Reflective tape on the lanyard

FIGURE 11-29: Reflective cord

FIGURE 11-30: A Glowring

Glowrings are designed to be attached to key rings to make them easy to find in the dark. They work because they contain a tiny vial of radioactive tritium gas. This radioactive gas emits electrons as it decays, and these electrons strike the phosphorescent coating inside the vial, causing a faint glow of light to be emitted. These devices have a very long life span (over ten years) and require no maintenance.

Note Glowrings come in a variety of colors, but green is usually the brightest.

All you need to do to add a Glowring element to your GPS is get yourself one (do an Internet search, which will bring up a whole raft of suppliers) and some good glue (epoxy is best).

When you get the Glowring, take a sharp knife and carefully split the casing in half along the join, as shown in Figure 11-31.

This exposes the fragile glass vial containing the tritium. Take great care not to break this! Set it aside safely for a moment.

When you have the two halves, carefully remove the lug from one of the halves to make a flat surface.

Epoxy the plastic, along with the glass vial, to the GPS case, as shown in Figure 11-32. Don't glue it to the screen, to the buttons, or over the antenna. Anywhere else should be fine.

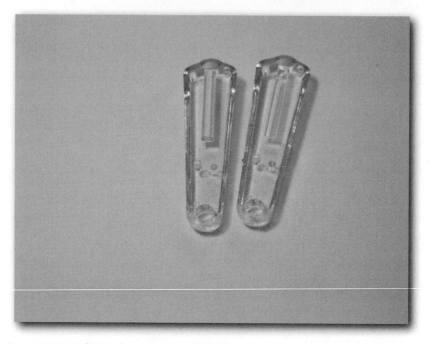

FIGURE 11-31: Splitting the outer case of the Glowring

FIGURE 11-32: Attaching the Glowring

Leave the glue to settle and dry (consult the instructions for the adhesive) before using the GPS. Once it is hard, you can use the GPS with the new glowlight!

Protect the Screen

The screen is a vulnerable point on the GPS. There's not much you can do to protect the screen from extremely heavy impact unless you get case designed for that purpose (such as those made by Otter; www.otterbox.com), but you can take steps to protect the screen from scuffs, scratches, and light damage. This topie is also discussed in Chapter 5, "Protecting Your GPS."

To protect it from bumps, the trick of adding a few dots of silicone sealant to the corners really helps, as does gluing on small rubber bumpers, as shown in Figure 11-33.

If you want to protect the screen from scratches, you can always get a set of screen protectors designed for a PDA, such as the iPAQ. These screen protectors are thin, plastic sheets with a light, easily removable adhesive as a backing. You will need to cut the screen protector to the appropriate size using a pair of scissors before sticking it on because you are unlikely to find any that fit your GPS screen exactly.

Note A good place to keep a GPS when not in use is a belt pouch. This way, you protect it from the scratches it will inevitably pick up in pockets and from the possibility of damage if you step on it while walking.

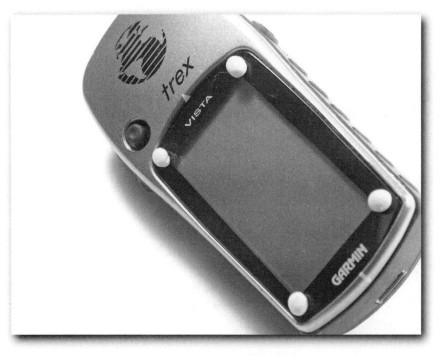

FIGURE 11-33: Rubber bumpers add simple screen protection.

Power Protection

A sudden jolt to the GPS receiver can cause the batteries to shift, causing it to lose power and switch off. This can be really annoying when you are on the move because you'll have to go through the restart process again. Protect against this by adding a small bit of foam behind the battery compartment door to cushion them, as shown in Figure 11-34.

FIGURE 11-34: Pad the battery compartment to prevent power loss.

Waterproofing

The easiest way to waterproof your GPS for geocaching is to use a specially designed case for the job (see Chapter 5).

Some of the best cases come from a company called Aquapac (www.aquapac.net), which makes some superb cases for both GPS units and PDAs. They even make cases that have a special waterproof opening for cables, and stylus holders for PDAs.

Figure 11-35 shows a case designed for an iPAQ that has a waterproof outlet for cables. This is ideal for connecting the iPAQ to a GPS via a cable connection.

FIGURE 11-35: This Aquapac case for the iPAQ enables cable connections.

 Note Zip-lock bags and other plastic bags don't provide reliable protection against the elements and should not be used to protect anything valuable.

Summary

In this chapter, we've looked at geocaching and the hacks, tweaks, and specific software that you can use to get to caches faster and easier than before.

We've looked at software that can help you plan your geocaching outings better and help you get to caches quicker, whether by car or on foot.

We've also looked at modifications you can make to your GPS and PDA, along with accessories that will help you protect your gear under all conditions. When it comes to being in the outdoors, there's no such thing as bad weather, just being badly equipped. If you take the time to properly equip yourself and your electronic gear, there's no need for geocaching to stop just because it is raining.

Do take great care, however, to protect your equipment from water, dirt, and especially impacts and being crushed. A moment of lost concentration could cause the destruction of hundreds of dollars of gear.

Remember that geocaching isn't all about the numbers and getting to the cache first (well, okay, for some people it is!). Do take the time to look around and enjoy your adventure. Take your time, take photos, enjoy the company you're with, and have a great time — after all, it is a hobby!

In the next chapter, you'll take a look at some other games you can play with your GPS.

GPS Games

I f anything drives the sales of electronic or consumer products, it's leisure. Yes, people buy a lot of things for work and because they have to, but nothing gets people spending money like when they are spending it on fun!

For years, GPS was merely a serious tool with serious applications, such as navigating, military, and surveying. This was partly because simple GPS receivers (simple by today's standards, at least) were considered specialist and were very expensive, but it was also hard to see what appeal they would have. However, there were certain hobbyists who waited anxiously for GPS units to fall to a sensible price. Hobbies that required people to know where they were on the planet at any given time were an obvious entry point for GPS to make headway into the civilian market.

A few companies (Garmin and Magellan in particular) took a gamble and released GPS receiver units aimed at the hobby market. They weren't cheap, with basic units costing in excess of $400 to $500, but for people with hobbies in which knowing your exact position could mean the difference between life and death, it was a worthwhile investment.

Outdoor enthusiasts were convinced, but the entry of GPS in the consumer electronics market was more of a ripple than a wave. Since then, interest has been slow but steady. When hikers, sailors, and pilots were beginning to become interested in GPS, its accuracy was still hindered by the deliberate error overlayed onto the civilian signal by the U.S. government. This Selective Availability, as it was called, meant that users had to put up with errors in accuracy of up to 100 meters. Figure 12-1 is a diagram showing just what this level of inaccuracy meant.

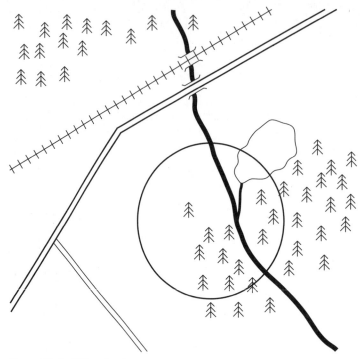

FIGURE 12-1: 100-meter inaccuracy

Those experienced at navigating by map and compass could already achieve this, so GPS was seen as an "emergency" device handy in bad weather or a device for those who weren't as competent at navigating using traditional methods.

However, in May 2000, things changed a lot in the GPS world when former President Clinton ordered the removal of the degrading Selective Availability error, transforming overnight the accuracy from a respectable 100 meters to an amazing 10 meters! Figure 12-2 compares this new accuracy level with the old.

Note

This wasn't the first time that Selective Availability had been switched off. It is ironic that an error designed to help deter others from using GPS for military purposes (the fear was that someone would build a nuclear missile and strap a cheap GPS to the front and thus gain immense precision) was actually first turned off during a time of war. This was during the Gulf War (1991), and the error was removed because of a shortage of military GPS units, forcing soldiers to use civilian units to navigate the deserts.

Even though these days the civilian GPS signal doesn't contain the deliberate error, the military (along with certain civilian applications) still uses a different encrypted signal (called P-code) that is in itself more accurate than the civilian signal (called CA-code) and less prone to jamming and spoofing (being interfered with by a fake signal).

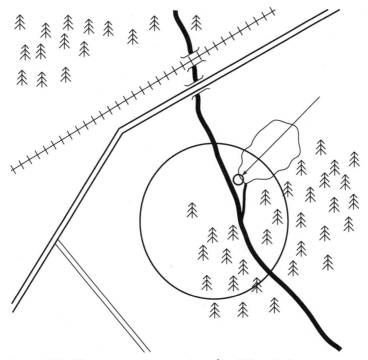

FIGURE 12-2: 10-meter inaccuracy compared to 100-meter inaccuracy

Now everyone was interested. This level of accuracy meant that you could determine exactly which road you were traveling on (even which side of the highway), which trail or footpath you were following, or which side of a ravine you were on. This marvelous level of accuracy suddenly available was something only previously dreamt about and something that was well worth the price tag.

The civilian GPS boom had now begun!

The Dawn of GPS Games

When new technology gets into the hands of enough people, eventually they will build a game around it, and it took only a few days for the game that is now called *geocaching* to be born (more on geocaching in Chapter 11). Geocaching is the game that most GPS users will have heard of, but it is not the only game. You can use GPS for many other games besides the directly navigation-related hobbies.

What kind of games can you play with a GPS? While most of them are related to location, not all of them are.

The following sections describe a few of the most popular games.

Points of Confluence

Points of confluence are places where lines of latitude and longitude intersect. They are purely artificial, being a by-product of the way maps have been created. Figure 12-3 shows an example of such a point.

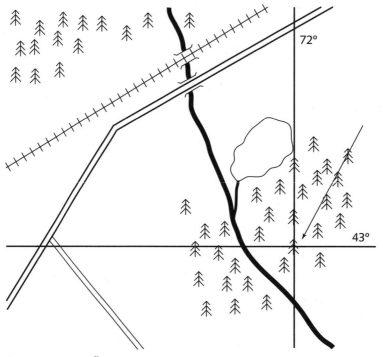

FIGURE 12-3: A confluence point

There is no significance to these locations other than human fascination with numbers, especially round numbers with a lot of zeros, but that hasn't stopped people from finding these locations, logging them, and commemorating their visit with a photo.

Of course, it didn't take long for someone to develop a website devoted to the cataloging of people's "finds" of these points of confluence. This site, `www.confluence.org`, is devoted to this sport.

It's more than just about logging a point of the Earth's surface. The project goes further than that. It encourages the searcher not only to post details of their finds, but to narrate the story of their find. Moreover, because the points are spread across the globe, with many in very remote areas, the logs of people's visits make interesting reading.

The first person to actively log a point of confluence is a man named Alex Jarrett, and he began doing this in 1996, visiting the points and then posting details of his finds on a website.

The first confluence found was 43 degrees north, 72 degrees west. This spot is in the state of New Hampshire. Alex bicycled 10 miles and walked an additional mile through woods before he came to the spot — an isolated place situated next to a swamp. This didn't deter him from continuing his pursuit of more points of confluence. It seems that if you provide some people with a point on the globe and an easy way to navigate there (and there aren't many easier ways than using GPS), people will go there — not for gain or greed, but purely out of a sense of adventure.

The sport is more than it first appears, however. Not only is it about logging points, it is also about seeing and recording how, over time, those spots change. This means that everyone who visits a point of confluence, whether it is one previously unlogged or one logged many times, is charting the changes made over time and contributing to the picture of our changing world.

How many points of confluence are there? A lot! There are 64,442 latitude and longitude degree intersections in the world (this includes both of the poles as one intersection). However, there's no point in logging points of confluence in the oceans, and many more points near the poles are not worth logging (unless you happen to be there!). Nonetheless, even after subtracting these, it still leaves us with a massive 16,167 confluences to find, with nearly 13,000 of them being on land.

Confluences are divided into two categories:

- Primary
- Secondary

Primary confluences are major intersections that are either on land or within sight of land (if they are on water or ice) on a clear day. All other confluences are secondary ones. There will be a confluence within 49 miles (79 km) of where you are, anywhere on the surface of the Earth, so there's no real reason for you not to visit one!

In the U.S., there are 1,095 primary confluences (with Texas having the most with 66) and 169 secondaries. In the U.K., there are 38 primary confluences and 18 secondary ones.

When heading out to find points of confluence, remember that they are not like geocaches and that there may not be trails or roads nearby. Follow these simple rules:

- Take care — follow sensible hiking rules such as leaving word of where you are going with someone responsible, taking provisions, maps, a compass, a cell phone, and so on.

- Remember that to find and log confluences, you will need a working GPS and camera, so be sure to take enough batteries with you or an alternative power supply!

- Don't trespass! When in doubt, ask the landowner's permission. The website www. confluence.org provides a letter that you can show to landowners to make it all look official, or at least organized.

- Plan your route, both in and out. Do this carefully and have alternatives in case you come across something you didn't expect. In addition, have escape routes planned and documented in case of bad weather.

- Respect the environment. Take nothing but photographs, leave nothing but footprints (and make those as soft as possible).

Note Using an application such as RoboGEO (www.robogeo.com) to incorporate GPS positional data into your digital photographs makes recording and documenting points of confluence easier.

Benchmarking/Trigpointing

We now move on to finding not points on the globe, but real things. Benchmarks and trigpoints are points used by mapmakers when surveying. They are known points of the Earth's surface that have been accurately marked. The benchmark is a physical object—usually a concrete pillar or a metal disc, as shown in Figure 12-4.

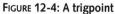
FIGURE 12-4: A trigpoint

Note Trigpoint—short for triangulation point—is the term commonly used in the U.K., but it is included here because it is now used in the U.S., too.

On these pillars or discs will be information that is used for logging. Sometimes it is just an ID for the marker, while other times it may be more. There is nothing inherently exciting about the actual marker or the places where they are located. It simply goes to show that if people are made aware of a given point somewhere, some of those people will want to seek it out.

Note It seems that the government departments responsible for keeping track of these markers (the United States Geological Survey in the U.S. and the Ordinance Survey in the U.K.) approve of benchmarking because benchmarkers visiting them can report on any damage that they have suffered, or that they are missing.

Finding benchmarks isn't hard. Some are marked on maps. However, the digital age has made finding them much easier, and now the main geocaching website (www.geocaching.com) lists benchmarks in the U.S.

Note For a listing of U.K. trigpoints, visit www.trigpointinguk.com.

Finding benchmarks is a matter of logging on to www.geocaching.com and doing a search. Start off by doing a search of your local area (you can search based on zip code). This should (hopefully) pull up a big list of them. For your first outing, it is advisable to pick a benchmark that has already been visited by others — this enables you to confirm that it is actually there (or was on the date of the last find). More important, the log might contain a photograph that you can use in your hunt.

After downloading the coordinates to your GPS, simply follow the pointer until you get close. However, now things get interesting. You are looking for something that is not hidden per se, but it might not be too obvious. Finding huge concrete pillars is easy, but finding a small nondescript bolt in the ground can be quite hard, so you may need to search for a while before you find it. Console yourself, however, with the knowledge that the more you find, the easier it becomes!

Once you have found the benchmark, you can log it. There are no logbooks to fill in or swaps for you to trade, but you can take the details off the marker. You can also take a picture of it (put your GPS in the shot if possible).

When you get back to your PC, you can log your find on the geocaching website.

Note Don't go out benchmarking expecting a find every time. Many benchmarks are old and damaged, missing, or in overgrown areas.

GPS Drawing

Many GPS units are now capable of displaying a map. This can either be a detailed map, showing roads, rivers, coastlines, and contours or it can be a very simple map showing nothing more than waypoints that you have entered. What both have in common is that they will be capable of displaying the trail you have navigated on the screen with the map. This trail, known as a *track* or *breadcrumb trail*, is the log of the path that you (or, more accurately, the GPS) took. When these units became more popular, they spawned a new GPS-related hobby — GPS drawing!

GPS drawing (sometimes called *geo art*) is an activity in which you walk around with a GPS switched on and track your position, and then you use the track or breadcrumb trail to create a picture on the screen of the GPS. Figure 12-5 shows an example.

Seems easy — but it isn't. You have to make really huge movements in order for them to appear on the screen, which means that you need a lot of space in which to work. It's also good to have a plan in advance.

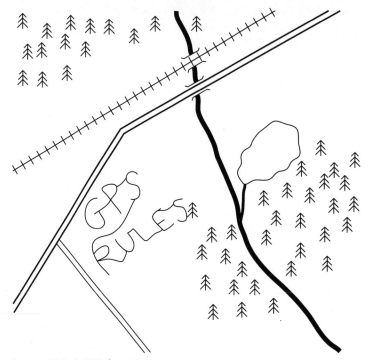

Figure 12-5: A GPS drawing

Of course, there is a website that is devoted to GPS drawing — called, unsurprisingly, www.gpsdrawing.com.

You can carry out GPS drawing in any activity that you do outdoors — walking, hiking, jogging. But why be restricted? What about having a go while skiing? Or cycling? In the car? You don't even have to be limited to being on the ground! Even pilots, sailors, and skydivers can enjoy GPS drawing!

Here are some tips for newcomers to GPS drawing:

- You need plenty of space to do even the simplest GPS drawing. Flat ground without hedges, walls, streams, and rivers is ideal.

- Steer clear of cliff edges, mountainsides, and other dangerous areas.

- You will need a mapping GPS unit — it's nearly impossible to use any other kind of unit (unless it is hooked up to an external device, such as a PDA).

- For the best drawings, you need a clear view of the sky. That rules out wooded areas and deep valleys or ravines.

- Make sure you start off with new (or freshly charged) batteries. Some GPS units will lose the breadcrumb trail if they shut down because of flat batteries.

- It might be a good idea to practice before trying something ambitious. Try following the markings on a football field or parking lot.

- Make faint lines by doing one pass. To make lines that are thicker or bolder, do multiple passes along the same route. The more passes you make, the darker and thicker the lines will appear. You can also use lines consisting of various numbers of passes as shading.

- The slower you go, the thicker and darker the line will appear. Therefore, the thicker lines will represent areas you've traversed several times slowly, and the faintest ones will represent areas you've covered only once, and fast.

- You might find it handy to use small markers as you draw. Depending on the area you are in, you could use stones, sticks, or golf tees. The easiest terrain to GPS draw in is sand.

- Don't worry if you make minor mistakes — these are common. Just pick up from where you went wrong and continue.

- After you are done, save the log of your track to prevent it from being deleted or over-written (consult your GPS manual for information on how to do this).

- Finally, if you have mapping software, import the log of the track into that for a better view.

Note For more information on GPS drawing visit www.gpsdrawing.com.

Hide-and-Seek

Why search solely for inanimate objects with your GPS? Geocaches and benchmarks are very well and good, but you can put a new twist on hide-and-seek with your GPS.

For this game, you need a GPS and a walkie-talkie. The walkie-talkie enables you to transmit your coordinates to the other players.

To play this game properly, you really need more than two people, preferably two teams. One team does the hiding while the other team does the seeking. You can add all sorts of variations to this game (such as playing it at night as a stalking game in which the seeking team has to sneak up undetected on the hiding team).

You can also employ some aids in this kind of game to help it along. One such aid is the Garmin Rino GPS receiver. This is a combination GPS receiver and walkie-talkie that enables you to transmit coordinates from one unit to the other (as well as transmitting voice). This is known as an Automatic Position Reporting System (APRS).

Note Garmin Rino GPS/walkie-talkie hybrids are also excellent for families that want to keep in touch while on the move outdoors.

You don't need Garmin Rino GPS receivers to do this, however. If you have a GPS such as a Garmin eTrex (in fact, all modern Garmin units as well as Magellan units will do) and two FRS (Family Radio Service) two-way radios (these need to have headphone and microphone connectors on them in order to interface), you can do the same thing — well, you do need two other kits: One is called a TinyTrak3 and the other is a Terminal Network Controller (TNC). You will also need to make a few cables.

To summarize, you will need the following:

- 2 GPS receivers
- 2 FRS two-way radios
- Set of cables for connecting the units together (covered shortly)
- 1 TinyTrak3 kit
- 1 TNC kit
- 1 PDA (for viewing locations). The only ones I tested are Palm devices running 3.01 they must have a serial port. Alternatively, a laptop will do.

The TinyTrak3 is a GPS position encoder and is available from www.byonics.com/tiny trak in various forms (kit or ready-made). Prices start from $36 for TinyTrak3 in kit form.

After you have assembled the TinyTrak3 (it requires soldering but nothing difficult is involved), you can program it by connecting it to a PC via a serial port and running the configuration software, shown in Figure 12-6.

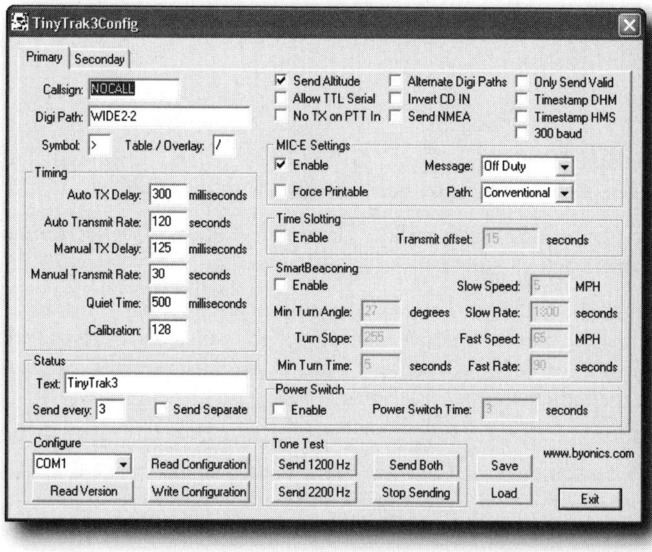

FIGURE 12-6: TinyTrak configuration software

Some important features of the configuration interface include the following:

- **Callsign:** If you are using the system with an amateur radio kit, this is where you would put your FCC callsign. If you are only using FRS two-way radios, you can put any six-character ID here.
- **Digi Path:** The default value of WIDE2-2 is correct for this.

- **Auto TX Delay:** This sets the delay (measured in milliseconds) between pressing the transmit key and sending the GPS data. Set this to 300.

- **Auto Transmit Rate:** This sets the interval between GPS updates. This can be whatever you want, but you should set it to a short interval initially so you know that the system is working. I recommend between 5 and 120 initially.

- **Quiet Time:** This sets the duration during which the radio channel must be quiet before the system transmits a location packet. If the channel is shared with voice, set this to 500.

- **MIC-E Settings:** Leave these options disabled.

Once the preceding settings are specified, the TinyTrak3 is ready for use.

Next, you will need to assemble the TNC. This is available in kit form from http://john. hansen.net (this is much cheaper than buying a readymade kit, which can be expensive). Currently, the kit retails at $45. Assembly of this kit is straightforward, but like the TinyTrak3, it requires some soldering.

Then you need to assemble the cables, of which there are three. Before you begin assembly, you need a conductor plug that fits the headphone and microphone socket for your radios. These are available from electrical outlets or you can cannibalize an old set of headphones and microphones for the job.

The first cable is a GPS-to-serial port cable, the assembly of which is described in Chapter 2.

Next is a cable to connect the TinyTrak3 to the radios. Figure 12-7 shows the wiring details for the cable to connect the radio to the TinyTrak3.

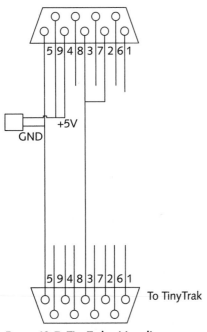

FIGURE 12-7: TinyTrak wiring diagram

The final cable is a gender changer for connecting the GPS cable to the TinyTrak3. The wiring diagram is shown in Figure 12-8.

You also need to wire the TNC to the radio and your PDA. These instructions vary depending on what devices you are using. Instructions will be provided with the TNC kit.

Now assemble all the parts. You will need mapping software running on the PDA. If you don't have a Palm PDA, you can use your laptop with whatever mapping software you run on that.

That's it! This sort of setup enables you to play a variety of hide-and-seek-style games, and extends the capabilities of your existing GPS receiver/walkie-talkie setup.

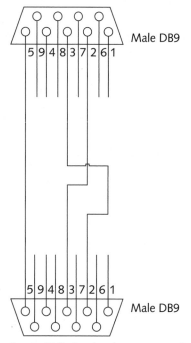

FIGURE 12-8: Gender changer connector

Foxhunt

Another variation on a theme is the foxhunt game. This can be played all sorts of ways, but one interesting, recent variation is to use a GPS connected to a cell phone to relay the coordinates.

You could use the system detailed in the previous section for this game, but the range of such radios isn't great, which limits the scope of the game. Much better are units known as *telematics* units, or GPS-based vehicle tracking systems.

The game is played something like this: You install a telematics unit in a vehicle. This vehicle then becomes the "fox" that others can chase. Each time someone wants to know where the fox is, he or she sends a message to the cell phone and gets a message back almost instantly indicating the position and speed of the fox. At random intervals, the fox stops for a few minutes of "rest." The object of the game is for those in pursuit of the fox to catch it.

The following ground rules are vital for the success and safety of the game:

- The fox must stop periodically to enable those hunting it to catch up.

- No driving carelessly, quickly, or dangerously. Put simply, no law breaking!

- Have a minimum of two people in all chase cars — one to drive and one to navigate and send the messages.

- Take good-quality road maps with you, whether you are the fox or in the chase vehicles. Using mapping software on your laptop connected to your GPS is a great idea for this!

- Make sure that your cell phone is fully charged — without it, it's all a waste of time!

If you are interested in a telematics device, a good place to start investigating them is www.global-telematics.com.

These units aren't cheap, but they offer great scope for games, especially using vehicles over reasonably large distances of several miles. In addition, when the unit isn't being used as a gaming device, it can be installed as a lo-jack so you can keep track of your vehicle in case it is stolen.

Other Games

This section describes two other games for which a GPS can be handy. This isn't a comprehensive list by far, but it gives you a handy starting point from which to start.

Follow the Leader

This is a simple game whereby you create a track on a GPS, making it as complex as possible (see Figure 12-9), and then pass that track to others who have to follow it. The person who can follow it closest in the best time is the winner.

FIGURE 12-9: Try to follow
this track!

Go Fetch!

This game is similar in style to geocaching (see Chapter 11), but there are differences. The main one is that geocaching is organized and the caches are permanent (or semi-permanent at least), whereas the finds in a game of Go Fetch! are temporary.

The game is played as follows: One person goes out and places several finds. Each find consists of a box containing a token (anything distinctive will do, use your imagination). These are hidden about the place and waypoints are taken on the GPS. You then take the coordinates for each find and write them on a piece of paper. The pieces of paper are put into a draw from which the coordinates are pulled out and pinned to a board.

Now the coordinates are in a different order from the way in which the finds were placed, which makes the game a little more complex, as each person has to choose the route between each of the finds that he or she thinks is best (print out a map of the area for each contestant but don't mark the finds on it).

The winner is the first person across the finish line with a token from each of the containers. This is useful for Easter egg hunts or party treasure hunts.

 Note For more information on GPS games, visit www.gpsgames.org.

Summary

This chapter has been all about having some fun with your GPS, getting some fresh air, and putting into good use a lot of the things that you have learned from the previous chapters.

There really is no better way to learn to use your GPS and get a grip on its advanced features than to go out and participate in some light-hearted competitive sport with others. This way, all the ins and outs you've learned will give you a competitive edge in winning whatever game you are playing!

GPS Primer

This appendix is a quick GPS primer for anyone who wants to know a little more about the GPS network and how it works; and how the little plastic box they have in their hand is capable of giving them such a tremendously accurate positional fix anywhere on the globe.

The GPS Network

The GPS network consists of three distinct levels, or segments:

- Space segment
- Control segment
- User segment

The Space Segment

The space segment consists of around 30 NAVSTAR satellites (also known as Space Vehicles, or SVs for short). The exact number varies, but is normally between 27 and 30. These satellites are the property of the U.S. Department of Defense and are operated and controlled by the 50th Space Wing, located at Schriever Air Force Base, Colorado.

Note NAVSTAR is an acronym for NAVigation Satellite Timing And Ranging.

Of these 30 SVs, about 24 are active, and three are kept as spares in case of problems with any of the others.

The spare satellites are positioned so that they can be quickly moved to the appropriate orbit in the event of a failure of one of the operational satellites. Satellites that are not working properly are considered *sick*, and you may occasionally notice such a satellite oddly labeled on your GPS screen (its icon might appear gray or the lock-on bar may show a good signal but no lock). This is likely to be during testing when the Department of Defense deliberately marks a "healthy" satellite as "sick" to see how the system copes.

The 24 operational satellites are arranged in six orbital planes around the Earth, with four satellites in each plane. The satellites have a circular orbit of 20,200 km (10,900 nm), and these orbits are arranged at an inclination angle of 55 degrees to each other.

Several incarnations of GPS satellites have been put into orbit. The first set, called Block I, were launched between 1978 and 1985, none of which are now operational. Replacements for these were called the Block II and Block IIA. Additional replacements are called Block IIR, and the latest satellites are called IIF.

The 27 satellites currently in use are a combination of Block II, Block IIA, Block IIR, and Block IIF satellites.

The satellites were built by a variety of U.S. defense contractors:

- Block II/IIA: Rockwell International (Boeing North American)
- Block IIR: Lockheed Martin
- Block IIF: Boeing North American

The orbital period (the time it takes for a satellite to orbit around the Earth) is twelve hours. This means that at any given location, each satellite appears in the sky four minutes earlier each day. The apparent groundtrack of the satellites (the path that their orbits would draw on the surface of the Earth) is not the same each day because it is shifted westward slightly with each orbit (a drift of 0.03 degrees each day).

The orbits of the satellites form a birdcage around the Earth such that there should always be four or more satellites above the horizon at any one time. Two places on the globe, however, do not fully benefit from the way in which the GPS satellite orbits are orientated: the north and south poles. The orbital coverage here is not as good (for example, satellites are never overhead at the poles), but this was considered a good compromise given the limited use that GPS would see at these locations.

Note Why 30 satellites? This is the number considered sufficient to ensure that at least four (and a maximum of twelve) satellites are always visible, at all sites on the Earth, at all times.

The GPS space segment was supposed to be activated in the late 1980s, but several incidents (one of which, sadly, was the Challenger Space Shuttle disaster on January 28, 1986) caused significant delays, and the full system of 24 SVs wasn't deployed until 1994.

Note Some of the SVs that you will be using are now well over a decade old. This exceeds their initial design life span of around 8 years!

The job of the satellites is multifold:

- To provide extremely accurate, three-dimensional location information (latitude, longitude, and altitude), velocity, and a precise time signal
- To provide a worldwide common grid reference system that is easily converted to any local grid in use

- To be capable of passive all-weather operations

- To provide continuous real-time information

- To provide support for an unlimited number of users and areas

- To provide high-precision information for military and government use

- To provide support to civilian users at a slightly less accurate level

Here are some interesting facts about the GPS SVs:

- **Power plant:**

    - The SVs are powered by solar panels generating 800 watts.

    - The panels on the newer Block IIFs have been upgraded to generate 2,450 watts.

- **Weight:**

    - Block IIA: 3,670 pounds (1,816 kilograms)

    - Block IIR: 4,480 pounds (2,217 kilograms)

    - Block IIF: 3,758 pounds (1,705 kilograms)

- **Height:**

    - Block IIA: 136 inches (3.4 meters)

    - Block IIR: 70 inches (1.7 meters)

    - Block IIF: 98 inches (2.4 meters)

- **Width** (includes wingspan)

    - Block IIA: 208.6 inches (5.3 meters)

    - Block IIR: 449 inches (11.4 meters)

    - Block IIF: approximately 116 feet (35.5 meters)

- **Design life:**

    - Block II/IIA: 7.5 years

    - Block IIR: 10 years

    - Block IIR-M (modernized): 8.57 years

    - Block IIF: 11 years

- **Date of first launch:** 1978

- **Launch vehicle:** Originally, the Delta II rocket was used; but for the bigger Block IIF SVs, the EELV launch vehicle was used.

The Control Segment

The control segment, just like the space segment, is U.S. Department of Defense property. Just as we have no direct access to the space segment, the same is true of the control segment. The control segment is made up of a worldwide network of monitoring stations, ground antennas, and a master control station.

There are five monitoring stations:

- Hawaii
- Kwajalein (on the Marshall Islands in the Pacific Ocean)
- Ascension Island (South Atlantic Ocean)
- Diego Garcia (Indian Ocean)
- Colorado Springs, Colorado

There are three ground antennas:

- Kwajalein (on the Marshall Islands in the Pacific Ocean)
- Ascension Island (South Atlantic Ocean)
- Diego Garcia (Indian Ocean)

There is also one master control station located at Schriever Air Force Base in Colorado.

This vast array of systems is used to passively track all satellites in view and gather ranging data. This information is passed on to the master control station where it is processed in order to determine precise satellite orbits and update each satellite's navigation message so that they are as accurate as possible. Updated information is transmitted to each satellite via the ground antennas.

The User Segment

The user segment is the part of the system to which you and I have access. This is where all the GPS receivers come in. There are many types of receivers in the user section:

- Handheld systems
- Car navigation systems
- Professional commercial systems used for navigation and surveying
- Military receivers

The satellites transmit two types of signal that can be received by the user segment:

- Standard Positioning Service (SPS)
- Precise Positioning Service (PPS)

Standard Positioning Service (SPS)

The SPS is a positioning and timing service that is available to all GPS users on a continuous, worldwide basis with no direct charge. SPS is provided on one of the frequencies that the GPS satellites use, called L1. It contains a coarse acquisition (C/A) code and a navigation data message.

Precise Positioning Service (PPS)

The Precise Positioning Service (PPS) is a highly accurate military positioning, velocity, and timing service that is available on a continuous, worldwide basis to users authorized by the U.S. The P(Y) code–capable military user equipment provides robust and predictable positioning accuracy of at least 22 meters (95 percent) horizontally and 27.7 meters vertically, and time accuracy to within 200 nanoseconds (95 percent).

PPS is the data transmitted on both GPS frequencies: L1 and L2. PPS was designed primarily for U.S. military use and access to it is controlled by encrypting the signal.

Anti-spoofing (A-S) measures guard against fake transmissions of satellite data by encrypting the P-code to form the Y-code. This is only activated periodically when deemed necessary.

How GPS Works

The basic principle behind GPS is straightforward: The GPS receiver picks up a signal from three or more of the satellites and then uses this information to calculate the distance to the satellites. This information is, in turn, used to determine a location on the globe where the receiver is at that time. This whole process is based on a system called *trilateration*.

Trilateration is easy to visualize. Looking at the map in Figure A-1, assume that you are positioned somewhere on it.

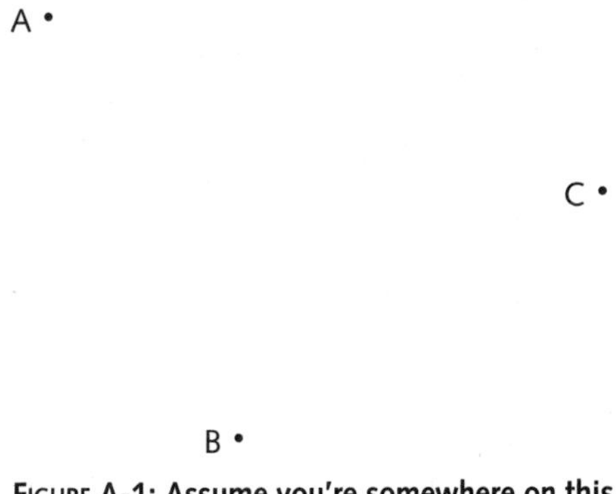

A •

C •

B •

FIGURE A-1: Assume you're somewhere on this map.

Now assume that you know that you are within a certain distance of Point A (see Figure A-2).

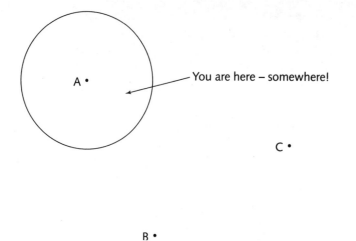

FIGURE A-2: Now assume you're somewhere within this circle.

The area you are in falls within the circle. It's still quite a big area, but it narrows it down quite a bit. Now suppose that you also know your distance from Point B (see Figure A-3).

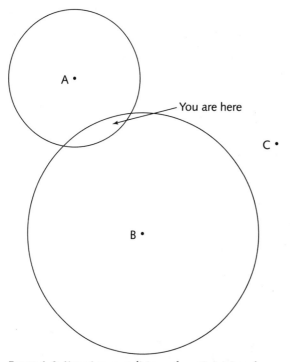

FIGURE A-3: Knowing your distance from Point A and Point B narrows the field.

Knowing your distance from Point C further refines the positional information (see Figure A-4).

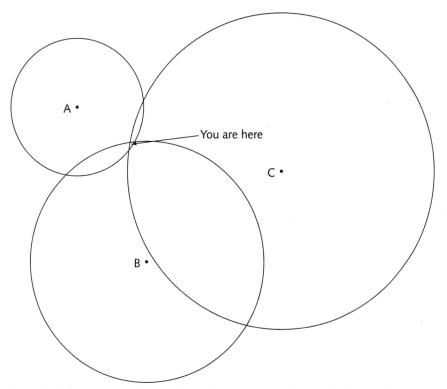

FIGURE A-4: Knowing your distance from three points provides a lot of information.

This is an example of two-dimensional trilateration (2-D trilateration). What GPS does is take this into three dimensions (3-D trilateration or triangulation).

In principle, three-dimensional trilateration doesn't differ much from two-dimensional trilateration, but it is trickier to grasp. What you need to do is imagine the radii of the circles from the preceding examples going off in all directions, so instead of a getting a series of circles, you get a series of spheres.

If you know you are fifteen miles from Point A (or satellite A in the sky), you could be anywhere on the surface of a huge, imaginary sphere with a fifteen-mile radius. If you also know you are eighteen miles from satellite B, you can overlap the first sphere with second, larger sphere. These spheres all intersect in a perfect circle. Finally, if you know the distance to satellite C, you get a third sphere, which will intersect with the other circles at two points, as shown in Figure A-5.

The Earth itself acts as another sphere. It is assumed that you are on the Earth, so you can eliminate the other point in outer space, as shown in Figure A-6.

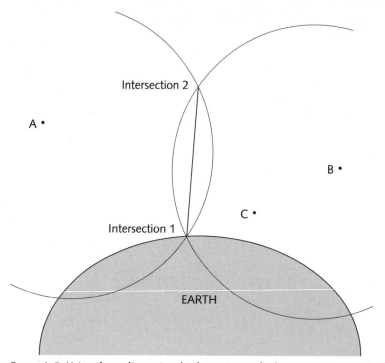

FIGURE A-5: Using three-dimensional trilateration to find your position on the Earth

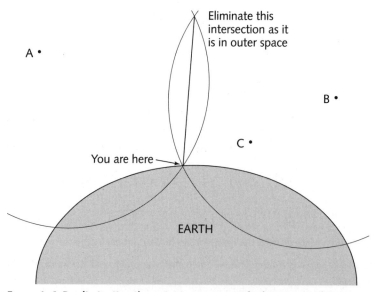

FIGURE A-6: By eliminating the point in space, you find your exact location.

Receivers generally use four or more satellites, however, to improve accuracy and provide precise altitude information.

In order to perform this simple calculation and determine where you are, the GPS receiver has to know two things:

- The location of at least three satellites above you
- The distance between you and each of those satellites

The more accurate these values are, the more accurate your position will be.

The GPS receiver determines both the location of the satellites and your distance from them by analyzing the high-frequency, low-power radio signals from the GPS satellites. Better units have multiple (or parallel) receivers, so they can pick up signals from several satellites simultaneously. If you buy a GPS receiver nowadays, it will be a multi-channel receiver (12 or even 14 channels simultaneously).

The radio waves from the GPS SVs, like all other radio waves, are electromagnetic energy, which means that they propagate at the speed of light (roughly 186,000 miles per second, or 300,000 km per second, in a vacuum). A GPS receiver can figure out how far a signal has traveled by timing how long it took the signal to arrive. The mechanism by which it does this is quite clever.

At a particular time (midnight, for example), the SVs begins transmitting a long digital pattern called a *pseudo-random code*. This code consists of a carrier wave that transmits the digital "chips" that make up the code. The receiver knows when this code starts (this information is transmitted to the GPS along with the signal) and begins running the same digital pattern at exactly the same time. When the satellite's signal reaches the receiver, its transmission of the digital pattern will lag slightly behind the digital pattern that the receiver would expect. This lag between the two corresponds to the time delay from the satellite sending the signal and the receiver receiving it.

Speed × Time = Distance

Therefore, if it takes 0.08 of a second for a satellite's signal to reach the GPS receiver, the distance between the two must be 14,880 miles (186,000 miles per second × 0.08 seconds = 14,880 miles). The GPS receiver must be located somewhere on an imaginary sphere that has a radius of 14,880 miles.

One thing that GPS relies on is accurate timing. To provide this, every GPS satellite carries four atomic clocks on board that provide an extremely accurate timing signal. The GPS receiver, however, doesn't contain an atomic clock (this would make it preposterously expensive!). Instead, it contains an inexpensive quartz clock, and the internal timekeeping is updated when the receiver is capable of locking on and receiving a signal from four or more SVs.

GPS Signal Errors

The GPS system isn't absolutely perfect, however, because the radio signal has to propagate through the atmosphere to the receiver. The receiver isn't perfect either. The following table describes the sources of the possible errors present.

Error	Amount of Error (feet/meters)
Ionosphere	13.1/4.0
Clock	6.9/2.1
Ephemeris	6.9/2.1
Troposphere	1.3/0.7
Receiver	1.6/0.5
Multipath	3.3/1.0
TOTAL	**33.1/10.4**

The errors resulting from the ionosphere and the troposphere are due to the slowing down of the signal (remember that the speed of light quoted is the speed of light in a vacuum). Clock errors are due to inaccuracies in timing. Even using atomic clocks, the speed of light is so fast and the distance that it has to travel is so short that small errors in timing add up. Ephemeris errors are due to the fact that it is impossible to know absolutely the orbits of the satellites. Slight variations cause small errors.

Receiver error is also significant; this is the error in the antenna and the delays in processing caused by the internal circuitry (also due to temperature changes affecting the internal clock).

Finally, there are multipath errors. This error is caused by the signal being reflected or bounced off things (such as a building or the ground).

There are other issues with the signal. Because it is a microwave signal, it is absorbed by water, so a GPS receiver won't work underwater. Fortunately, not many people need to use it underwater, so this isn't a huge problem, but water can affect the system in other ways:

- Leaves contain water and can absorb the GPS signal, dramatically reducing signal strength and quality. The denser the leaves, the more the signal is degraded. Worse than leaves are pine needles. These not only contain water, but are the right size and shape to act as mini-antennas, catching the signal. This usually means that if you are traveling though dense forests (especially conifers), you will need to find a clearing to gain a good signal lock.

- Humidity in the air, such as rain, snow, or fog, can also weaken the signal. In addition, areas of high mist (such as near waterfalls) can be problematic because the high water content of the air exacerbates the problem.

- A layer of water on the antenna can dramatically reduce the signal's quality.

Summary

This appendix provided a brief look at the GPS network and what makes it work. GPS is a vastly complex multi-billion-dollar system, and certain key parts of it are classified. Nonetheless, this appendix should give you a good working knowledge of the system and what can affect its accuracy.

Websites/Internet Resources

Here is a list of useful GPS-related websites, categorized according to type.

GPS Manufacturers

Site	Description
www.garmin.com	Garmin website
www.magellangps.com	Magellan website
www.delorme.com	DeLorme website
www.lowrance.com	Lowrance website
www.laipac.com	Laipac website
www.haicom.com.tw	Haicom website
www.navman.com	Navman website
www.miogps.com	Mio Technology website
www.emtac.com.tw	Emtac website
www.trimble.com	Trimble website

Digital Map Makers

Site	Description
www.memory-map.com	Memory-Map (U.S.)
www.memory-map.co.uk	Memory-Map (U.K.)
www.maptech.com	Maptech website
www.fugawi.com	Fugawi website

Continued

Digital Map Makers *(continued)*

Site	Description
www.destinator1.com	Destinator website
www.tomtom.com	TomTom website
www.garmin.com/cartography	Garmin cartography
www.magellangps.com/en/products	Magellan mapping

Geocaching

Site	Description
www.geocaching.com	Premier geocaching site
www.navicache.com	Geocache listing site
shop.groundspeak.com	Geocaching store
www.brillig.com/geocaching	Geocaching site

Software

Site	Description
www.robogeo.com	RoboGEO enables you to insert GPS coordinate information into digital photographs.
www.teletype.com	Navigating software for PDAs
www.oziexplorer.com	Excellent mapping software
www.expertgps.com	Excellent mapping software
javagps.sourceforge.net	Java application that enables communication with attached GPS receivers
www.gartrip.de	GARTrip enables you to take control over waypoints and routes. Works with Garmin and Magellan receivers.
www.gpsassist.net	Helper application for TomTom Navigator software
www.sping.com/seaclear	SeaClear provides a chart plotter and navigation software for the PC.

Site	Description
www.wherify.com	Personal GPS locator
www.topofusion.com	GPS mapping for Windows
www.compegps.com	Tracking and routing software
www.gpsu.co.uk	GPS utility created to enable easy management, manipulation, and mapping of GPS data
www.easygps.com	Import/export waypoints easily
www.geopainting.com	This is the home of GPSMapEdit, which enables you to create your own maps.

Hardware

Site	Description
www.pfranc.com	Cable connectors for GPS receivers
www.lynks.co.uk	Cables, connectors, and GPS accessories
www.ram-mount.com	Mounts for GPS receivers for all occasions
www.stormcase.com	Stormcase—the ultimate rugged outdoor case for all your electronics
www.otterbox.com	Rugged, waterproof, dustproof, crushproof boxes for your GPS and other electronics
www.smartsolar.com	Portable solar power solutions
www.aquapac.net	Waterproof bags for GPS

Information

Site	Description
www.gpsinformation.net/	Extensive GPS information
www.ultimategps.com	GPS news and information
www.gpsworld.com	GPS news and technology website
www.mobilegpsonline.com	A site concentrating on GPS and mobile computers
www.gpspassion.com	Information and discussion forum

Continued

Information *(continued)*

Site	Description
www.travelbygps.com	Information for the traveler using GPS
www.gpsnuts.com	GPS information and reviews
www.trailregistry.com	Plan your hiking and backpacking trips here!
www.confluence.org	Interesting GPS game
gpsgames.org	The name says it all—GPS games!
www.nomad.ee/micros/etrex.shtml	Extensive information on Garmin GPS
www.keenpeople.com	Large, very active GPS community
www.gps-practice-and-fun.com	A lot of good GPS information
www.pocketgps.co.uk	Good information and a great selection of international points of interest
groups.yahoo.com/group/ Magellan_Meridian/	Group-specific discussion on the Magellan Meridian
groups.yahoo.com/group/GarminF	Group-specific discussion on the Garmin GPS units
finance.groups.yahoo.com/group/etrex/	Group-specific discussion on the Garmin eTrex units

Glossary

12-channel   A GPS receiver that can keep a lock on 12 satellites simultaneously.

14-channel   A GPS receiver that can keep a lock on 14 satellites simultaneously.

Accuracy   A measure of how close the position given by the GPS is to the true position.

Acquisition time   The time it takes for the GPS receiver to determine its initial position.

Active antenna   An antenna that amplifies the GPS signal before feeding it to the GPS receiver.

Active leg   The segment of a route that is currently being traveled.

Almanac   A data file that contains orbit information on the GPS satellites, clock corrections, and atmospheric delay information. The almanac is transmitted by the GPS satellites to a GPS receiver to enable it to keep a lock and reacquire a lost signal quickly.

Atomic clock   A very accurate clock that uses the decay of elements such as cesium or rubidium to measure the passage of time. A typical cesium clock has an error of about one second per million years. GPS satellites make use of multiple atomic clocks.

Availability   The number of hours that a particular location has sufficient satellites to allow a GPS receiver to work.

Breadcrumb trail   A visual representation of a path taken, shown on a map. Also known as a *track*.

C/A-code   Short for "Coarse/Acquisition" or "S-code," a name given to the civilian GPS signal.

COG   *See* Course over ground.

Cold start   The power-on sequence in which the GPS receiver downloads almanac data before establishing a fix.

Constellation   The set of GPS satellites in orbit around the Earth.

Control segment   The Earth-based component of the GPS network (the satellite control system).

Coordinates A unique numeric or alphanumeric scheme used to describe a precise location.

Course over ground The direction in which the GPS receiver is traveling.

Course to steer The direction to take in order to return on course.

Crosstrack Error The distance you are off a desired course in either direction.

CTS *See* Course to steer.

Cutoff angle *See* Mask angle.

Datum A position for which an accurate measurement of latitude and longitude is known. This is used in map-making and in GPS for determining coordinates across the whole map. It is used in mapping and surveying to ensure map accuracy.

DOP Dilution of Precision. An estimate made by the GPS of how much error exists in the reading.

Ephemeris The predictions of current satellite positions that are transmitted to the GPS receiver.

External antenna An antenna designed to be attached and detached from a GPS receiver.

Fix A single position that includes latitude, longitude, altitude, time, and date.

GLONASS This is the Russian counterpart to GPS.

GPS Global Positioning System.

GPSr Another term for a GPS receiver.

Healthy A term used to describe an orbiting GPS satellite suitable for use. "State" can also be used to refer to satellite health.

Latitude A north-south measurement of position perpendicular to the Earth's polar axis.

Longitude An east-west measurement of position. This is measured in relation to the prime meridian (the line corresponding to 0° longitude), an imaginary circle that passes through both the north and south poles.

Magnetic north The direction in which the north end of the compass needle points.

Mask angle The minimum elevation of a satellite above the horizon to ensure a good signal. This can be between 5 degrees and 15 degrees. GPS receivers usually ignore satellites below this elevation.

Multipath error Error caused by the interference of a GPS signal. It occurs when a signal from one satellite has reached the receiver antenna more than once because it has taken two or more different paths. It is generally caused when one signal has been bounced or reflected.

P-code Short for "Precision," a name given to the encrypted military GPS signal.

Position The latitude, longitude, and altitude of a particular point. Often, an estimate of error is associated with a position.

SA *See* Selective availability.

Satellite constellation The arrangement of the GPS satellites at any particular time.

Selective availability   An intentional random error in the clock time of the civilian GPS signal that was intended to degrade the signal and thereby only allow the military/government to have access to precise location information. This was removed in May 2000.

Space segment   The satellite component of the GPS network.

SPS   Another name given to the civilian C/A code.

SV   Space vehicles. Another name for the GPS satellites.

Track   The plot of a route taken or a route to be followed, stored on a GPS.

True north   The direction to the north pole.

User segment   The receivers using the GPS signals.

UTC   Universal Coordinated Time. The time system formerly known as Greenwich Mean Time (GMT).

WAAS   Wide Area Augmentation System. A system of ground-based beacons or additional satellites that improve the baseline GPS system. To make use of this, you need a WAAS-enabled GPS receiver.

Warm start   The power-on sequence in which the GPS receiver does not need to download the almanac data before establishing a fix.

Waypoint   A position stored in the GPS.

XTE   *See* Crosstrack error.

Y-code   Another name given to the encrypted P-code.

Index

Continued